2001 150

DOUGLAS LOVELL

XSL Formatting Objects

DEVELOPER'S HANDBOOK

SAMS 800 East 96th Street, Indianapolis, Indiana 46240

XSL Formatting Objects Developer's Handbook

International Standard Book Number: 0-672-32281-1

Library of Congress Catalog Card Number: 2001092018

Printed in the United States of America

First Printing: November 2002

08 07 06 4 3 2

Trademarks

All terms mentioned in this book that are known to be trademarks or service marks have been appropriately capitalized. Sams Publishing cannot attest to the accuracy of this information. Use of a term in this book should not be regarded as affecting the validity of any trademark or service mark.

Warning and Disclaimer

Every effort has been made to make this book as complete and as accurate as possible, but no warranty or fitness is implied. The information provided is on an "as is" basis.

Executive Editor
Michael Stephens

Acquisitions Editor
Carol Ackerman

Development Editor
Kevin Howard

Managing Editor
Charlotte Clapp

Project Editor
George E. Nedeff

Copy Editor
Barbara Hacha

Indexer
Sharon Shock

Proofreader
Linda Seifert

Technical Editor
Frank Neugebauer

Team Coordinator
Lynne Williams

Multimedia Developer
Dan Scherf

Interior Designer
Gary Adair

Cover Designer
Alan Clements

Page Layout
Julie Parks

Contents at a Glance

Table of Contents

Preface

Doug has written a book about XSL and Formatting Objects that is both great fun to read and chock full of examples and other useful bits of information. Why is such a book necessary? There is a tremendous hurdle for most people in sorting out the alphabet soup of just XML—let alone adding the intricacies of XSL, XSLT, XPath, and all the other Xs.

When XML on the Web was just beginning, I was asked many questions of the form, "Can you do…with XML?" You fill in the blank. My answer was typically the same: "Yes, but not alone." When it comes to formatting data and content, particularly with complicated layouts suitable for print and other media, you need XSL. To help you understand XSL, you need to start with Doug's book.

For more than 15 years, the "doom and gloom" crowd said it couldn't be done. They didn't have the necessary tenacity and perseverance. XSL is a formatter-independent style-sheet language for producing high-quality paginated output. And it works—the large number of interoperable implementations proves the point. Reading the W3C Recommendation is a daunting task; it's written as a "contract" for implementers. What we've needed all along is a book for users that can fill in the gaps and put the legalese into everyday English.

Doug spends an entire chapter setting up the conceptual framework for the methodology implicit in all good XML applications; that is, separate the processing information from the data itself while keeping the data free from the artifacts of a particular format, for a particular media. This allows the data to be reused in many forms—reports, invoices, specifications, bills of materials—on many different platforms and devices.

I don't want to rewrite the whole book here in the preface, so I will just point you to Chapter 2, "From Content to Presentation." You can see the same data from the National Weather Service transformed to HTML, XSL Formatting Objects, and WML (for cell phones and other wireless devices). Enjoy working with this and all other examples.

Another chapter I want to highlight is on implementations and tools. Although it has the potential to become out-of-date quickly, users need to know that there are a variety of implementation choices available to them—both for experimentation and for production-quality usage. It thrills me to see—even as I write this—that both RenderX and Antenna House are making announcements for new versions that allude to being the biggest, best, and most complete XSL implementations in the world. And then there's the Arbortext Epic editor and XFC from IBM alphaWorks. These and all other commercial implementations, as well as the critically important open source and free implementations, make it great for the industry and the user community as a whole. I love them all.

Sharon Adler

Chair, W3C XSL Working Group

September 2002

About the Author

Doug Lovell taught himself the Basic programming language on a PDP-11 time-sharing terminal when he was a young, impressionable freshman in high school. He saved his programs on punched paper tape, which he rolled up, banded, and stored in tobacco tins supplied by his pipe-smoking mathematics teacher. After becoming a certified flight instructor in Ohio and then moving to New York City to earn a fine arts degree in photography, Doug joined the electronic prepress and digital typesetting facility at Time, Inc. He picked up typesetting and prepress knowledge by working for a few years making *Time*, *Life*, *Fortune*, *People*, and *Sports Illustrated* ready for the presses.

While working prepress, he partnered in building and operating a business selling graphics tablets for the Commodore Amiga computer; he also wrote a program for animated cartoon drawing, for which he procured his first patent. He left Time to become a resident computer whiz for an engineering firm and to attend graduate school for a degree in computer science.

Now Doug works as a software engineer for IBM Research. Typesetting got a grip on him again when he pulled duty to satisfy all the hard-copy requirements of the AutoLoan Exchange project. The project pioneered the process of applying for, approving, and closing automobile loans on the Internet. Doug applied the TeX typesetting language to typeset individualized loan contracts on demand. TeX was most popularly used to typeset mathematics, physics, chemistry, and computer science journals; this may have been the most commercial application of TeX ever undertaken.

Doug's most recent program is an implementation of XSL Formatting Objects written with Java. He also has written several tools for working with XML and XSLT, early versions of which appeared on IBM's alphaworks new technologies Web site, and invented TeXML—an XML vocabulary for expressing TeX typesetting documents. He lives and breathes in the beautiful mid-Hudson Valley of New York, loves to hike the mountaintops, and flies aerobatics wherever he's allowed.

Dedication

For Kate and Maggie. Being your Dad and watching you become who you are makes it all worthwhile.

Acknowledgments

Thanks to Carol Ackerman at Sams for asking me five or six times to do this book and to Sharon Adler for her incredible confidence and encouragement—both on the job at IBM and in my undertaking to explain XSL to its broadest audience. Thanks to the editors and technical reviewers who contribute so much to making this a good read and exorcising the devil in the details.

Thanks to Mimi Jett for being such a wonderful, charismatic, welcoming, and encouraging leader in the TeX community, which itself deserves acknowledgment as a standard-bearer for computer typesetting, which sets the bar for collegial spirit, technical accomplishment, and skill, and where I have learned so very much. Thanks to Chris Rowley at Open University, who joined me as comrade in arms for first readings and understanding of the Candidate Recommendation, and especially to Christine Hu, Paul Fernhout, Anders Berglund, and others who have worked with me to understand the details and create an implementation. Thanks to all my colleagues. No one could hope for better.

Thanks to my family—parents, aunts, uncles, and cousins who've watched patiently and supportively while I've gone through many or more of the struggles and trials most of us face navigating this ocean of existence.

Some of us are fortunate to know someone of true genius who inspires us to our best. I'm fortunate to know Kate Curren. Thank you, Kate, and thanks to all of my friends. You listen when I need an ear and share the many good times and adventures that are the payoff from all our hard work.

We Want to Hear from You!

As the reader of this book, *you* are our most important critic and commentator. We value your opinion and want to know what we're doing right, what we could do better, what areas you'd like to see us publish in, and any other words of wisdom you're willing to pass our way.

As an executive editor for Sams Publishing, I welcome your comments. You can email or write me directly to let me know what you did or didn't like about this book—as well as what we can do to make our books better.

Please note that I cannot help you with technical problems related to the *topic* of this book. We do have a User Services group, however, where I will forward specific technical questions related to the book.

When you write, please be sure to include this book's title and author as well as your name, email address, and phone number. I will carefully review your comments and share them with the author and editors who worked on the book.

Email: `feedback@samspublishing.com`

Mail: Executive Editor
Sams Publishing
800 East 96th Street
Indianapolis, IN 46240 USA

For more information about this book or another Sams Publishing title, visit our Web site at `www.samspublishing.com`. Type the ISBN (excluding hyphens) or the title of a book in the Search field to find the page you're looking for.

CHAPTER 1

Introduction

XSL Formatting Objects. Love 'em. They're the answer to getting to print from XML. Sooner or later, your XML applications will want to put something down on paper. Maybe that old legacy app is just dying to write its life story. Perhaps your customer doesn't want to browse a statement online. Maybe your customer doesn't browse. That's what assistants are for. Suppose your customer wants a printed statement on demand, with all the latest transactions accounted in the document. Suppose you want to deliver print quality. You want to deliver PDF. You can pull the SQL query as XML. You're going to use FO.

XSL is eXtensible Stylesheet Language. It became a recommendation of the World Wide Web Consortium (W3C) on October 15, 2001. Its primary goal is to define a presentation language for XML. XSL goes beyond the capabilities of the Cascading Style Sheets (CSS) standard used to style HTML while remaining compatible with it. The most exciting aspect of XSL is that it creates a formatting standard rich enough to typeset any of the world's written languages.

The operative word here is "typeset." Typesetting implies a whole lot more than wrapping text in a window and throwing up scrollbars. It means more than font family, size, and color. It means tightly controlled ink on paper. It means pagination, hyphenation, running heads, and footers. It means high-quality presentation worthy of print.

This book provides comprehensive coverage of the XSL recommendation. It is a book about typesetting XML.

Who Needs FO?

Anyone who needs to translate a dynamic data stream into on-demand printed documents might consider using XML and XSL.

Anyone responsible for managing content delivery over multiple channels might consider using XML and XSL.

Dynamic data streams include databases, schedule data, traffic data, transactions, contracts, and inventories. Content delivery channels include Web browsers, cell phones, mail, books, articles, and help systems.

If you're an IT or information development professional, Web designer, manager, publisher, or an author producing reports, custom documents, catalogs, directories, itineraries, schedules, form letters, target mailings, books, reports, specifications, or product documentation, you might consider using XML and XSL.

XML and XSL provide an on-demand presentation solution for static or dynamic content accessed over multiple channels.

In addition, some of you out there have enough technical savvy to handle markup with a text editor, and you don't want to trust your family history or your first novel to a proprietary word processor. XML and XSL are for you.

What Do You Need to Know?

There are a few related standards that will be helpful, but not mandatory, for understanding this book. They are XML, HTML, CSS, and XSLT. The operative word is "helpful." Don't buy six more books and spend a year with them before coming back to buy this one. Don't crawl away in abject despair over accumulating enough background to make it through. Presumably you want typeset output from XML. Dive into that right away. Use this book. You'll pick up the rest on a need-to-know basis. Wing it.

There are about a zillion introductions to XML in print and on the Web. Here's what you need to know about XML to start this book: XML uses *elements*. You write elements using *tags*, which place the element name inside angle brackets, like this: `<element>`. Tags come in pairs—a start tag and an end tag. You have already seen a start tag. The end tag looks just like it, except that it has a slash after its opening bracket, like this: `</element>`. An element may have *attributes*. Attributes are name-value pairs. Write attributes within the start tag, after the element name, and before the closing bracket, like this: `<element name="value">`. Text or other elements may appear between the start and end tags. That is the *content* of the element. Here is a complete example: `<element name="value"> content </element>`. An element with no content may be written in shorthand, like this: `<element name="value"/>`. That may be the shortest introduction to XML ever published.

Anyone familiar with HTML markup and CSS properties will have a leg up on this book. That is because HTML markup is a lot like XML and provides an introduction to structured document markup. CSS properties form a subset of the properties available from XSL. If you never wrote an HTML tag and guess that CSS means Consolidated Savings and Securities, don't despair. You can still use this book to get a handle on FO.

The book presents examples as XSL Transformations (XSLT) that output XSL FO. Some understanding of XSLT may be helpful, but is not mandatory. Appendix A, "Basics of the XSL Transform," provides a short introduction to XSLT that contains more than you need to know to understand this book.

That's all you need to know. Get started.

Overview of the Book

We try to breeze through FO, covering everything in sufficient detail to make you productive in a hurry. You'll find an example for many, if not most, common typesetting tasks here, with the XSL markup required to produce the desired output.

Chapter 2, "From Content to Presentation," presents an extended example in detail. It presents style sheets that generate HMTL, WML, and XSL typeset output from a single content markup. It illustrates advantages of separating content from style and explains why that separation is useful.

Chapter 3, "Tools and Implementations," provides an overview of several tools and implementations known at the time of writing. It includes pointers to implementations that you may use to try the examples in the book and to resources for finding the latest information.

Chapters 4–7 will get you quickly on your feet producing typeset output. You'll have some fun along the way. The remaining chapters cover specific topics that you may someday need to cover. Read them in any order, when you need them.

As previously mentioned, Appendix A is an introduction to transforms. Appendixes B and C are comprehensive reference presentations of all the FOs, properties, and the property values available in XSL.

Fine Print

Much of the book will focus on print presentation. FO is not limited to print, but it stands out as a markup of choice for print. One of the features of printed works is that they are composed of many pages. The page concept is foreign to the scrolling computer display.

Printers still produce the finest detail in presentation. That is one of the reasons we still use a printer. It's easier on the eyes. Paper reports and books are easy to hold. They persist when we toss them on the desk. Turning a page, we keep our place. Try scrolling a large document, such as the XSL recommendation in your browser. It's easy to get lost. You have no finger in the page.

When our laptops can display many millions of pixels rather than half a million, our expectations for display will begin to match our expectations for print. Whether the page paradigm will replace the scrolling paradigm on the desktop is perhaps an open question. The popular Adobe Acrobat PDF viewer supports a hybrid. The continuous viewing option scrolls the bottom of one page as if it's attached to the top of the next page.

The text of this book was printed with about 12 times more resolution than what you see on the display of your computer. That's only about one order of magnitude greater (two if you square it, three if you count pixels). When a computer display rivals print in detail, we may have less interest in resorting to print, but more reason to have typeset quality visuals. XSL Formatting Objects provide the typesetting edge.

CHAPTER 2

From Content to Presentation

This chapter describes a simple application that exhibits the benefits of separating content from presentation. It provides a detailed view of an application that converts an aviation weather summary to HTML for online viewing, to XSL FO for printing, and to Wireless Markup Language (WML) for display on wireless devices.

Readers already familiar with transforms to HTML may find it helpful to see an HTML and an FO example side by side from the same input.

The WML portion illustrates the power of XSL to tailor presentations to radically different target devices given a single markup. This is a primary advantage of designing applications that leverage XML and XSL to separate data content from data presentation.

Aviation Weather Example

Data for aviation weather comes through the National Weather Service (NWS) National Meteorological Center (NMC) in Washington, D.C. from weather reporting sites around the country. Regional NWS offices, such as Weather Service Forecast Offices, (WSFO) use charts, reports, and raw data from NMC meteorologists to produce local forecasts.

The Federal Aviation Administration (FAA) distributes vital weather information to pilots through a number of channels. Pilots can call published numbers at airports for automated weather observations or the latest airport information. They can listen to hazardous weather advisories broadcast from navigational facilities. They can call a weather briefer at an FAA-operated Flight Service Station (FSS) for a full preflight aviation briefing.

Many pilots now go online for their weather. The FAA contracts through DynaCorp to provide directly to the pilot much of the same data that is available to a weather briefer. This is a tremendous benefit. A briefer can read and a pilot can copy only so much of the relevant data in a phone conversation. The Direct User Access Terminal Service (DUATS) lets a pilot view or print a standard briefing and then review details on the phone with a briefer.

A great deal of effort has gone into the Web interface for DUATS aviation weather. Pilots use the best and latest user-interface technology to enter time, location, and other details about their flights and requested weather. The results come back looking much like they came off a Teletype terminal in the 1970s. Figure 2.1 shows an example.

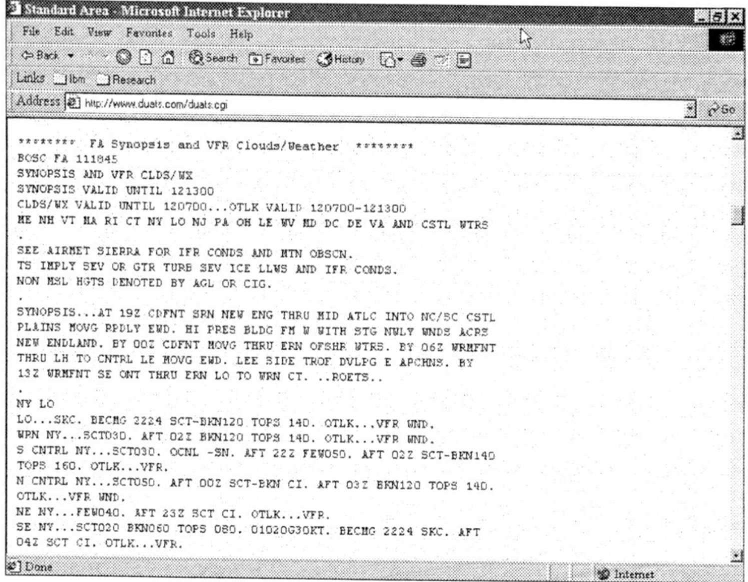

Figure 2.1

Boston area forecast, February 11, 2002.

This is an area forecast generated on February 11, 2002. The designator, BOSC, indicates that Boston Center developed the forecast. Boston Center operates the WSFO for much of the Northeastern United States. The forecast shown in Figure 2.1 came from a DUATS session on the Internet available to holders of a current aviation medical. All pilots receive periodic physical exams from FAA designated physicians. The aviation medical is proof of this exam. All pilots must have one to fly.

These reports are actually easy to read after you learn the abbreviations and get some practice. Professionals can read them as easily as you can read this text. The abbreviations make them very concise; when you understand them, you can quickly get a lot of useful weather information.

That economy of presentation is more of a holdover from another age of computing, however. It was extremely important in the days when these reports printed on 300-baud Teletype terminals. Those terminals had rolls of yellow paper about 10 inches wide. They printed by impact through a ribbon and had only uppercase characters. The 300-baud transmission rate meant that a person could read as fast as the terminal typed.

In these days of high-speed DSL and cable access in which 56K baud phone lines seem slow, the purpose for that economy of letters seems only to mystify the uninitiated.

We can use XML to present the data in abbreviated format, as plain English, and in any number of other formats. One area where some need for economy still exists is in the display on cell phones and other wireless devices. Only a few characters are available on small cell phone displays. The abbreviated presentation allows more words to fit into the smaller space. We'll use the abbreviated report for the cell phone display.

Figure 2.2 shows a translated output of the same forecast. This was produced by a computer program that translates the abbreviations from a table into the full words in English. However, some problems occur with this; for example, in translating NC/SC, the program could not distinguish "no change" from "North Carolina" or "stratocumulus" (a meteorological term for a cloud type) from "South Carolina."

The plain-language forecast is something most of us would consider a vast improvement over the initial report. Old timers might find it more than a little verbose. Can we improve on this a little? Maybe not, but we can make it easy to work with this data in a number of formats.

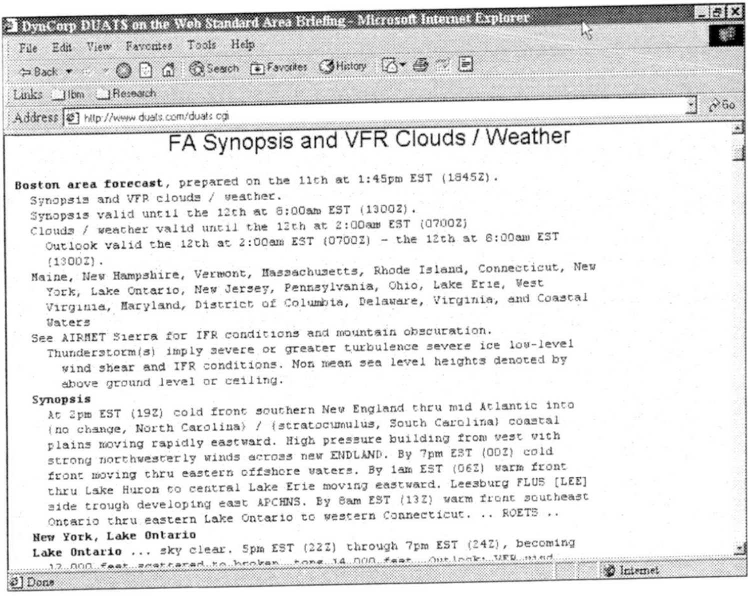

Figure 2.2

Plain-language translation of the Boston area forecast.

XML Encoded Weather

Suppose for a few minutes that aviation weather data is available as an XML-encoded data stream. You can now apply a style sheet to produce nicely formatted HTML. If the pilot would like to print the weather for in-flight reference, you could use FO to deliver PDF on demand.

You can even envision an abbreviated presentation of this data on a PDA or cell phone. A digital communication module in the flight-management system on the aircraft could display in-flight updates. A third style sheet could convert the same data to WML for display on those smaller devices.

Following is some XML source markup to drive the scenario. It begins with some data about the source and coverage:

```
<?xml version='1.0'?>
<wx>
  <area-forecast source="BOSC"
   day="11" hour="18" minute="45"
   expire-day="12" expire-hour="13" wx-expire="07">
    <area>
      <region id="NY"/>
      <region id="NH"/>
      <region id="Coastal waters"/>
    </area>
    <sigs id="SIERRA"/>
```

It continues with the synopsis. Note that conditions include both the abbreviated and plain-language text:

```
    <synopsis>
      <at hour="19">
        <condition>
          cdfnt srn new eng thru mid atlc into
          nc/sc cstl plains movg rpdly ewd
          <text>
            A cold front extending from southern New England
            through the Mid-Atlantic states into the North and
            South Carolina coastal plains will be moving rapidly
            eastward.
          </text>
        </condition>
        <condition>
```

```
      hi pres bldg fm w with stg nwly wnds acrs new eng
      <text>
        High pressure is building from the west
        with strong northwesterly winds across New England.
      </text>
    </condition>
  </at>
  <by hour="00">
    <condition>
      cdfnt movg thru ern ofshr wtrs.
      <text>
        The cold front will be moving through the eastern
        offshore waters.
      </text>
    </condition>
  </by>
```

The synopsis has divisions organized by time. It tells a story about what will happen to these weather systems in the future, with specific predictions about when changes will occur:

```
  <by hour="06">
    <condition>
      wrmfnt thru lh to cntrl le movg ewd
      <text>
        A warm front extending through Lake Huron to central
        Lake Erie will be moving eastward.
      </text>
    </condition>
    <condition>
      lee side trof dvlpg e apchns
      <text>
        A lee-side trough will develop behind the cold front
        in the eastern Appalachians.
      </text>
    </condition>
  </by>
  <by hour="13">
    <condition>
      wrmfnt se ont thru ern lo to wrn ct
      <text>
        The warm front will reach from southeastern Ontario
        through eastern Lake Ontario to western Connecticut.
      </text>
```

```
      </condition>
    </by>
    <forecaster id="roets"/>
  </synopsis>
```

After the synopsis, the data contains detailed cloud and weather forecasts for smaller regions in the coverage area. It starts with the big picture and then gives more detail. The first is for Lake Ontario:

```
  <clouds-wx>
    <area id="lo"/>
    <sky cover="clr"/>
    <at hour="22" minute="24">
      <sky cover="sct-bkn" height="120" tops="140"/>
    </at>
    <outlook conditions="VFR">
      <factor>wind</factor>
    </outlook>
  </clouds-wx>
```

The second describes predicted weather for south-central New York:

```
  <clouds-wx>
    <area id="s-cntrl-ny"/>
    <sky cover="sct" height="030"/>
    <condition>
      ocnl -sn.
      <text>
        occasional light snow
      </text>
    </condition>
    <after hour="22">
      <sky cover="few" height="050"/>
    </after>
    <after hour="02">
      <sky cover="sct-bkn" height="140" tops="160"/>
    </after>
    <outlook conditions="VFR"/>
  </clouds-wx>
 </area-forecast>
</wx>
```

This is not to redesign the NWS systems; it is inspiration for an example. This markup could have been produced automatically from the NWS report in a manner similar to that used to expand the report into plain English, but it wasn't. It was made by hand from the reports in Figures 2.1 and 2.2.

Some Common Templates

The rest of this chapter will focus on the XSL presentations of the XML encoded weather. The presentations for HTML and FO include some common templates, described next.

Templates are the working units of XSLT style sheets. They match something in the source document and produce something else in the result. Appendix A gives more detail about the working of XSLT. Templates work to add presentation markup to XML content. They select portions of the content and decorate that with style commands. For example, a template may match a title element and output a command to present the title in italic.

Some templates are useful for more than one presentation. The first template in the example that follows changes 1 to 1st and 3 to 3rd. Both our HTML and our FO presentations will use that template. We typically place common templates of this sort into modules that we can include in multiple style sheets. These modules start with requisite XSLT boilerplate:

```
<?xml version='1.0'?>
<xsl:stylesheet version="1.0"
 xmlns:xsl="http://www.w3.org/1999/XSL/Transform">
```

We follow that with a utility template that puts the correct English suffix on a number. That is the "st" in "1st." The number itself comes as a parameter to the template. The `<xsl:choose>` element brackets a number of tests. It executes the content of first test, which passes the following:

```
  <xsl:template name="ord">
    <xsl:param name="number"/>
    <xsl:choose>
      <xsl:when test="$number='3'">
        <xsl:text>rd</xsl:text>
      </xsl:when>
      <xsl:when test="$number='2'">
        <xsl:text>nd</xsl:text>
      </xsl:when>
      <xsl:when test="$number='1'">
        <xsl:text>st</xsl:text>
      </xsl:when>
      <xsl:otherwise>
        <xsl:text>th</xsl:text>
```

```
      </xsl:otherwise>
    </xsl:choose>
  </xsl:template>
```

The next template outputs introductory material for the forecast. That includes the identity of the forecast office, the time of the forecast, and expiration times. These lines work nicely to format the dates and times:

```
  <xsl:template name="ident-info">
    <xsl:text> prepared on the </xsl:text>
    <xsl:value-of select="@day"/>
    <xsl:call-template name="ord">
      <xsl:with-param name="number" select="@day"/>
    </xsl:call-template>
    <xsl:text> at </xsl:text>
    <xsl:value-of select="@hour"/>
    <xsl:text>:</xsl:text>
    <xsl:value-of select="@minute"/>
    <xsl:text> Zulu, valid until the </xsl:text>
    <xsl:value-of select="@expire-day"/>
    <xsl:call-template name="ord">
      <xsl:with-param name="number" select="@expire-day"/>
    </xsl:call-template>
    <xsl:text> at </xsl:text>
    <xsl:value-of select="@expire-hour"/>
    <xsl:text>:00 Zulu</xsl:text>
    <xsl:value-of select="@expire-minute"/>
    <xsl:text>. Clouds and weather valid until </xsl:text>
    <xsl:value-of select="@wx-expire"/>
    <xsl:text>:00 Zulu</xsl:text>
    <xsl:text>.</xsl:text>
  </xsl:template>
```

These two templates list the regions covered by the forecast. The first works in the synopsis portion, the second in the clouds and weather portion. They list the region elements with a comma after all but the last:

```
  <xsl:template match="region">
    <xsl:value-of select="@id"/>
    <xsl:if test="position()!=last()">
      <xsl:text>, </xsl:text>
    </xsl:if>
```

```
</xsl:template>

<xsl:template match="area[parent::clouds-wx]">
  <xsl:value-of select="@id"/>
  <xsl:if test="following-sibling::area">
    <xsl:text>, </xsl:text>
  </xsl:if>
</xsl:template>
```

The outlook is a broad designation that indicates whether the weather will be nasty or nice. The technical terms are IFR, MVFR, and VFR. IFR stands for Instrument Flight Rules. This is the condition when cloud cover, fog, or other reduced visibility requires pilots to fly by instruments in coordination with Air Traffic Control. VFR stands for Visual Flight Rules, which is the opposite; pilots can see the world outside the cockpit. The M in MVFR means Marginal. Factors such as wind or ice may be mentioned in the outlook.

The `<xsl:value-of>` element pulls the outlook condition from the `conditions` attribute of the `outlook` element:

```
<xsl:template match="outlook">
  <xsl:text>Outlook</xsl:text>
  <xsl:value-of select="@conditions"/>
  <xsl:text>. </xsl:text>
  <xsl:apply-templates/>
</xsl:template>

<xsl:template match="factor">
  <xsl:value-of select="text()"/>
  <xsl:choose>
    <xsl:when test="position() != last()">
      <xsl:text>, </xsl:text>
    </xsl:when>
    <xsl:otherwise>
      <xsl:text>.</xsl:text>
    </xsl:otherwise>
  </xsl:choose>
</xsl:template>
```

The HTML and FO templates call this template to translate the name of elements `from`, `by`, `at`, and `after` into text in the result document:

```
<xsl:template name="from-by-at">
  <xsl:choose>
```

```
      <xsl:when test="name()='from'">
        <xsl:text>From </xsl:text>
      </xsl:when>
      <xsl:when test="name()='by'">
        <xsl:text>By </xsl:text>
      </xsl:when>
      <xsl:when test="name()='at'">
        <xsl:text>At </xsl:text>
      </xsl:when>
      <xsl:when test="name()='after'">
        <xsl:text>After </xsl:text>
      </xsl:when>
    </xsl:choose>
    <xsl:value-of select="@hour"/>
    <xsl:text>:00 Zulu</xsl:text>
  </xsl:template>
```

This is where the style sheet outputs the long, plain-language descriptions and translates sky conditions:

```
  <xsl:template match="text">
    <xsl:value-of select="text()"/>
  </xsl:template>

  <xsl:template match="sky">
    <xsl:choose>
      <xsl:when test="@cover='clr'">
        <xsl:text> Sky clear</xsl:text>
      </xsl:when>
      <xsl:when test="@cover='sct-bkn'">
        <xsl:text> Clouds scattered to broken</xsl:text>
      </xsl:when>
      <xsl:when test="@cover='sct'">
        <xsl:text> Clouds scattered</xsl:text>
      </xsl:when>
      <xsl:when test="@cover='bkn'">
        <xsl:text> Clouds broken</xsl:text>
      </xsl:when>
      <xsl:when test="@cover='ovc'">
        <xsl:text> Overcast</xsl:text>
      </xsl:when>
    </xsl:choose>
    <xsl:if test="@height">
      <xsl:text>, layer at </xsl:text>
```

```
      <xsl:value-of select="@height"/>
      <xsl:text>00 feet MSL </xsl:text>
    </xsl:if>
    <xsl:if test="@tops">
      <xsl:text>, tops at </xsl:text>
      <xsl:value-of select="@tops"/>
      <xsl:text>00 feet MSL </xsl:text>
    </xsl:if>
  </xsl:template>
```

The last template of the style sheet suppresses any odd bits of text not explicitly called out by the other templates:

```
  <xsl:template match="text()"/>

</xsl:stylesheet>
```

A Style Sheet to Produce HTML

Following is an XSL style sheet that produces HTML from the report. It begins with the XSL style sheet declaration:

```
<?xml version='1.0'?>
<xsl:stylesheet version="1.0"
 xmlns:xsl="http://www.w3.org/1999/XSL/Transform">
```

These are processing instructions. The first causes the processor to strip leading and trailing spaces from the text of the XML input. The second indicates that the output will be HTML rather than XML. The third includes the common templates described in the preceding section:

```
  <xsl:strip-space elements="*"/>
  <xsl:output method="html"/>
  <xsl:include href="wxcommon.xsl"/>
```

The root rule outputs the HTML outer structure, the `html` root element, and the body:

```
  <xsl:template match="/">
    <html>
    <body>
      <xsl:apply-templates/>
    </body>
    </html>
  </xsl:template>
```

The style sheet begins in earnest here. This outputs the title and introductory material. The last few lines order the remainder of the output: first, the areas of coverage, then the significant weather advisory, the synopsis, and the detailed cloud and weather forecasts:

```
<xsl:template match="area-forecast">
  <h2>FA Synopsis, VFR Clouds and Weather</h2>
  <p><b>
    <xsl:choose>
      <xsl:when test="@source='BOSC'">
        Boston
      </xsl:when>
    </xsl:choose>
    <xsl:text> area forecast</xsl:text>
  </b>
  <xsl:call-template name="ident-info"/>
  <br/>
  <xsl:apply-templates select="area"/>
  <xsl:apply-templates select="sigs"/>
  </p>
  <xsl:apply-templates select="synopsis"/>
  <xsl:apply-templates select="clouds-wx"/>
</xsl:template>
```

The source XML has `region` element children of the `area` element in the area forecast. This template matches the `area` element, outputs some text, and then processes the `region` children with `<xsl:apply-templates/>`. The section in this chapter titled "Some Common Templates" presented the template that matches the `region` child elements. That template outputs each region name. It places a comma and a space after every name but the last.

```
<xsl:template match="area[parent::area-forecast]">
  <xsl:text>Valid in </xsl:text>
  <xsl:apply-templates/>
  <br/>
</xsl:template>
```

The significant weather advisory is always the same. Only the name of the AIRMET changes. AIRMET comes from the words aircraft and meteorological. An AIRMET is a special advisory that notes locations of thunderstorm activity, tornadoes, and other severe weather conditions that might be hazardous to aircraft.

```
<xsl:template match="sigs">
```

```
    <xsl:text>See AIRMET </xsl:text><xsl:value-of select="@id"/>
    <xsl:text> for IFR conditions and mountain obscuration.</xsl:text>
    <br/>
    <xsl:text>Thunderstorms imply severe or greater turbulence,
    severe icing, low level wind shear, and IFR conditions.</xsl:text>
    <br/>
    <xsl:text>Non-MSL heights denoted by "AGL" or "CIG."</xsl:text>
    <br/>
  </xsl:template>
```

These templates provide the headings and spacing between the major sections of the report. The first starts the synopsis of major weather systems. The second puts a header on the cloud and weather detail forecasts for each region:

```
  <xsl:template match="synopsis">
    <h3>Synopsis</h3>
    <xsl:apply-templates/>
  </xsl:template>

  <xsl:template match="clouds-wx">
    <h3>
      <xsl:apply-templates select="area"/>
      <xsl:text>: </xsl:text>
      <xsl:apply-templates select="outlook"/>
    </h3>
    <xsl:apply-templates select="sky"/>
    <xsl:apply-templates select="conditions"/>
    <xsl:apply-templates select="after|from|by|at"/>
  </xsl:template>
```

The forecaster divides the report into periods, after which he predicts a change in the weather.

```
  <xsl:template match="after|from|by|at">
    <p>
      <b>
        <xsl:call-template name="from-by-at"/>
      </b>
      <xsl:apply-templates/>
    </p>
  </xsl:template>
</xsl:stylesheet>
```

An XSLT processor, such as those discussed in Chapter 3, "Tools and Implementations," reads the XML encoded weather data, applies the style sheet, and outputs the HTML presentation. The result appears in the browser similar to what is shown in Figure 2.3. The example used the default HTML styling. A graphic designer could create a CSS style sheet to make it look more distinguished. The take-away message is that this HTML presentation was produced with an XSL style sheet from the XML markup.

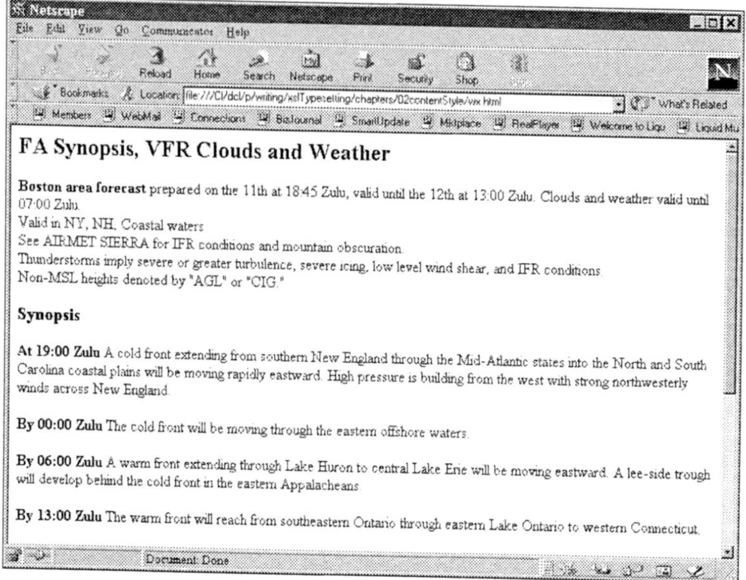

FA Synopsis, VFR Clouds and Weather

Boston area forecast prepared on the 11th at 18:45 Zulu, valid until the 12th at 13:00 Zulu. Clouds and weather valid until 07:00 Zulu.
Valid in NY, NH, Coastal waters
See AIRMET SIERRA for IFR conditions and mountain obscuration.
Thunderstorms imply severe or greater turbulence, severe icing, low level wind shear, and IFR conditions.
Non-MSL heights denoted by "AGL" or "CIG."

Synopsis

At 19:00 Zulu A cold front extending from southern New England through the Mid-Atlantic states into the North and South Carolina coastal plains will be moving rapidly eastward. High pressure is building from the west with strong northwesterly winds across New England.

By 00:00 Zulu The cold front will be moving through the eastern offshore waters.

By 06:00 Zulu A warm front extending through Lake Huron to central Lake Erie will be moving eastward. A lee-side trough will develop behind the cold front in the eastern Appalacheans.

By 13:00 Zulu The warm front will reach from southeastern Ontario through eastern Lake Ontario to western Connecticut.

Figure 2.3

The forecast formatted as HTML.

The style sheet may seem elaborate, but remember that you need to write it only once. You can process another markup with the new forecast, issued 12 hours later, to produce a new HTML output. You can get a lot of mileage, every twelve hours, out of the style sheet before you ever have to change it again.

A Style Sheet to Produce XSL FO

HTML output to a printer from a browser is not something you would put on letterhead and mail to a client. It isn't something you would print in a book or publish as a white paper. Publishers don't typeset magazines with it.

How do you get something from an XML data stream that you would be proud to see in print? Let's try a style sheet that produces XSL FO and then taste the pudding.

The FO style sheet is similar in many ways to the HTML style sheet. The reason is that it navigates the same input and produces a result document with similar structure. Here's all of it as proof.

The beginning declares that anything beginning with `fo:` is Formatting Objects. Anything beginning with `xsl:` is XSL transform. The XML namespace recommendation defines this syntax. Namespaces in a style sheet distinguish XSLT control elements from the formatting objects:

```
<?xml version='1.0'?>
<xsl:stylesheet version="1.0"
 xmlns:xsl="http://www.w3.org/1999/XSL/Transform"
 xmlns:fo="http://www.w3.org/1999/XSL/Format">

  <xsl:strip-space elements="*"/>
  <xsl:output method="xml"/>
  <xsl:include href="wxcommon.xsl"/>
```

Chapter 4 discusses in detail the fundamental FO document structure produced by this template, which matches the root of the input document:

```
  <xsl:template match="/">
    <fo:root>
      <fo:layout-master-set>
        <fo:simple-page-master
         master-name="page">
          <fo:region-body
           region-name="body"
           margin-top="0.5in"
           margin-bottom="1in"
           margin-left="0.5in"
           margin-right="0.5in"/>
        </fo:simple-page-master>
      </fo:layout-master-set>
      <fo:page-sequence master-reference="page">
        <fo:flow flow-name="body">
          <fo:block>
            <xsl:apply-templates/>
          </fo:block>
```

```
      </fo:flow>
    </fo:page-sequence>
  </fo:root>
</xsl:template>
```

The template that follows is the one that formats the dates and times. It calls the `ident-info` template defined in the common templates file. A few elements prefixed with `fo:` remind us that we're speaking a new tongue:

```
<xsl:template match="area-forecast">
  <fo:block
    font-weight="bold"
    font-size="16pt">
    <xsl:text>FA Synopsis, VFR Clouds and Weather</xsl:text>
  </fo:block>
  <fo:block><fo:wrapper font-weight="bold">
    <xsl:choose>
      <xsl:when test="@source='BOSC'">
        Boston
      </xsl:when>
    </xsl:choose>
    <xsl:text> area forecast</xsl:text>
  </fo:wrapper>
  <xsl:call-template name="ident-info"/>
  </fo:block>
  <xsl:apply-templates select="area"/>
  <xsl:apply-templates select="sigs"/>
  <xsl:apply-templates select="synopsis"/>
  <xsl:apply-templates select="clouds-wx"/>
</xsl:template>
```

These list the forecast regions, as before. The significant weather advisory follows:

```
<xsl:template match="area[parent::area-forecast]">
  <fo:block><xsl:text>Valid in </xsl:text>
  <xsl:apply-templates/>
  </fo:block>
</xsl:template>

<xsl:template match="sigs">
  <fo:block><xsl:text>See AIRMET </xsl:text>
```

```
    <fo:wrapper font-weight="bold">
      <xsl:value-of select="@id"/>
    </fo:wrapper>
  <xsl:text> for IFR conditions and mountain obscuration.</xsl:text>
  </fo:block>
  <fo:block>
    <xsl:text>Thunderstorms imply severe or greater turbulence,
    severe icing, low level wind shear, and IFR conditions.</xsl:text>
  </fo:block>
  <fo:block>
    <xsl:text>Non-MSL heights denoted by "AGL" or "CIG."</xsl:text>
  </fo:block>
</xsl:template>
```

In HTML `P`, `H1`, `H2`, and similar elements all represent a block division of the output. The differences are presentational, or stylistic. FO does not mix structural markup with styles. There is essentially one stacking structure, the `block`. Attributes of the block determine the appearance.

This set of attributes defines what we need to make a block appear as a subheading. This is the equivalent of the `H3` in the HTML style sheet.

```
<xsl:attribute-set name="subhead">
  <xsl:attribute name="font-weight">bold</xsl:attribute>
  <xsl:attribute name="font-size">14pt</xsl:attribute>
  <xsl:attribute name="space-before.maximum">24pt</xsl:attribute>
  <xsl:attribute name="space-before.optimum">14pt</xsl:attribute>
  <xsl:attribute name="space-before.minimum">12pt</xsl:attribute>
  <xsl:attribute name="keep-with-next">always</xsl:attribute>
</xsl:attribute-set>
```

These next two templates apply the subhead styling to the blocks that separate major sections of the forecast. Note the use of `xsl:use-attribute-sets`. That attribute acts to copy all the attributes from the `attribute-set` just defined:

```
<xsl:template match="synopsis">
  <fo:block
   xsl:use-attribute-sets="subhead">Synopsis</fo:block>
  <xsl:apply-templates/>
```

```
  </xsl:template>

  <xsl:template match="clouds-wx">
    <fo:block
     xsl:use-attribute-sets="subhead">
      <xsl:apply-templates select="area"/>
      <xsl:text>: </xsl:text>
      <xsl:apply-templates select="outlook"/>
    </fo:block>
    <xsl:apply-templates select="sky"/>
    <xsl:apply-templates select="conditions"/>
    <xsl:apply-templates select="after|from|by|at"/>
  </xsl:template>
```

The template at the end of the style sheet formats the forecast cloud and weather conditions. The common templates already described carry out most of the work:

```
  <xsl:template match="after|from|by|at">
    <fo:block>
      <fo:wrapper font-weight="bold">
        <xsl:call-template name="from-by-at"/>
      </fo:wrapper>
      <xsl:apply-templates/>
    </fo:block>
  </xsl:template>

</xsl:stylesheet>
```

Figure 2.4 shows PDF generated by the Apache FOP formatter given the FO style sheet and XML weather data. Not only does it look better on the page than printed HTML does, it will paginate better as well.

Better pagination means that no lines of text will be sliced in half horizontally at the bottom or top of a page. No header sections will be separated at the bottom of a page from their content that appears on the page following. You can even prevent a paragraph from starting if only one or two lines will print before the page break.

FA Synopsis, VFR Clouds and Weather

Boston Area forecast prepared on the 11th at 18:45 Zulu, valid until the 12th at 13:00 Zulu.
Clouds and weather valid until 07:00 Zulu.
Valid in NY, NH, Coastal waters
See AIRMET **SIERRA** for IFR conditions and mountain obscuration.
Thunderstorms imply severe or greater turbulence, severe icing, low level wind shear, and IFR conditions.
Non-MSL heights denoted by "AGL" or "CIG."

Synopsis

At 19:00 Zulu A cold front extending from southern New England through the Mid-Atlantic states into the North and South Carolina coastal plains will be moving rapidly eastward. High pressure is building from the west with strong northwesterly winds across New England.
By 00:00 Zulu The cold front will be moving through the eastern offshore waters.
By 06:00 Zulu A warm front extending through Lake Huron to central Lake Erie will be moving eastward. A lee-side trough will develop behind the cold front in the eastern Appalachians.
By 13:00 Zulu The warm front will reach from southeastern Ontario through eastern Lake Ontario to western Connecticut.

lo: OutlookVFR. wind.

Sky clear
At 22:00 Zulu Clouds scattered to broken, layer at 12000 feet MSL, tops at 14000 feet MSL

s-cntrl-ny: OutlookVFR.

Clouds scattered, layer at 03000 feet MSL
After 22:00 Zulu, layer at 05000 feet MSL
After 02:00 Zulu Clouds scattered to broken, layer at 14000 feet MSL, tops at 16000 feet MSL

Figure 2.4
PDF forecast output produced with the XSL FO style sheet.

A Style Sheet to Produce WML

WML is a markup designed for wireless applications. It is an XML presentation markup for cell phones, personal digital assistants, pagers, and other devices that may link to a data source, such as a Web site, with a wireless radio connection.

The primary design point for WML is this. The devices that display it have small screens, little memory, restricted processing power, and limited input mechanisms. WML emphasizes navigation among small portions of data. The wireless connection discourages making many transactions with the data source to retrieve the data. WML therefore provides markup to place all the small data portions and the navigation among them into a single document.

The style sheet for producing WML has some very different structures from the prior two style sheets. This is because it reduces the major sections into many small pages, or *cards*, for the portable display. It produces two content pages that assist the reader in finding and navigating those pieces. Let's see how it works.

The `xsl:output-method` element in the style sheet header declares the WML document type that will appear in the XML document type declaration of the result.

WML requires

```
<?xml version='1.0'?>
<xsl:stylesheet version="1.0"
 xmlns:xsl="http://www.w3.org/1999/XSL/Transform">

  <xsl:strip-space elements="*"/>

  <xsl:output method="xml"
   doctype-public="-//WAPFORUM//DTD WML 1.3//EN"
   doctype-system="http://www.wapforum.org/DTD/wml13.dtd"/>
```

The `title` variable declaration defines title text used by more than one template in the document. The templates use a dollar sign before the name, `$title`, to refer to the variable:

```
<xsl:variable name="title">
  <xsl:value-of
   select="/wx/area-forecast/@source"/>
  <xsl:text> FA </xsl:text>
  <xsl:value-of select="/wx/area-forecast/@day"/>
  <xsl:text> </xsl:text>
  <xsl:value-of select="/wx/area-forecast/@hour"/>
  <xsl:text>:</xsl:text>
  <xsl:value-of select="/wx/area-forecast/@minute"/>
  <xsl:text>Z</xsl:text>
</xsl:variable>
```

WSFO stands for Weather Service Forecast Office. The office identifier comes to the template as parameter `oid`. The `<xsl:choose>` element selects the correct translation of the forecast office identifier into a place name. This example shows only one translation:

```
<xsl:template name="wsfo">
  <xsl:param name="oid"/>
  <xsl:choose>
    <xsl:when test="$oid='BOSC'">
      <xsl:text>Boston</xsl:text>
    </xsl:when>
    <xsl:otherwise>
      <xsl:value-of select="$oid"/>
    </xsl:otherwise>
  </xsl:choose>
</xsl:template>
```

This template formats times. The Z stands for Zulu. It is a designation that indicates that the time is expressed in Greenwich Mean Time (GMT). GMT is the time in Greenwich, England. Aviators and forecasters use it because it allows time comparisons and calculations independent of changes in time zones:

```
<xsl:template name="time">
  <xsl:value-of select="@hour"/>
  <xsl:text>:</xsl:text>
  <xsl:choose>
    <xsl:when test="@minute">
      <xsl:value-of select="@minute"/>
    </xsl:when>
    <xsl:otherwise>
      <xsl:text>00</xsl:text>
    </xsl:otherwise>
  </xsl:choose>
  <xsl:text>Z</xsl:text>
</xsl:template>
```

The root rule outputs the WML root element. The template that follows, matching the `area-forecast` element, outputs the structure of the remainder of the document.

The top card of the template, output here, contains the forecast identifier, a link to the cloud and weather portions, and links to each forecast period in the synopsis. The link to the cloud and weather portion may be navigated by pressing the 1 key. The 9 key links the first card of the synopsis.

The template invokes processing of the synopsis, clouds, and weather portions after closing the initial indexing card:

```
<xsl:template match="/">
  <wml>
    <xsl:apply-templates/>
  </wml>
</xsl:template>

<xsl:template match="area-forecast">
  <card id="fa">
    <p>
      <xsl:value-of select="$title"/>
      <xsl:text> expires </xsl:text>
      <xsl:value-of select="@expire-day"/>
      <xsl:text> </xsl:text>
      <xsl:value-of select="@expire-hour"/>
```

```
        <xsl:text>:00Z</xsl:text>
      </p>
      <xsl:apply-templates select="area"/>
      <xsl:apply-templates select="sigs"/>
      <p>
        <a>
          <xsl:attribute name="href">#cwx</xsl:attribute>
          <xsl:attribute name="accesskey">1</xsl:attribute>
          <xsl:text>Clds/Wx</xsl:text>
        </a>
      </p>
      <xsl:apply-templates select="synopsis" mode="toc"/>
      <p><a>
        <xsl:attribute name="href">#syn1</xsl:attribute>
        <xsl:attribute name="accesskey">9</xsl:attribute>
        <xsl:text>next</xsl:text>
      </a></p>
    </card>
    <xsl:apply-templates select="synopsis" mode="synopsis"/>
    <xsl:call-template name="cwx-index"/>
    <xsl:apply-templates select="clouds-wx"/>
  </xsl:template>
```

The list of regions defining the area for the forecast will appear separated by commas in a single paragraph:

```
<xsl:template match="area[parent::area-forecast]">
  <p>
    <xsl:apply-templates/>
  </p>
</xsl:template>

<xsl:template match="region">
  <xsl:value-of select="@id"/>
  <xsl:if test="position()!=last()">
    <xsl:text>, </xsl:text>
  </xsl:if>
</xsl:template>
```

A paragraph places the significant weather AIRMET identifier on a line by itself:

```
<xsl:template match="sigs">
  <p>
```

```
      <xsl:text>Airmet </xsl:text>
      <xsl:value-of select="@id"/>
    </p>
  </xsl:template>
```

The toc mode matches forecast periods of the synopsis to produce a link for each one. The `<xsl:number>` element produces the quick access key for each period, from 2 to 8. Recall that the 9 key was reserved to navigate to the next card. The anchor for each link contains the time of the forecast period:

```
<xsl:template match="synopsis" mode="toc">
  <xsl:apply-templates
   select="at|by|from|after" mode="toc"/>
</xsl:template>

<xsl:template name="syn-id">
  <xsl:text>syn</xsl:text>
  <xsl:number value="position()"/>
</xsl:template>

<xsl:template match="at|by|from|after" mode="toc">
  <p>
    <a>
      <xsl:attribute name="href">
        <xsl:text>#</xsl:text>
        <xsl:call-template name="syn-id"/>
      </xsl:attribute>
      <xsl:if test="position() &lt; 7">
        <xsl:attribute name="accesskey">
          <xsl:number value="position()+1"/>
        </xsl:attribute>
      </xsl:if>
      <xsl:value-of select="name()"/>
      <xsl:text> </xsl:text>
      <xsl:call-template name="time"/>
    </a>
  </p>
</xsl:template>
```

This template places a link associated with the 1 key on the cards defined for each of the forecast periods and on the card defined for the clouds and weather forecast index:

```
<xsl:template name="home-link">
  <p><a>
```

```
      <xsl:attribute name="href">#fa</xsl:attribute>
      <xsl:attribute name="accesskey">1</xsl:attribute>
      <xsl:value-of select="$title"/>
    </a></p>
  </xsl:template>
```

The style sheet now defines templates to output the synopsis. The second template will match each time an `at`, `by`, `from`, or `after` element appears in the synopsis. It will output a card for each forecast period matched. Each card contains a 9 link to the following card. The last of the cards for the synopsis contains a 9 link to the clouds and weather portion:

```
<xsl:template match="synopsis" mode="synopsis">
  <xsl:apply-templates
   select="at|by|from|after" mode="synopsis"/>
</xsl:template>

<xsl:template match="at|by|from|after" mode="synopsis">
  <card>
    <xsl:attribute name="id">
      <xsl:call-template name="syn-id"/>
    </xsl:attribute>
    <xsl:call-template name="home-link"/>
    <p><b>
    <xsl:text>Synopsis </xsl:text>
    <xsl:choose>
       <xsl:when test="name()='from'">
         <xsl:text>From </xsl:text>
       </xsl:when>
       <xsl:when test="name()='by'">
         <xsl:text>By </xsl:text>
       </xsl:when>
       <xsl:when test="name()='at'">
         <xsl:text>At </xsl:text>
       </xsl:when>
       <xsl:when test="name()='after'">
         <xsl:text>After </xsl:text>
       </xsl:when>
    </xsl:choose>
    <xsl:call-template name="time"/>
    </b></p>
```

```
    <xsl:apply-templates
     select="condition" mode="synopsis"/>
    <p>
      <a>
        <xsl:attribute name="href">
          <xsl:choose>
            <xsl:when test="position() = last()">
              <xsl:text>#cwx</xsl:text>
            </xsl:when>
            <xsl:otherwise>
              <xsl:text>#syn</xsl:text>
              <xsl:number value="position() + 1"/>
            </xsl:otherwise>
          </xsl:choose>
        </xsl:attribute>
        <xsl:attribute name="accesskey">9</xsl:attribute>
        next
      </a>
    </p>
  </card>
</xsl:template>

<xsl:template match="condition" mode="synopsis">
    <p><xsl:value-of select="text()"/></p>
</xsl:template>
```

Both the index and the individual card templates call the template named `cwx-id` to set link references and targets. The template manufactures the identifier from the position of the element within the clouds and weather portion of the forecast:

```
<xsl:template name="cwx-id">
  <xsl:text>cwx</xsl:text>
  <xsl:number value="position()"/>
</xsl:template>
```

These templates output an index to the detailed forecasts for each region in the forecast area. The sample data contains two regions: one for Lake Ontario and one for south-central New York:

```
<xsl:template name="cwx-index">
  <card>
```

```
      <xsl:attribute name="id">cwx</xsl:attribute>
      <xsl:call-template name="home-link"/>
      <p><b>
        <xsl:text>Clds/Wx valid until </xsl:text>
        <xsl:value-of select="/wx/area-forecast/@wx-expire"/>
        <xsl:text>:00Z</xsl:text>
      </b></p>
      <xsl:apply-templates select="clouds-wx" mode="toc"/>
      <p><a>
        <xsl:attribute name="href">#cwx1</xsl:attribute>
        <xsl:attribute name="accesskey">9</xsl:attribute>
        <xsl:text>next</xsl:text>
      </a></p>
    </card>
  </xsl:template>

  <xsl:template match="clouds-wx" mode="toc">
    <p><a>
      <xsl:attribute name="href">
        <xsl:text>#</xsl:text>
        <xsl:call-template name="cwx-id"/>
      </xsl:attribute>
      <xsl:if test="position() &lt; 7">
        <xsl:attribute name="accesskey">
          <xsl:value-of select="position()+1"/>
        </xsl:attribute>
      </xsl:if>
      <xsl:apply-templates select="area"/>
    </a></p>
  </xsl:template>
```

The `clouds-wx` template outputs a card for each regional detailed forecast. The 1 key links back to the index. The 9 key links to the next card. The conditional test `<xml:if test="position() != last()">` omits the next card link on the last card:

```
  <xsl:template match="clouds-wx">
    <card>
      <xsl:attribute name="id">
        <xsl:call-template name="cwx-id"/>
      </xsl:attribute>
```

```
      <p>
        <a>
          <xsl:attribute name="href">#cwx</xsl:attribute>
          <xsl:attribute name="accesskey">1</xsl:attribute>
          <xsl:text>Clds/Wx</xsl:text>
        </a>
      </p>
      <p>
        <b>
          <xsl:apply-templates select="area"/>
          <xsl:text>: </xsl:text>
        </b>
        <xsl:apply-templates select="outlook"/>
      </p>
      <p>
        <xsl:apply-templates select="sky" mode="clouds-wx"/>
        <xsl:apply-templates
         select="condition" mode="clouds-wx"/>
      </p>
      <xsl:apply-templates
       select="at|by|from|after" mode="clouds-wx"/>
      <xsl:if test="position() != last()">
        <p>
          <a>
            <xsl:attribute name="href">
              <xsl:text>#cwx</xsl:text>
              <xsl:number value="position() + 1"/>
            </xsl:attribute>
            <xsl:attribute name="accesskey">9</xsl:attribute>
            next
          </a>
        </p>
      </xsl:if>
    </card>
  </xsl:template>
```

These four templates format lists of the conditions, areas, and outlook factors that appear on each of the cloud and weather forecast cards:

```
  <xsl:template match="condition" mode="clouds-wx">
    <xsl:value-of select="text()"/>
```

```
    <xsl:if test="following-sibling::area">
      <xsl:text>, </xsl:text>
    </xsl:if>
  </xsl:template>

  <xsl:template match="area[parent::clouds-wx]">
    <xsl:value-of select="@id"/>
    <xsl:if test="following-sibling::area">
      <xsl:text>, </xsl:text>
    </xsl:if>
  </xsl:template>

  <xsl:template match="outlook">
    Outlook <b><xsl:value-of select="@conditions"/>. </b>
    <xsl:apply-templates/>
  </xsl:template>

  <xsl:template match="factor">
    <xsl:value-of select="text()"/>
    <xsl:if test="position() != last()">
      <xsl:text>, </xsl:text>
    </xsl:if>
  </xsl:template>
```

Each predicted change in weather appears in a separate paragraph. The nature and time of the predicted weather change begins the paragraph in bold:

```
  <xsl:template match="at|by|from|after" mode="clouds-wx">
    <p>
      <b>
        <xsl:choose>
           <xsl:when test="name()='from'">
             <xsl:text>Frm </xsl:text>
           </xsl:when>
           <xsl:when test="name()='by'">
             <xsl:text>By </xsl:text>
           </xsl:when>
           <xsl:when test="name()='at'">
             <xsl:text>At </xsl:text>
           </xsl:when>
```

```
        <xsl:when test="name()='after'">
          <xsl:text>Aft </xsl:text>
        </xsl:when>
      </xsl:choose>
      <xsl:call-template name="time"/>
    </b>
    <xsl:text> </xsl:text>
    <xsl:apply-templates mode="clouds-wx"/>
  </p>
</xsl:template>

<xsl:template match="sky" mode="clouds-wx">
  <xsl:value-of select="@cover"/>
  <xsl:if test="@height">
    <xsl:text> </xsl:text>
    <xsl:value-of select="@height"/>
  </xsl:if>
  <xsl:if test="@tops">
    <xsl:text>, tops </xsl:text>
    <xsl:value-of select="@tops"/>
  </xsl:if>
</xsl:template>
```

The rule to suppress any text from the source not explicitly called for completes the style sheet.

```
  <xsl:template match="text()"/>
</xsl:stylesheet>
```

The style sheet enables a small wireless device to receive materially the same weather information available from a Web browser or in print form from a server on the Internet. Imagine getting detailed weather forecasts on your wrist.

Figure 2.5 reproduces a series of screen shots of a phone emulated by the UP.SDK WML emulator program provided by Openwave Systems, Inc. You can find the emulator at the company's developer support Web site, `http://developer.openwave.com`.

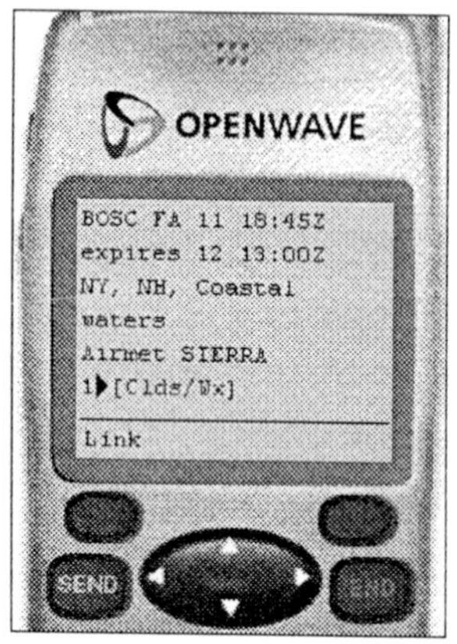

The initial display of the forecast. Scroll down.

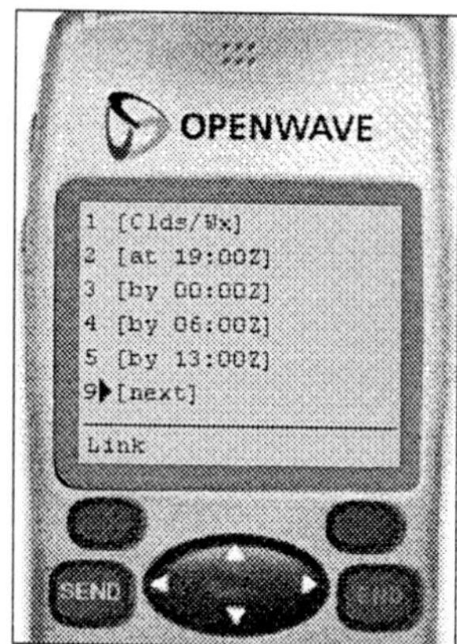

Menu provides access to portions of the synopsis. Press 9.

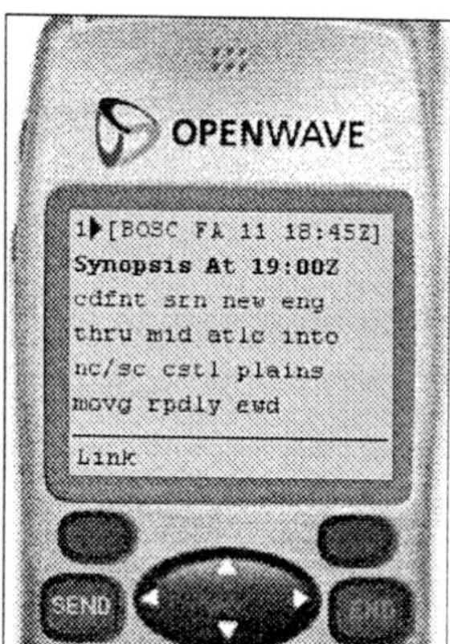

The first portion of the synopsis. Press 9.

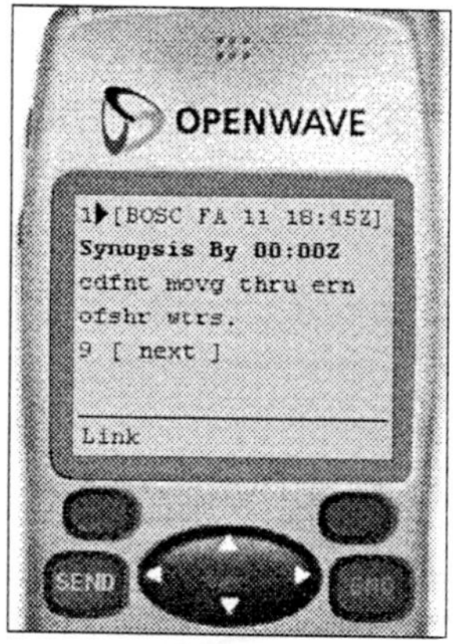

Location of the front at midnight in England. Press 1.

Figure 2.5

Storyboard interaction with the WML presentation.

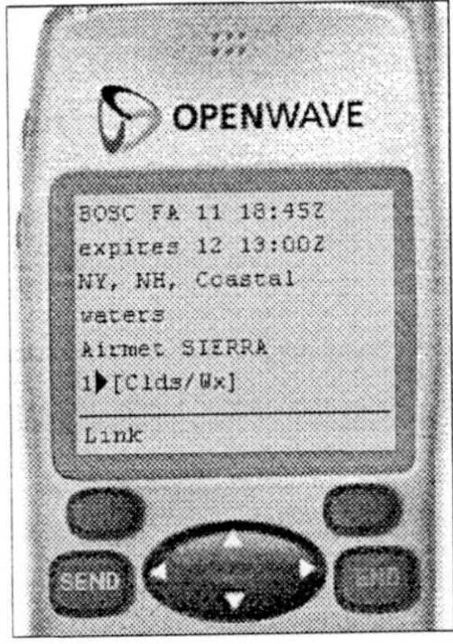

Return to the initial presentation. Press 1.

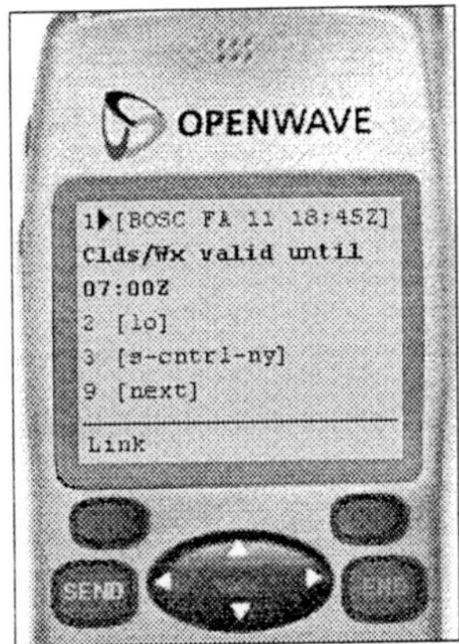

Forecast details menu. Press 9.

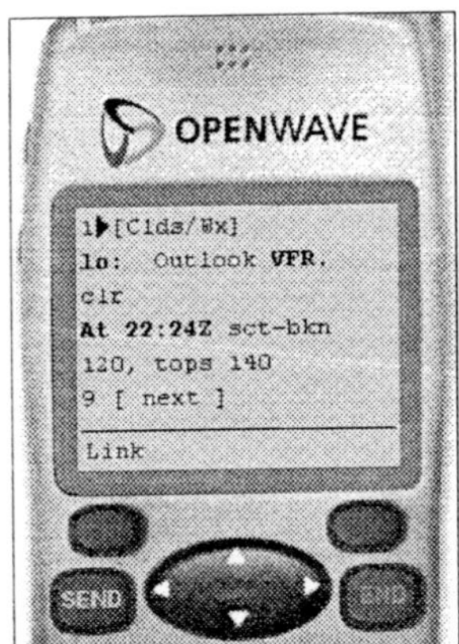

Detailed forecast for Lake Ontario. Press 9.

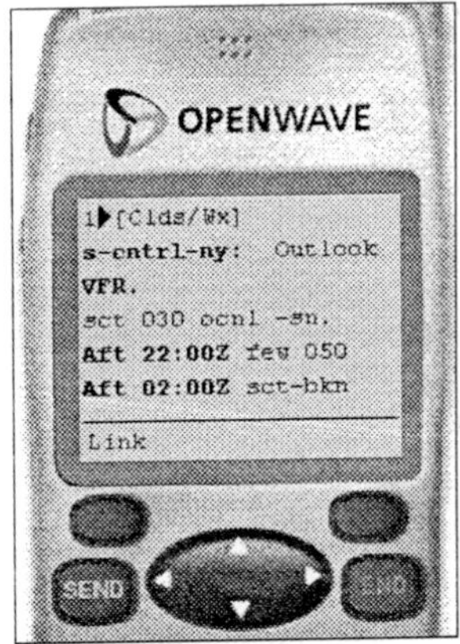

Detailed forecast for south-central New York.

Figure 2.5 Continued

Images of UP.SDK courtesy Openwave Systems Inc. "Openwave," the Openwave logo, and UP.SDK are trademarks of Openwave Systems Inc. All rights reserved.

Summary

You have now seen three presentations from a single markup. This is the power of separating content from presentation. The markup provides rich information about the meaning of the data. That enables a great deal of flexibility in transformation. Presentation can omit or reorder elements, highlight elements, combine them, change their format, group them or separate them visually, and tailor the appearance for the device on which they will appear.

All the examples in this book illustrate content markup translated to style. The advantages of that approach should become more and more evident with each new example. Chapter 4 presents a simple first example that you can type and try for yourself. Before that, you'll read some discussion of the tools available to process and display XSL Formatting Objects.

CHAPTER 3
Tools and Implementations

This is a brief review of many sources of XSL information, tools, and implementations available at the time of writing. No such review printed in a book can be completely up to date. Most, or at least many, of the things mentioned here have a reasonable chance of surviving at least as long as there is interest in this book. Developments occurring after this writing will be missing. The future will be just like today, only different.

No review of resources, tools, and implementations can hope to be complete. Enough pointers should be here to help you find a good deal of what is available for XSL. Certainly, you will be able to use the "Formatters" section to find and download a formatter that will help you experiment with the examples in this book.

Online Resources

The first thing to know about tools and implementations for XSL is `www.w3.org/Style/XSL/`. This Web site maintained by the World Wide Web Consortium (W3C) contains up-to-date links to many XSL resources. New information appears from time to time. This W3C site acts as a portal for much of the best information about XSL.

A current discussion group on Yahoo! averages about 100 posts per month. The posts center around practical usage issues. The locator for that group is `http://groups.yahoo.com/group/xsl-fo/`. Subscribe to it by sending an empty mail message to `XSL-FO-subscribe@yahoogroups.com`.

The locator for the FO interest mailing list at the W3C is `http://lists.w3.org/Archives/Public/www-xsl-fo/`. This list is somewhat less active than the list at Yahoo!, but it has similar content.

The XML.org Web site hosted by Oasis at `http://www.xml.org/xml` contains a great deal of XML-related materials. It currently places CSS and XSL related links at `http://www.xml.org/xml/resources_focus_cssxslfo.shtml`.

Dave Pawson has placed many pointers about FO at `http://www.dpawson.co.uk/xsl/sect3/index.html`. He gleaned these from the XSL interest list at Mulberry Technologies, `http://www.mulberrytech.com/xsl/`. He also placed a draft of a book about FO online at `http://www.dpawson.co.uk/xsl/sect3/bk/index.html`.

Many useful articles about XML in general and XSL in particular may be found at IBM's developerWorks Web site located at `http://www.ibm.com/developerworks/xml/`.

Transform Engines

Transform engines implement the XSL Transformations (XSLT) Recommendation. This recommendation, made in November 1999, has found general utility as a language for specifying transformations from one XML language to another. It is fundamental to XSL because it is the language used to transform content markup into FO.

There are several implementations of XSLT. Most formatters now incorporate one of them to complete an end-to-end typesetting solution for XML, which means that you will not have to download a transform engine separately and integrate it with a formatter to get going with FO.

Transform engines and the formatters that incorporate them will accept a style sheet and a source document as input. The transform engines output a result document as a file. XSL processors stream the result directly into the typesetting engine to produce formatted output, such as PDF. Figure 3.1 shows the general model. The transformation step produces FO from an input source document and style sheet. The formatting step takes FO to some output. Most of the formatters mentioned in the next section will function given FO data from a separate transformation step or as complete XSL processors that directly incorporate the transformation step.

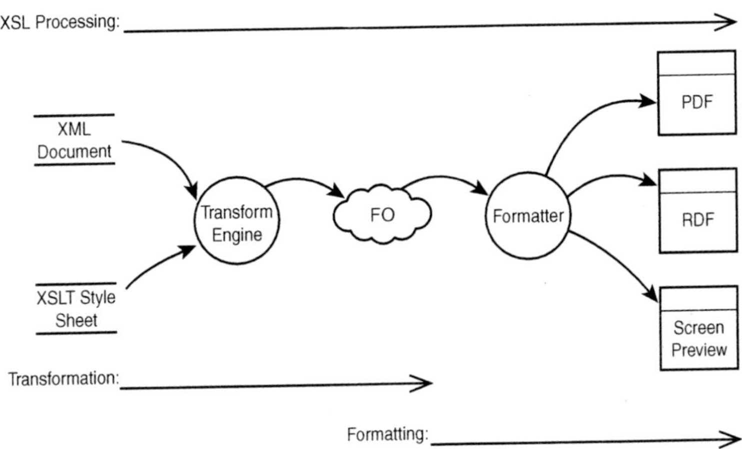

Figure 3.1
General XSL processing stream model.

The transform engines by themselves may be of interest for diagnostic purposes, experimentation, and for understanding the transformation component incorporated into a formatter. Two major transform engines are Xt and Xalan.

Xt was written by James Clark, the editor of the XSLT recommendation. It is very fast and capable. Download Xt from `www.jclark.com/xml/`.

Xalan was originally written in Java by Scott Boag at Lotus. It is now an open source project at Apache with Java and C++ implementations. You will find them at `xml.apache.org/xalan-j` and `xml.apache.org/xalan-c`.

Formatters

Formatters process XML conforming to the XSL Formatting Objects Recommendation to output some presentation form. Many formatters are available for XSL. The most supported output presentation forms are PostScript, PDF, and onscreen display.

The following sections discuss where to find several implementations and how to get them. All the formatters mentioned have evaluation versions that may be downloaded for experimentation without charge. The FOP formatter is free to download and is developed with an open source model.

Antenna House

Nearly all the examples in this book were typeset with an evaluation copy of the Antenna House formatter version 2.0.1 downloaded from `www.antennahouse.com`. Figure 3.2 shows a screen shot of the formatter in action.

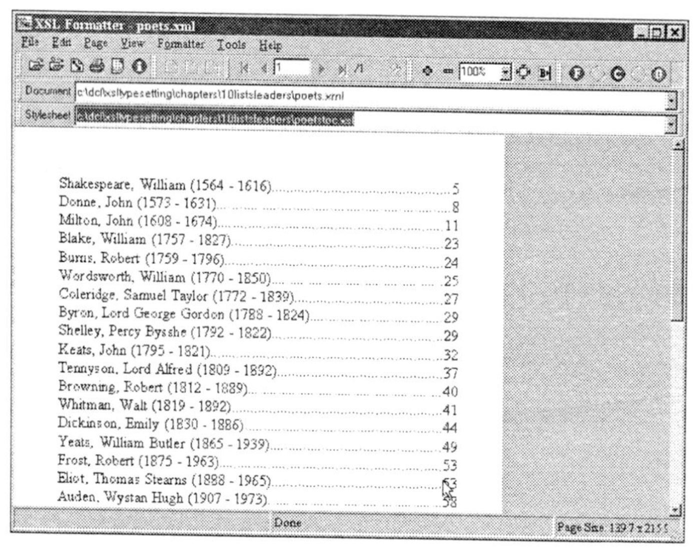

Figure 3.2

Antenna House XSL formatter screen shot.

The two fields below the menu and toolbar allow selection of a source document and a style sheet. The program displays a preview of the formatted document. The view contains tools to enlarge the display for a closer look or otherwise adjust the scaling of a page in the display. Another function will output the formatted result as a PDF file.

The program includes a configuration dialog that enables customization of all the defaults left to the formatter by the W3C recommendation. That includes the default font family, fonts for the generic font-family names, such as `serif`, the default text color, widths of `thin`, `medium`, and `thick` borders, the default page size, and so forth.

The formatter uses the Microsoft MSXML3 or MSXML4 XSLT parser that may be downloaded for the Windows platform from `msdn.microsoft.com/downloads`. Type **`MSXML`** into the search field. The Antenna House formatter may also be configured to use an external XSLT processor, in which case the FO result must go to an intermediate file.

XEP

XEP is a very capable commercial implementation of FO. It is the one that the editors of the W3C recommendation chose to typeset the PDF format version available at the W3C.

The free XEP download available from `www.renderx.com` is for experimentation only. Their literature indicates that it prints "sample" across each page and quits after typesetting a limited number of pages. To get all the benefits of these programmers' hard work, you will have to pay them.

I was unable to try the XEP formatter because the license for the evaluation version required that I accept confidential intellectual property. This was fortunately not a handicap because the Antenna House formatter was able to typeset most of the examples.

FOP

FOP is an open source effort supported by the Apache Software Foundation. It has been available since some of the earliest public drafts of the XSL recommendation. Judging from the posts to the interest lists, many people are using FOP to experiment with XSL. It is not currently as complete as either the XEP or the Antenna House formatters, especially with respect to the formatting of tables. That may have changed by the time you read this.

One feature of FOP is its support for Scalable Vector Graphics (SVG). SVG is an XML format for drawing graphs, charts, and other graphical presentations expressible using line drawing and fill. FOP will render an SVG source referred to from FO.

Download FOP from `xml.apache.org/fop`. It has a user interest mailing list that you can subscribe to by sending mail to `fop-user-subscribe@xml.apache.org`. The formatter uses the Xalan transform engine, which is included in the download.

XFC

The IBM XSL Formatting Objects Composer (XFC) was written by this author and others at IBM Research. We've tried some ambitious things with this formatter, such as implementations for `writing-mode`, `multi-property-set`, and `multi-case`. The free download may provide some value to people experimenting with FO. The alphaworks license requires a fee for any commercial use. The license bought for that fee is an as-is license that does not include any promise of support.

XFC uses the Xalan transform engine, which is included in the download. Download the processor from `www.alphaworks.ibm.com/tech/xfc`.

jFor

SourceForge hosts an open source implementation of FO as well as Apache. The jFor project outputs only Rich Text Format (RTF). RTF is useful for import into Microsoft Word or the WordPad application shipped with Microsoft Windows. You will find the project, including download links, at `sourceforge.net/projects/jfor/`. The document located at `www.jfor.org/` contains some description of the project as well.

Arbortext

Arbortext, `www.arbortext.com`, is a long-time player in the SGML formatting world that had strong participation in preparing the XSL recommendations. They produce end-to-end, complete industrial solutions for content authoring and formatting. The Arbortext Epic Editor provides structured content editing for publishing to multiple output media. The editor includes a capable implementation of FO. It enables formatting for delivery on the Web, in print, over wireless devices, or as a CD-ROM interactive application.

Editors

A simple text editor will work fine for editing XML, including XSL style sheets. A number of structured editors are available that are designed with XML in mind.

If you're using a text editor, you will sometimes have the problem of finding an error in the source, such as a missing end tag or a missing close quote. Errors of that type are known as *well-formedness errors*. They break the syntax of XML. The processing application may not be helpful in pinpointing well-formedness errors.

Microsoft Internet Explorer Version 5.5 (IE 5.5) has a mode for displaying XML content that is very helpful in pinpointing well-formedness errors. It gives the exact line where an expected end tag was not found, for example.

If you're having trouble pinpointing an error in an XML source, try loading it with IE5.5.

XSL Spy has is now a complete XSL editing environment. With version 4.4, the editor introduced an FO formatter extension based on XEP. This means that the editor will preview a style sheet with result elements in the FO namespace. XSL Spy is a commercial product. Refer to `www.xmlspy.com/` for further information about XSL Spy.

The oXygen XML editor incorporated FOP with version 1.2 so that you can generate a PDF or PostScript output directly from the editor. The oXygen editor is a commercial product. The locator for oXygen is `oxygen.sync.ro/`.

SourceForge has an open source project titled Formatting Objects Authoring (FOA), located at `foa.sourceforge.net/`. The tool has an interactive preview that uses the FOP formatter.

jCatalog Software AG sells an editor for FO that lets you graphically lay out a document. The editor will store the document as a style sheet to format input XML data. The product is called XSLFast, located at `www.xslfast.com`.

The IBM Websphere Studio Application Developer contains editors for XML and XSLT. Find that at `www.ibm.com/software/ad/studioappdev/`.

SoftQuad, recently acquired by Corel Corp., produces an XML editor called XMetal `www.xmetal.com`. This is not strictly an XSL editor, but it is highly acclaimed as a general-purpose editor for markup.

Microsoft Word

The HTML export and import functions of Microsoft Word offer some capability for XML editing. Word has a styling feature that enables you to name combinations of font, paragraph, layout, and alignment settings. Word will output a class attribute on paragraphs containing the name of the style for that paragraph. It outputs CSS definitions that match each class. Following is an example of a CSS definition output by MS Word:

```
p.HA, li.HA, div.HA
        {mso-style-name:HA;
        mso-style-parent:"";
        margin-top:0in;
        margin-right:0in;
        margin-bottom:12.0pt;
        margin-left:0in;
        line-height:12.0pt;
        mso-pagination:widow-orphan;
        font-size:12.0pt;
        mso-bidi-font-size:10.0pt;
        font-family:Courier;
        mso-fareast-font-family:"Times New Roman";
        mso-bidi-font-family:"Times New Roman";
        font-weight:bold;
        mso-bidi-font-weight:normal;}
```

This style definition will match for all `<p>`, `<li>`, or `<div>` elements that have `class="HA."` The mso-prefixed names are Microsoft proprietary names. Word uses those to capture internal settings not otherwise expressible with CSS. The other settings, such as `font-weight`, `line-height`, and `margin-top`, are all CSS defined. The following HTML output typesets a title element using the properties defined by the style named `HA`:

```
<p class=HA>(b)Tools and Implementations</p>
```

The bottom line of all this is that you can apply the style settings within a Microsoft Word document, save that as HTML, and then use a style sheet to convert it to FO or any other XML result. A style sheet template that matched the title element just shown would look like this:

```
<xsl:template match="p[@class='HA']">
  <!— template body —>
</xsl:template>
```

SourceForge has a project called WH2FO at `wh2fo.sourceforge.net/` that accepts the Microsoft Word HTML output and produces XSL FOs.

Summary

Several viable implementations of XSL are available that you are free to download and experiment with. There are also industrial strength products that support the recommendation. If you need a robust, reliable, full implementation to support your business, you will have to pay for it. You will also find versions to freely experiment with as proof of concept or to improve your skills.

At this point, you might like to download the Antenna House evaluation copy used by the author, one of the free implementations or an evaluation copy of another commercial implementation and begin experimenting with the simple example in the next chapter, "Hello XSL World."

CHAPTER 4

Hello XSL World

It's time to dust off the keyboard and get rolling with a live example. You'll download some XSL software, type a minimal typeset XSL example, and watch it fly. This will be your first detailed look at the XSL FO language and how it is used. This chapter will let you test a processor installation and understand the basic format of XSL FO documents.

A First XML/XSL Pair

Here's the XML data that will drive your first test:

```
<?xml version='1.0'?>
<hello>Hello XSL World</hello>
```

Simple, eh? All examples from here on will leave out that repetitive first line, `<?xml version='1.0'?>`. That is the XML declaration. It should be the first line of any XML data. From now on, you fill it in.

Now here's a style sheet that will typeset that data using FO. Remember, you supply the XML declaration:

```
<xsl:stylesheet version="1.0"
 xmlns:xsl="http://www.w3.org/1999/XSL/Transform"
 xmlns:fo="http://www.w3.org/1999/XSL/Format">
  <xsl:template match="hello">
    <fo:root>
      <fo:layout-master-set>
        <fo:simple-page-master
         master-name="page">
          <fo:region-body
           region-name="body"
           margin-top="0.5in"
           margin-bottom="1in"
           margin-left="0.5in"
           margin-right="0.5in"/>
        </fo:simple-page-master>
      </fo:layout-master-set>
      <fo:page-sequence master-reference="page">
        <fo:flow flow-name="body">
          <fo:block>
            <xsl:value-of select="text()"/>
          </fo:block>
        </fo:flow>
      </fo:page-sequence>
    </fo:root>
  </xsl:template>
</xsl:stylesheet>
```

That seems like a lot of typing to typeset a few words. Let's run it and then go over the sample line by line.

The previous chapter described tools for processing and displaying XSL. Download something, install it, and test that it works using this example.

Run the transform and compose the result. If you name the sample XML `hello.xml` and the sample style sheet `hello.xsl`, your command to display FO might be **xfc hello.xml hello.xsl**. With FOP the command line would be **fop -xml hello.xml -xsl hello.xsl -awt.** The result should look something like Figure 4.1.

Figure 4.1
Another FO presentation is born.

Let's look in detail at the example.

Analyzing the Code

The style sheet declaration is boilerplate. It must appear exactly as shown:

```
<xsl:stylesheet version="1.0"
 xmlns:xsl="http://www.w3.org/1999/XSL/Transform"
 xmlns:fo="http://www.w3.org/1999/XSL/Format">
```

The first line provides the style sheet element that encloses the entire style sheet. The second and third lines declare namespaces used in the style sheet.

The first namespace is the one for XSL transform. We have chosen the namespace prefix `xsl` for elements that compose directives about the transformation.

The second namespace is the one for XSL FO. We have chosen the namespace prefix `fo` for elements that compose directives for formatting.

As you look at the sample, you will see a mix of elements in the transform namespace, such as `xsl:template`, and elements in the FO namespace, such as `fo:root`. The namespace simply aids the XSL transform processor in distinguishing transform directives from the stuff it will output—FO in this case.

Use these three lines as boilerplate. Remember to close the transform with the end tag for the style sheet element, `</xsl:stylesheet>`.

The first line following the style sheet declaration begins a transform template, `xsl:template`. A transform template matches some part of the input XML as a selection. This template matches the single `hello` element in the input.

We call everything contained within the template the *template body*. The transform will output the template body whenever it matches something in the input. The transform will execute any transform directives in the body as it encounters them.

The only transform directive in the body of the template in this example is `xsl:value-of`:

```
<fo:block>
  <xsl:value-of select="text()"/>
</fo:block>
```

The `xsl:value-of` directive evaluates the XML data referred to by its `select` attribute. In this case, `select="text()"` causes the `xsl:value-of` directive to evaluate the text of the matched input. Here it evaluates the text of the `hello` element: Hello XSL World.

Note

If you're familiar with XSL transform, this discussion is review. If you're not familiar with it, be aware that the explanation so far forms the primary basis of what you need to know about transforms to read the examples in this book. The rest is just FO.

Now let's look at the body of the template more closely to discuss the formatting objects.

The body of the template that matches `hello` contains a single `<fo:root>`. This is the FO equivalent of the `<HTML>` element. It brackets the entire output. The transform processor will add the FO namespace declaration to this element.

The FO root element contains two child elements. Those are the `layout-master-set` and the `page-sequence`. Every FO data stream will contain one `layout-master-set`. It may contain one or more instances of `page-sequence`. The `layout-master-set` must come first so formatters can efficiently process the data stream.

The `layout-master-set` contains declarations of page layouts. Let's examine it more closely:

```
<fo:layout-master-set>
  <fo:simple-page-master
   master-name="page">
    <fo:region-body
     region-name="body"
     margin-top="0.5in"
     margin-bottom="1in"
```

```
        margin-left="0.5in"
        margin-right="0.5in"/>
    </fo:simple-page-master>
  </fo:layout-master-set>
```

The content of the `layout-master-set` is a set of layout masters. This example defines only one layout master. Many more could be specified. The `master-name` property uniquely identifies each layout master. The single master declared here has the inventive name `page`. Figure 4.2 illustrates the basic structure of a formatting objects document and shows the references in the `page-sequence` to elements of the `layout-master-set`.

This page layout declaration describes a simple page with margins all around. The top, left, and right margins are half an inch. The bottom margin has a width of one inch. Chapter 8, "Page and Style," covers page layouts in great detail. This single master will serve you well until that time. (It's always nice to have a master who serves.)

The `page-sequence` follows the `layout-master-set` and contains the actual textual content of the pages:

```
<fo:page-sequence master-reference="page">
  <fo:flow flow-name="body">
    <fo:block>
      <xsl:value-of select="text()"/>
    </fo:block>
  </fo:flow>
</fo:page-sequence>
```

You will look later at elements that define content that repeats on every page. For now, use a single `flow` element within the `page-sequence`. The `flow` element defines the content that will flow from page to page.

The formatter places as much of the content of the `flow` as it can fit onto one page. It then finds an appropriate place to end the page and start a new one. It continues placing the remaining content on a new page until that is filled. It goes on in this way, typesetting one or one hundred pages, until it has exhausted all the content within the `flow`.

The formatter does not place the content of the flow anywhere on the page. It places it within a particular region of the page. You will recall that the `simple-page-master` contained a region-body whose `region-name` attribute had the value `body`.

The flow has a `flow-name` attribute, which also has the value `body`. This is not an accident. The formatter matches the `flow-name` to a region in the master selected by the page-sequence. That is the region where the flowed text appears.

The `master-reference` attribute on the `page-sequence` matched the `master-name` attribute on the single `simple-page-master` defined in the `layout-master-set`.

You will learn more about this in Chapter 8. Let it suffice for now that the `page-sequence` selects a master by matching the value of `master-reference` to a `master-name`. The `flow` selects a region by matching the value of `flow-name` to a `region-name`. Figure 4.2 shows the basic structure of an XSL FO document. It contains annotations to point out the matching attributes in the layout-master-set and page-sequence.

```
<fo:root
 <fo:layout-master-set>
  <fo:simple-page-master
  master-name="page">
   <fo:region-body
   region-name="body">
...
  </fo:simple-page-master>
 </fo:layout-master-set>
 <fo:page-sequence master-reference="page">
  <fo:flow flow-name="body">
...
  </fo:flow>
 </fo:page-sequence>
</fo:root>
```

Figure 4.2

Matching masters and regions.

The content in the example, the part inside the `flow`, is a single `block` element with some text inside. A block is equivalent to one paragraph of text. The paragraphs of this book, for example, would be coded in FO as blocks with space before or after them.

An FO `block` element may contain zero or a few dozen words or more. It doesn't matter how many. The formatter will break those words into lines of text and stack those lines into a paragraph. Much of the rest of this book is about the content of those blocks.

A Style Sheet for the Root Rule

This book develops quite a few style sheets, just about all of them can use the definition for the layout-master-set developed here for the Hello XSL World example. Listing 4.1 gives the content of an XSL file named `rootrule.xsl` that many of the examples in the following chapters include avoiding repetition. This may be the single most useful style sheet in the entire book:

Listing 4.1 *Root Rule Defines a Reusable Layout-Master-Set*

```
<?xml version='1.0'?>
<xsl:stylesheet version="1.0"
 xmlns:xsl="http://www.w3.org/1999/XSL/Transform"
 xmlns:fo="http://www.w3.org/1999/XSL/Format">

  <xsl:template match="/">
    <fo:root>
      <fo:layout-master-set>
        <fo:simple-page-master
         master-name="page">
          <fo:region-body
           region-name="body"
           margin-top="0.5in"
           margin-bottom="1in"
           margin-left="0.5in"
           margin-right="0.5in"/>
        </fo:simple-page-master>
      </fo:layout-master-set>
      <fo:page-sequence master-reference="page">
        <fo:flow flow-name="body">
          <xsl:apply-templates/>
        </fo:flow>
      </fo:page-sequence>
    </fo:root>
  </xsl:template>

</xsl:stylesheet>
```

The template matches the root of the input and outputs the root of the FO result. The `apply-templates` command processes the remainder of the input inside of the flow. This will not cover the needs of every document, but it covers the needs of many.

The XSL include mechanism will bring this definition into many of the examples we develop in later chapters. The line to include this file looks like this:

```
<xsl:include href="rootrule.xsl"/>
```

Summary

That is the extent of this simple XSL example. It has provided an introduction to the two major sections of an FO data stream: the `layout-master-set` and the `page-sequence`. You have seen a simple page layout definition that defines a body region with some margins. You watched the formatter place the content of a flow within the body region and display it on the page.

The last section, A Style Sheet for the Root Rule, developed a style sheet component called `rootrule.xsl` that subsequent chapters of the book will use in examples to avoid repetition.

If you have been able to format the Hello XSL World example, you now have the tools necessary to work with all the remaining examples in the book. In the next chapter, you'll learn about the many ways FO will let you decorate a block and the text within it.

CHAPTER 5

Color, Fonts, and Rules

If you ask me what made the Xerox STAR, Apple Macintosh, and Microsoft Windows the way of the present, it wasn't pointing and clicking with a mouse. It wasn't that maze of overlapping rectangles we call windows. It was fonts and color.

Green screens were ghastly. Typewriter text marched in lines as pedantic as starched white shirts, dark ties, and horn-rimmed glasses. It was color and fonts that put a computer in every middle-class teenage bedroom. Do you think it was the applications? No. Instant messaging is a frill. Put instant messaging on a green screen with a Ctrl+G bell. No one but the geeks in the math lab would touch it.

With that in mind, we'd better figure out how to make our XML angle brackets run racy in red, slip on stripes, and tango in Tahoma. We'll make a sample document and manipulate the style sheet to put XSL fonts, colors, and rules through their paces.

A Bulletin

The example to motivate our further explorations of style is this slightly irreverent bulletin from the fictional Society for Legends and Olde Stories.

Bulletin for a Fictional Society
They are currently busy recounting heroic Irish legends. We find the famous Deirdre of the Sorrows lamenting her beloved Naisi. Fergus swears vengeance for his honor and for the sons of Usna. Maeve, queen of Connacht covets the brown bull of Quelgny. The fairy Fedelma warns Maeve about the unstoppable warrior of Ulster, Cuchulain.

Listing 5.1 has the content of the bulletin. These stories are told in T. W. Rolleston's *Celtic Myths and Legends*, published by Dover. They're classics in some circles, as classic as the legends of the Greeks.

Listing 5.1 *Bulletin of the Society for Legends and Olde Stories*

```
<?xml version="1.0" ?>
 <bulletin number="7" year="2002">
  <theme>Heroic tales of Ireland</theme>
  <old-business dateline="April">
   <item>
     <headline>
      <character>Deirdre</character>
      tells of her sorrows
     </headline>
     <story>
      <character>Naisi</character>
      fought with honor. We lived in peace at
      <place>Glen Etive</place>
      . For my sake
      <character>Conor</character>
       murdered my only love.
      </story>
     </item>
       <headline>
        <character>Fergus</character>
        rails against
        <character>Conor</character>
       </headline>
       <story>
        <quote>Leacherous betrayer, your foul, wanton massacre blackens
         my kin with blood of fair youth. Treacherous drunkard, I shall
         make of my sword a spit to turn you before the fire.</quote>
       </story>
      </item>
     </old-business>
 <news>
  <item>
```

Listing 5.1 *(continued)*

```
    <headline>Brown bull gets royal attention</headline>
    <story>
     In
     <place>Quelgny</place>
     ,
     <character>Dara</character>
     , son of the famous
     <character>Fachtna</character>
     , displayed the finest bull ever seen in
     <place>Ulster</place>
     .
     <quote>His back is broad as a football field. He's savage and mighty
     as a storm tossed sea,</quote>
     said the steward,
     <character>mac Roth</character>
     .
     <quote>
     I wouldn't trade him for all the land in
      <place>Connacht</place>
      ,
      </quote>
      said.
      <character>Dara</character>
      .
     </story>
   </item>
  </news>
  <up-and-coming dateline="August">
   <item>
    <story>
     <character>Maeve</character>
     and
     <character>Fergus</character>
     bond to raid
     <place>Ulster</place>
     .
     <character>Ailell</character>
     tags along.
    </story>
   </item>
   <item>
    <story>
```

Listing 5.1 *(continued)*

```
      <character>Fedelma</character>
      the prophetess warns
      <character>Maeve</character>
      of
      <character>Cuchulain</character>
      .
      <quote>A stripling young and modest, but in battle a dragon. He
      doth wondrous feats with his weapons. By him your slain shall lie
      thickly.</quote>
     </story>
    </item>
   </up-and-coming>
   <queries>
    <query>
     Wanted. Original Editions by
     <author>Standish James O'Grady</author>
     (
     <dates>1846-1928</dates>
     ).
     <title>History of Ireland - Heroic Period</title>
     . Two volumes published
     <date>1878</date>
     and
     <date>1881</date>
     . Also
     <title>The Triumph and the Passing of Cuchulain</title>
     published
     <date>1919</date>
     .
    </query>
   </queries>
  </bulletin>
```

The markup for the bulletin is content markup. Tags such as `<old-business>`, `<news>`, `<headline>`, and `<story>` denote parts of the content. Tags such as `<character>` and `<place>` denote content with special meaning.

The society cares about things such as authors, characters, places, dates, and titles. It doesn't care about bold and italic, `<H1>`, or `<DIV>`. It certainly doesn't care about `<block>` and `<wrapper>`. Content tags have meaning to the consumers of the content and little to do with presentation.

The content tags facilitate searching. If a `<title>` and a `<place>` are both presented in italic, the `<i>` tag does not distinguish the two. A society librarian could easily search for all the places mentioned in last year's bulletins. The search is for everything contained in a `<place>` element. If these were contained in `<i>` elements, the search would find titles and any other italicized content as well.

Users of XML customize markup to form meaningful tags that distinguish portions of the content important to them. XSL does the job of translating content markup into presentation. That's what we're about to do here. Let's get started.

Skeletons in the Closet

You can't get anywhere with this markup until you have an XSL transform to put it into FO. Before that, you must have some idea of the layout you would like for the document. With a layout in mind, you can rough in a skeleton of the transform. The skeleton forms the basic structure. It isn't pretty to look at, yet. We'll keep it in the closet until we dress it up a little. It provides a foundation from which to apply styling.

The layout for the bulletin will be very simple. It provides a title in a banner at the top, together with issue identification. The theme of the newsletter appears next, followed by the major sections—the old business, news, up and coming, and queries. Each major section gets a heading. The items in the first two sections each get a title before their content.

That simple design yields several basic styles:

Base—Settings applicable to most of the document

Title—For the title of the newsletter

Issue—For the number and year of the bulletin

Theme—For the topic below the banner

Section—For section headings

Item—For item titles

Content—For the body text within the newsletter

Query— For the query section.

You'll use the XSLT `attribute-set` element to encapsulate property settings used in the style sheet. Empty attribute sets hold a place for later styling. The style sheet contains one for each of the basic styles just listed. Each attribute set differs only in the value of the `name` attribute. Nothing more is needed, now. You want to get the basic structure working before fiddling with properties to style the document.

```
<xsl:attribute-set name="base"/>
<xsl:attribute-set name="title"/>
<xsl:attribute-set name="theme"/>
<xsl:attribute-set name="section"/>
<xsl:attribute-set name="item"/>
<xsl:attribute-set name="content"/>
<xsl:attribute-set name="query-box"/>
```

The following template rule outputs the layout masters, now familiar from Chapter 4, "Hello XSL World." New content within the `flow` element outputs the banner using two `block` elements. The first `block` contains text generated by the style sheet for the title of the newsletter. The second `block` contains the issue identification. The attribute `xsl:use-attribute-sets` on each of those blocks applies style properties from the attribute set definitions. Web page designers will find a familiar pattern here. In Web design, HTML elements tagged with the `class` attribute refer to styles defined in a CSS style sheet.

```
<xsl:template match="bulletin">
  <fo:root>
    <fo:layout-master-set>
      <fo:simple-page-master
       master-name="page">
        <fo:region-body
         region-name="body"
         margin-top="0.5in"
         margin-bottom="1in"
         margin-left="0.5in"
         margin-right="0.5in"/>
      </fo:simple-page-master>
    </fo:layout-master-set>
    <fo:page-sequence master-reference="page">
      <fo:flow flow-name="body" xsl:use-attribute-sets="base">
        <fo:block xsl:use-attribute-sets="title">
          Bulletin of the Society for Legends and Olde Stories
        </fo:block>
        <fo:block xsl:use-attribute-sets="issue">
          Issue <xsl:value-of select="@number"/>,
          <xsl:value-of select="@year"/>
        </fo:block>
        <xsl:apply-templates/>
      </fo:flow>
    </fo:page-sequence>
  </fo:root>
</xsl:template>
```

The next template matches the `theme` element and outputs its content within a `block` styled as `theme`. In an HTML style sheet, the `block` element might be a `p`, or `div`. The `use-attribute-sets` attribute would be the `class` attribute.

```
<xsl:template match="theme">
  <fo:block xsl:use-attribute-sets="theme">
    <xsl:apply-templates/>
  </fo:block>
</xsl:template>
```

The rest of the templates in the style sheet have the same structure. The content of the `match` attribute and the name of the attribute set change in each template.

```
<xsl:template match="old-business">
  <fo:block xsl:use-attribute-sets="section">
    From our <xsl:value-of select="@dateline"/> gathering:
  </fo:block>
  <xsl:apply-templates/>
</xsl:template>

<xsl:template match="news">
  <fo:block xsl:use-attribute-sets="section">
    Breaking stories:
  </fo:block>
  <xsl:apply-templates/>
</xsl:template>

<xsl:template match="up-and-coming">
  <fo:block xsl:use-attribute-sets="section">
    Coming in <xsl:value-of select="@dateline"/>:
  </fo:block>
  <xsl:apply-templates/>
</xsl:template>

<xsl:template match="queries">
  <fo:block xsl:use-attribute-sets="section">
    Member queries:
  </fo:block>
  <xsl:apply-templates/>
</xsl:template>

<xsl:template match="headline">
```

```
    <fo:block xsl:use-attribute-sets="item">
      <xsl:apply-templates/>
    </fo:block>
  </xsl:template>

  <xsl:template match="story|query">
    <fo:block xsl:use-attribute-sets="content">
      <xsl:apply-templates/>
    </fo:block>
  </xsl:template>
```

That's all that is needed at present. The style sheet formats the XML source document as a series of styled block elements. It provides the framework, or skeleton, that you can now decorate with FO styling properties. Run it through your formatter to verify that it outputs the content of the bulletin. Your result should look something like that in Figure 5.1. The Apache FOP processor version 0.20.3rc output the figure. The default font will depend on the formatter.

Bulletin of the Society for Legends and Olde Stories
Issue 7, 2002
Heroic tales of Ireland
From out April gathering:
Deirdre tells of her sorrows
Naisi fought with honor. We lived in peace at Glen Etive. For my sake Conor murdered my only love.
Fergus rails against Conor
"Lecherous drunkard, I shall make of my sword a spit to turn you before the fire."
Breaking stories:
Brown bull gets royal attention
In Quelgny, Dara, son of the famous Fachtna, displayed the finest bull ever seen in Ulster. "His back is broad as a football field. He's savage and mighty as a storm tossed sea." said the steward, mac Roth. "I wouldn't trade him for all the land in Connacht," said Dara.
Coming in august:
Maeve and Fergus bond to raid Ulster. Ailell tags along.
Fedelma the prophetess warns Maeve of Cuchulain. "A stripling you and modest, but in battle a dragon. He doth wondrous feats with his weapons. By him your slain shall lie thickly."
Member queries:
Wanted. Original Editions by Standish James O'Grady (1846-1928). History of Ireland - Heroic Period. Two volumes published 1878 and 1881. also The Triumph and the Passing of Cuchulain published 1919.

Figure 5.1
Skeleton output.

Font Selection

A number of the XSL properties coordinate to select a font. They are all properties in the Common Font Properties group—`font-family`, `font-model`, `font-selection-strategy`, `font-size`, `font-size-adjust`, `font-stretch`, `font-style`, `font-variant`, and `font-weight`. This chapter talks about them all.

Font installations are system and implementation dependent. A font that exists on one system may not exist on another. One system may have capability to produce a given size, weight, or style combination. Another may not. FO markup must be portable from one system to the next. How can that be?

The answer is this: It is impossible to explicitly select a given system font using FO markup. A FO processor must take the combination of font-selection properties as clues or constraints. It locates a font on the system that most closely meets those constraints. On the surface, that sounds like it gives you a frightening lack of control. The formatter won't typeset using the fonts you want! In practice, however, it works quite well. If you specify 10-point Helvetica Bold, that's almost always exactly what you get.

Let's begin with the basic four font properties. They are `font-family`, `font-size`, `font-style`, and `font-weight`. You'll use these more than any others. Following is a styling for the title of your bulletin:

```
<xsl:attribute-set name="base">
  <xsl:attribute name="font-family">
    Book Antiqua,Bookman Old Style,Times Roman,serif
  </xsl:attribute>
  <xsl:attribute name="font-style">oblique</xsl:attribute>
  <xsl:attribute name="font-weight">bold</xsl:attribute>
  <xsl:attribute name="font-size">18pt</xsl:attribute>
</xsl:attribute-set>
```

font-family

The `font-family` property accepts a list of font family names. Font families, such as Book Antiqua, Bookman Old Style, or Times Roman, are groups of fonts with similar design characteristics. They are what we commonly think of when we think of a font. We think of things like the size of the font and whether it is bold as variants. In typesetting parlance, a font is something more specific. It is a collection of *glyphs*, or markings, that have the same size, boldness, obliqueness, and characteristic properties. The collection of fonts with the same characteristic properties forms a font family.

That may seem like splitting hairs, but it's important to realize that fonts on your system with such names as Baskerville, Baskerville Bold, Baskerville Bold Italic, and Baskerville Italic all belong to the same font family—namely, Baskerville.

When it comes to specifying the font family, it is always best to provide a list. The formatter will search the system for a font using the names provided, in order. If the first does not exist on the system, the formatter tries the next, and so forth. At the end of the list, it is best to provide a generic font name.

XSL defines five generic `font-family` names that implementations must map to some font on the system. Each generic font name refers to a characteristic that the selected system font should satisfy. The `monospace` font should have letters that all take the same amount of space, for example. Figure 5.2, output with Antenna House XSL Formatter 2.0, presents samples of each of the generic font families. The default family is any font the implementation chooses to make the default.

serif: What a thing it is, not to have a head when a body wants it worst.

sans-serif: What a thing it is, not to have a head when a body wants it worst.

cursive: *What a thing it is, not to have a head when a body wants it worst.*

fantasy: *What a thing it is, not to have a head when a body wants it worst.*

monospace: `What a thing it is, not to have a head when a body wants it worst.`

Figure 5.2
Sample generic families.

font-style

Every font has style, except maybe Helvetica. Poor, straight-laced Helvetica doesn't seem very stylish. The `font-style` property means something else. Use this property to select an `italic`, a `backslant`, or an `oblique` font. The default is `normal`. In an italic font, the tops of the characters slant to the right of the bottoms. They look like they're racing off to a party. An oblique font has a slightly drunken tilt, but it's happy, like coming home from the party. Sometimes oblique looks identical to italic. A backslant leans to the left. It looks like it's screeching to a halt. Figure 5.3, shown later in this chapter, demonstrates various styles.

Use the italic style for the titles of books or for emphasis. This attribute set calls for italic text. The template calls on it to italicize title markup:

```
<xsl:attribute-set name="italicize">
  <xsl:attribute name="font-style">italic</xsl:attribute>
</xsl:attribute-set>

<xsl:template match="title">
  <fo:wrapper xsl:use-attribute-sets="italicize">
    <xsl:apply-templates/>
  </fo:wrapper>
</xsl:template>
```

font-weight

Use the `font-weight` property to get dark, heavy looking type that stands out boldly. FO allows a range of weights specified in increments of 100 from `100` to `900`. A weight of 400 is effectively `normal`, which is the default. A weight of 700 is effectively bold. The values `bolder` and `lighter` will increase or decrease the weight by an increment of 100, up to the maximum or down to the minimum.

The most useful value for `font-weight` is simply `bold`. Figure 5.3 demonstrates a bold weight.

font-stretch="condensed": This is the valiant Cornish man who slew the giant Cormoran.
font-stretch="expanded": This is the valiant Cornish man who slew the giant Cormoran.
font-style="backslant": This is the valiant Cornish man who slew the giant Cormoran.
font-style="oblique": This is the valiant Cornish man who slew the giant Cormoran.
font-style="italic": *This is the valiant Cornish man who slew the giant Cormoran.*
font-variant="small-caps": THIS IS THE VALIANT CORNISH MAN WHO SLEW THE GIANT CORMORAN.
font-weight="bold": **This is the valiant Cornish man who slew the giant Cormoran.**

Figure 5.3
Sample font stretch, style, variant, and weight.

font-size

The `font-size` property lets you choose characters that are larger or smaller. The usual unit for specifying the size of a font is the point. You select `font-size="9pt"`, `font-size="12pt"`, or `font-size="36pt"`. XSL also allows you to specify the size in words, in increasing order of size, from xx-small to x-small, small, medium, large, x-large, and xx-large. It's just like buying a T-shirt.

If the current font size is `large` and you specify `font-size="smaller"`, you will get the next lower font size, `medium`. If you specify `font-size="larger"`, you will get the next higher font size, `x-large`. The default size is `medium`, which may be about equivalent to 12 points. The scaling suggested by the recommendation from one size to the next is 1.2. That suggests that `large` might have a size of about 14.4 points and `small`, 10 points. These values are implementation defined. The implementation may choose different values. It may even choose different values for each font.

Conventional usage provides point sizes for fonts, but that is not a requirement. Font size specifications of 2 cm, 1.25 inches, or 3 em are also valid. The font in use for the parent FO determines the size of one em unit. A numeric size specification without units is valid and is equivalent to using em units. The formatter also takes a value specified as a percentage against the size of the parent font. If the parent FO has a font with size equal to 10 points, `font-size="3em"` will translate to 30 points, and `font-size="1.2"` and `font-size="120%"` will translate to 12 points. Use whatever you like best.

font-size-adjust

The size of a font refers to the size of its em square. The *em square* is a square with sides of length roughly equal to the width of the character "m" in that font. We tend to think of font size as the height of letters in a font; it's a little disconcerting to find that the measure is actually the width of the "m" character. The *ex height*, which is the height of an "x" character, might seem like a better choice. But that isn't the way it is.

Measuring size with the em square means that two fonts with the same value for `font-size` may not appear to be the same size at all. Consider Verdana and Times Roman. Verdana appears much larger than Times Roman. Its em is narrower relative to the height of its ex.

A font with a wide em substituted by a font with a narrower em at the same size will look too large. This leaves the problem of selecting a font size that will work for all the fonts listed on the `font-family` property. It can't be done. If Verdana is the first choice and Times Roman is the second, the font size coded for Verdana will be too large for Times Roman.

The ratio of the em square to the ex height defines the *aspect ratio* for a font. Every font family has one. A formatter can use the difference in the aspect ratios of two families to calculate an adjusted font size that will make both families appear to be the same size.

Use the `font-size-adjust` property to compensate for differences in the aspect ratios of the fonts listed by the `font-family` property. Code the desired aspect ratio. That should generally be equal to the aspect ratio of the first font. The formatter uses the coded aspect ratio to compute the ex height of the first font family listed on the `font-family` property. It selects a `font-size` for all other font families in the list such that they match ex height with the first. The default value is none, meaning the formatter makes no adjustment to font sizes.

Recall that implementations are free to choose font sizes given the font-size names, xx-small through xx-large. It would be a pleasant surprise to find that an implementation selected sizes so that medium in one font had the same ex height as medium in another. That would make things very convenient, indeed.

font-variant and font-stretch

Figure 5.3 contains samples for `font-variant` and `font-stretch`. They are the special-effects team for fonts.

XSL defines only one font variant, `small-caps`. With `small-caps`, uppercase and lowercase characters both look like capitals, except that the lowercase characters are smaller. The default value is `normal`.

The `font-stretch` property adjusts the spacing and the width of characters. Values range from `ultra-condensed`, in which 60 words will pack into a Volkswagen Beetle, to `ultra-expanded`, which provides first-class airline seating for every character. The values `wider` and `narrower` select the next wider or narrower setting than the inherited setting.

font-selection-strategy

Unicode support in XSL complicates font selection because every font does not contain every character. Most European languages, including English, use Latin characters. They have a Latin "script." Chinese, Japanese, and Korean, among others, use CJK ideographs. Languages in India and Pakistan use Indic scripts. Arabic languages have their own script. Figure 5.4 shows examples of some different scripts.

Figure 5.4
Some scripts of the world.

A font may be on the system that exactly matches the font selection properties specified for a block of text. That font might not contain a glyph to represent every one of the Unicode characters in the text of that block. Many of the fonts on a system might contain glyphs for the Latin script, for example. Those fonts will not contain glyphs for CJK, Indic, or Arabic characters that appear in the paragraph.

In practice, it may be better to use a wrapper or inline formatting object (detailed in Chapter 6) to alter the font family for embedded scripts, like this:

```
<fo:block font-family="Times Roman, serif">
  Here is some text with Latin script
  <fo:wrapper font-family="SimHei, serif">
    Some CJK ideorgaphs
  </fo:wrapper>
  and more Latin script.
</fo:block>
```

That may not always be so obvious. An odd character or two might exist that is not present in every font family specified by the `font-family` property. A formatter might look globally at all the characters and select the font that contains most of them. A setting of `font-selection-strategy="auto"` (which is the default) allows the formatter to do so, perhaps achieving a more consistent appearance to the text in the block. A setting of `font-selection-strategy="character-by-character"` restricts the formatter to consideration of each character individually when selecting the font.

Placement and Inheritance

The font-selection properties may appear on any element. They all inherit from the parent. This means that a font setting affects the FO on which it is specified and all FO beneath or within that FO.

Basic font settings may appear on the page-sequence, flow, or static-content FO. Place specific settings at the highest level where they apply.

Consider filling in the rest of the styles for the bulletin as an example.

```
<xsl:attribute-set name="title">
  <xsl:attribute name="font-size"20pt</xsl:attribute>
</xsl:attribute-set>
```

```
<xsl:attribute-set name="issue">
  <xsl:attribute name="font-size">14pt</xsl:attribute>
</xsl:attribute-set>

<xsl:attribute-set name="theme">
  <xsl:attribute name="font-size">16pt</xsl:attribute>
</xsl:attribute-set>

<xsl:attribute-set name="section">
  <xsl:attribute name="font-size">16pt</xsl:attribute>
</xsl:attribute-set>

<xsl:attribute-set name="item">
  <xsl:attribute name="font-size">14pt</xsl:attribute>
</xsl:attribute-set>

<xsl:attribute-set name="content">
  <xsl:attribute name="font-style">normal</xsl:attribute>
  <xsl:attribute name="font-weight">normal</xsl:attribute>
</xsl:attribute-set>

<xsl:attribute-set name="noun">
  <xsl:attribute name="font-family">
    Lydian,LilyUPC,Helvetica,sans-serif
  </xsl:attribute>
</xsl:attribute-set>

<xsl:attribute-set name="italicize">
  <xsl:attribute name="font-style">italic</xsl:attribute>
</xsl:attribute-set>
```

The base style specified on the `flow` element sets the font family, style, and weight for most of the document. The other styles override the size, primarily on `block` elements within the document. They inherit everything else from the `flow` element. The bulletin should now look something like that shown in Figure 5.5.

Bulletin of the Society for Legends and Olde Stories

Issue 7, 2002

Heroic tales of Ireland

From our April gathering:

Deirdre tells of her sorrows

Naisi fought with honor. We lived in peace at Glen Etive. For my sake Conor murdered my only love.

Fergus rails against Conor

" *Leacherous betrayer, your foul, wanton massacre blackens my kin with blood of fair youth. Treacherous drunkard, I shall make of my sword a spit to turn you before the fire.* "

Breaking stories:

Brown bull gets royal attention

In Quelgny, Dara, son of the famous Fachtna, displayed the finest bull ever seen in Ulster. "*His back is broad as a football field. He's savage and mighty as a storm tossed sea,*" said the steward, mac Roth. "*I wouldn't trade him for all the land in Connacht,*" said Dara.

Coming in August:

Maeve and Fergus bond to raid Ulster. Ailell tags along.

Fedelma the prophetess warns Maeve of Cuchulain. "*A stripling young and modest, but in battle a dragon. He doth wondrous feats with his weapons. By him your slain shall lie thickly.*"

Member queries:

Wanted. Original Editions by Standish James O'Grady (1846-1928). *History of Ireland - Heroic Period.* Two volumes published 1878 and 1881. Also *The Triumph and the Passing of Cuchulain* published 1919.

Figure 5.5

Pretty with fonts.

Rules and Borders

Lots of rules exist in this world. When it comes to typesetting, we draw the line. In typesetting, a rule is a line drawn with a straight edge, usually horizontal or vertical.

The only way to get a vertical rule with FO is to draw it on the vertical border of a block or inline element. Horizontal rules may be drawn on the horizontal borders of an element or within a `leader`. This is not at all a limitation because block and inline elements may be empty. It's perfectly reasonable to output a block for the sole purpose of drawing the rule on its border.

There are four attributes of borders and a property for every combination of the four. The attributes are the border position, color, width, and style. The property `border-top-color` sets the color of the top border. The properties `border-top-style` and `border-left-style` set the style of the top and left borders, respectively.

The section "The Colorful Truth" later in this chapter covers color, and everything it says is applicable to border color. Here you will learn about the position, width, and style. You will modify the style sheet for the bulletin used in this chapter to demonstrate some of the border settings.

Border Position

The FO recommendation provides eight positions for borders. There are only four sides to a rectangle. Somehow, somewhere, something must overlap. The eight positions are `before`, `after`, `start`, `end`, `top`, `bottom`, `left`, and `right`. The first four—`before`, `after`, `start`, and `end`—are relative directions. The second four—`top`, `bottom`, `left`, and `right`—are absolute directions.

Chapter 6, "Block and Inline," will go into depth about relative and absolute directions. For now, assume that `top` is the same as `before`, `bottom` is the same as `after`, `left` is the same as `start`, and `right` is the same as `end`.

The recommendation contains 24 border property names that cover width, style, and color for each of the eight border positions. They have the format `border-<position>-<design>`, in which `<position>` is the side of the rectangle and `<design>` is either `style`, `width`, or `color`. You will need to use 12 of them to completely specify 4 borders. Which 12 you choose depends on whether you want to specify relative or absolute directions. Let's do an example using `top`, `bottom`, `left`, and `right`.

Border Style

At minimum, you must override the default style of a border to see a border formatted in the result. Here is a change to the template that applies special formatting to the query section of the bulletin:

```
<xsl:template match="queries">
  <fo:block xsl:use-attribute-sets="section">
    Member queries:
  </fo:block>
  <fo:block xsl:use-attribute-sets="query-box">
    <xsl:apply-templates/>
  </fo:block>
</xsl:template>
```

This attribute set fleshes out the skeletal definition established at the beginning of the chapter. It formats a medium width, black border around the queries:

```
<xsl:attribute-set name="query-box">
  <xsl:attribute name="border-top-style">solid</xsl:attribute>
  <xsl:attribute name="border-bottom-style">solid</xsl:attribute>
  <xsl:attribute name="border-left-style">solid</xsl:attribute>
  <xsl:attribute name="border-right-style">solid</xsl:attribute>
</xsl:attribute-set>
```

The medium width is the default. The default color is black. The default border style is none, which explains why all blocks do not have borders. Overriding the border style with one of dotted, dashed, solid, double, groove, ridge, inset, or outset causes the formatter to render the border. The example uses solid.

The groove, ridge, inset, and outset styles provide three-dimensional effects. A groove style may provide a chiseled look, like a channel running around the outside of the block. A ridge is the opposite. It may appear like a rounded frame. The outset and inset styles may make the entire box appear to be raised or depressed, like the buttons of a software program.

Border Width

Specify the width of a border using a length measure or one of the keywords thin, medium, or thick. The standard typesetting convention for border widths is 0.5pt, 1pt, or 2pt. XSL FO provides your choice of length units, however. It is perfectly okay to specify a border width in millimeters or even inches.

The only constraint on thin, medium, and thick borders is that the width of a thin border is less than the width of a medium border, which is less than the width of a thick one. In practice, we expect a thin border to be one-half to one point. A thick border might be two or three points.

These attributes added to the query-box attribute set introduced in the prior section will provide a more specific width than that given by the default. Note that the left border has the following:

```
<xsl:attribute name="border-top-width">1.5pt</xsl:attribute>
<xsl:attribute name="border-bottom-width">1.5pt</xsl:attribute>
<xsl:attribute name="border-left-width">2pt</xsl:attribute>
<xsl:attribute name="border-right-width">2pt</xsl:attribute>
```

Padding the Books

Padding in FO is far less labyrinthine than in corporate finance. It is simply the space between the content of a block and its border. Typically, it's not any fun to have the text in a box run right up against the border. It needs a little breathing space. Padding is like the mat that surrounds a picture inside its frame.

Padding, like border, may be independently positioned for each of the four sides using relative or absolute directions. Use lengths to specify the amount of padding. Here is the final query-box attribute set. Figure 5.6 demonstrates the result:

```
<xsl:attribute-set name="query-box">
  <xsl:attribute name="border-top-style">solid</xsl:attribute>
  <xsl:attribute name="border-bottom-style">solid</xsl:attribute>
  <xsl:attribute name="border-left-style">solid</xsl:attribute>
  <xsl:attribute name="border-right-style">solid</xsl:attribute>
  <xsl:attribute name="border-top-width">1.5pt</xsl:attribute>
  <xsl:attribute name="border-bottom-width">1.5pt</xsl:attribute>
  <xsl:attribute name="border-left-width">2pt</xsl:attribute>
  <xsl:attribute name="border-right-width">2pt</xsl:attribute>
  <xsl:attribute name="padding-top">3pt</xsl:attribute>
  <xsl:attribute name="padding-bottom">3pt</xsl:attribute>
  <xsl:attribute name="padding-left">6pt</xsl:attribute>
  <xsl:attribute name="padding-right">6pt</xsl:attribute>
</xsl:attribute-set>
```

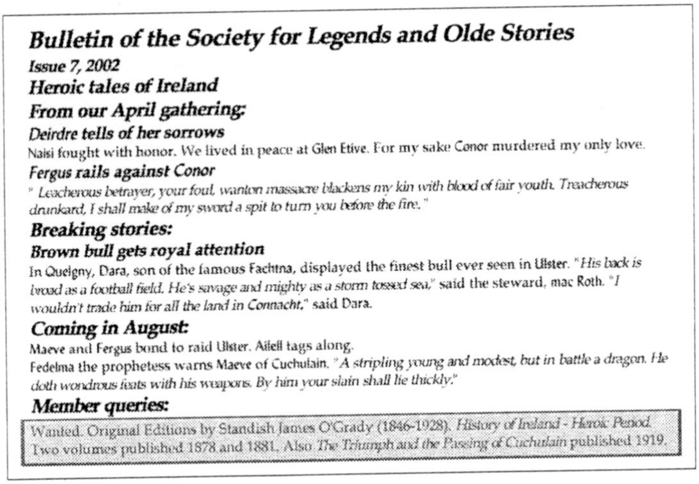

Bulletin of the Society for Legends and Olde Stories

Issue 7, 2002

Heroic tales of Ireland

From our April gathering:

Deirdre tells of her sorrows

Naisi fought with honor. We lived in peace at Glen Etive. For my sake Conor murdered my only love.

Fergus rails against Conor

" *Leacherous betrayer, your foul, wanton massacre blackens my kin with blood of fair youth. Treacherous drunkard, I shall make of my sword a spit to turn you before the fire.*"

Breaking stories:

Brown bull gets royal attention

In Quelgny, Dara, son of the famous Fachtna, displayed the finest bull ever seen in Ulster. "*His back is broad as a football field. He's savage and mighty as a storm tossed sea,*" said the steward, mac Roth. "*I wouldn't trade him for all the land in Connacht,*" said Dara.

Coming in August:

Maeve and Fergus bond to raid Ulster. Ailell tags along.

Fedelma the prophetess warns Maeve of Cuchulain. "*A stripling young and modest, but in battle a dragon. He doth wondrous feats with his weapons. By him your slain shall lie thickly.*"

Member queries:

Wanted. Original Editions by Standish James O'Grady (1846-1928). *History of Ireland - Heroic Period.* Two volumes published 1878 and 1881. Also *The Triumph and the Passing of Cuchulain* published 1919.

Figure 5.6

Finished appearance with border and padding.

The Colorful Truth

FO has only three places where you may specify a color: the background of a box, a rule, and the text. The `background-color` property sets the color of the background of a box. The `border-<position>-color` properties set the color of rules. The `color` property sets the color of text.

Each of these properties accepts color values specified in the same way, which is the way specified by CSS2. CSS2 allows a color name, an rgb numeric triplet, or a triplet of hexadecimal pairs. Let's look at these in detail.

The rgb numeric triplets designate intensity of red, green, and blue in combination. The lowest intensity value is 0, which is no color. The highest is 255, which is as bright as possible. The value `rgb(255, 0, 0)` yields red. You also can specify intensities as percentages from 0 to 100. The value `rgb(25%, 0, 25%)` yields purple.

A series of three or six hexadecimal digits preceded by the pound sign (#) will designate a color as well. The digits designate intensity of color in the same order—red, green, and then blue. The value `#fff` is equivalent to `#ffffff` or `rgb(100%, 100%, 100%)`, which is `white`. The value `#c80` is equivalent to `#c08000` is equivalent to `rgb(192, 64, 0)`, or `rgb(75%, 25%, 0)`.

FO recognizes the same color names recognized by CSS2 and HTML 4.01. They are `black`, `silver`, `gray`, `white`, `maroon`, `red`, `purple`, `fuchsia`, `green`, `lime`, `olive`, `yellow`, `navy`, `blue`, `teal`, and `aqua`. Capitalization is not supposed to be significant.

The following table, taken from HTML 4.01, provides the hexadecimal notation and the red, green, and blue numeric values for each of these color names. This should aid in determining new colors.

Table 5.1 *HTML 4.01 Hexadecimal Notation and Numeric Color Values*

Name	Hex	Red	Green	Blue
Black	#000000	0	0	0
Silver	#C0C0C0	192	192	192
Gray	#808080	64	64	64
White	#FFFFFF	255	255	255
Maroon	#800000	64	0	0
Red	#FF0000	255	0	0
Purple	#800080	64	0	64
Fuchsia	#FF00FF	255	0	255
Green	#008000	0	64	0
Lime	#00FF00	0	255	0
Olive	#808000	64	64	0
Yellow	#FFFF00	255	255	0
Navy	#000080	0	0	64

Table 5.1 *(continued)*

Name	Hex	Red	Green	Blue
Blue	#0000FF	0	0	255
Teal	#008080	0	64	64
Aqua	#00FFFF	0	255	255

Determine the hex values for a new color by first selecting a known color closest to the one you would like. Make the color darker or lighter by decreasing or increasing the values proportionately. Change the hue by increasing or decreasing one value only.

The first four "colors," black, silver, gray, and white, give an idea of the intensity resulting from different channel values. Zero (`00`) is black, `FF` is white. `80` and `C0` provide two levels of intensity in between. The color green, `#008000`, looks like a natural intensity, whereas lime, `#00FF00`, is neon bright.

To get a lighter purple (`#800080`) without going all the way to fuchsia (`#FF00FF`), try `#C000C0`. To get a darker red (`#FF0000`) without going all the way to maroon (`#800000`), try `#C00000`. Try `#FF00C0` to make fuchsia just a little bit more red.

To make an example in Celtic colors, try adding the following color properties to the attribute set of the query-box.

```
<xsl:attribute name="border-top-color">green</xsl:attribute>
<xsl:attribute name="border-bottom-color">green</xsl:attribute>
<xsl:attribute name="border-left-color">green</xsl:attribute>
<xsl:attribute name="border-right-color">green</xsl:attribute>
<xsl:attribute name="background-color">rgb(80%, 90%, 0)</xsl:attribute>
<xsl:attribute name="color">#800080</xsl:attribute>
```

Summary

You've gone from "Hello World" to a styled bulletin with fonts, borders, and color. You've seen how to use XSL templates and attribute sets to structure an FO output and describe its styling. The attribute sets provide separate, manageable units. The templates apply them consistently to the content. A designer can create the styles and alter the style attributes. A programmer can write the templates that structure the content and apply the styles.

Writers of content provide the appropriate markup but need not concern themselves with font families, rule widths, and other style details. This might all be faster with a word processor or page-makeup program if you have to write only one of a kind. The advantage becomes clear if you have to produce a bulletin every week to appear in typeset copy, large-print copy, and online as HTML.

We've waved our hands a little so far when discussing blocks and boxes. The next chapter provides details about the box model underlying block and inline elements of FO. It will tie up the loose ends regarding direction that we deferred in the discussion of rules and borders earlier in this chapter.

CHAPTER 6
Block and Inline

Now we've had about all the fun we can have without understanding a bit more about the formatting model.

Box Model

Just about everything in Formatting Objects (FO) has a rectangular box invisibly drawn on the page. The page itself is a box. It contains boxes for the regions at the edges of the page and the body region in the center. Regions contain boxes for blocks, which in turn contain more boxes for lines. Lines contain boxes for inline areas and text. The boxes that make marks on the page are deeply nested within more boxes that divide the page and herd them into place. Boxes, blocks, or areas—by any name it all reduces to rectangles nested within rectangles on the page.

The W3C XSL FO recommendation calls this nesting of rectangles the *area model.* Call them areas or call them boxes. Either works. An area seems like a playground or a park. It can have any shape. That sounds nice, but the formatting model is much less permissive. The word "box" is restrictive. A box has parallel lines and right angles. It holds things within bounds. XSL areas are boxes, plain and simple.

Every box has two directions—no more, no less. It has a `block-progression direction` and an `inline-progression direction`. When you specify limits of travel in these directions, you talk about the `block-progression dimension` and the `inline-progression dimension`. The convenient shorthand for these is `bpd` and `ipd`. You choose the word for the `d`, direction or dimension. The important words, the words that really matter, are the words block and inline. Master block and inline and the world of typesetting is at your feet.

Reference Orientation

In the good old humdrum, day-to-day world of Latin scripts, everything reads from left to right and from top to bottom. Lines of text start at the left and end at the right. Paragraphs and pages stack lines from top to bottom. Lines at the top read before lines at the bottom. Lines at the bottom read after lines at the top. In this world, we say that the `inline-progression direction` is left to right. The `block-progression direction` is top to bottom. Figure 6.1 demonstrates the default block and inline progression directions.

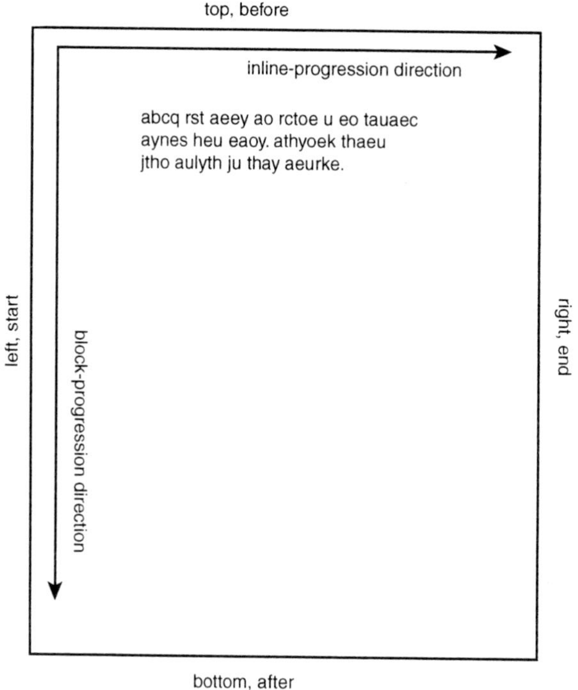

Figure 6.1
Left to right, top to bottom.

Every once in a while, we try to make things exciting and turn the page sideways. The familiar term for this is *landscape*. Lines of text still start at the left and end at the right. They still stack from top to bottom, but we've turned the page 90 degrees to put the long edge on top (see Figure 6.2).

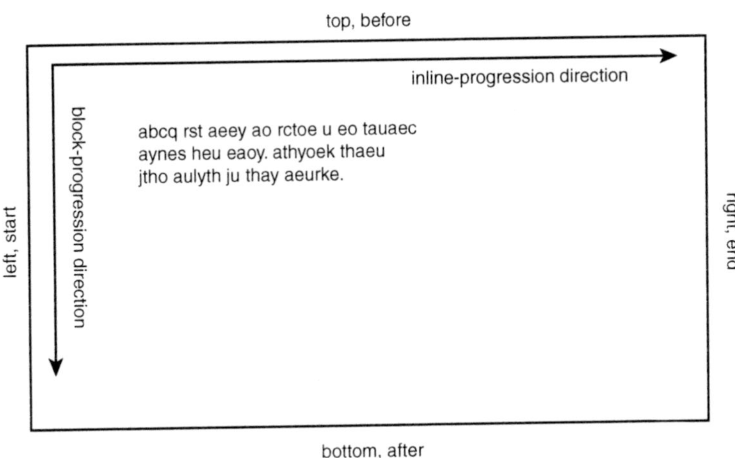

Figure 6.2
Reference orientation at 90 degrees.

Use the `reference-orientation` property to rotate the page so that a different edge is on top. Set the `reference-orientation` property equal to `90`. That setting rotates the page so that the right edge is the top. That's it. The `reference-orientation` property determines which edge of the paper is the top. It does nothing else.

Refer again to Figures 6.1 and 6.2. The edge opposite the top is the bottom. The edge 90 degrees counterclockwise from the top is the left edge. The edge 90 degrees clockwise from the top and opposite the left is the right edge. Here is an FO fragment that sets the reference-orientation. The setting appears on the page master to rotate the entire page:

```
<fo:simple-page-master master-name="page"
  reference-orientation="90">
  <fo:region-body region-name="body"
    margin-top="0.5in" margin-bottom="1in"
    margin-left="0.5in" margin-right="0.5in" />


</fo:simple-page-master>
```

Writing Direction

Some languages in some countries use scripts that do not follow the left-to-right, top-to-bottom convention of Latin scripts. In traditional Chinese, for example, lines read from top to bottom. Paragraphs and pages stack lines from right to left (see Figure 6.3).

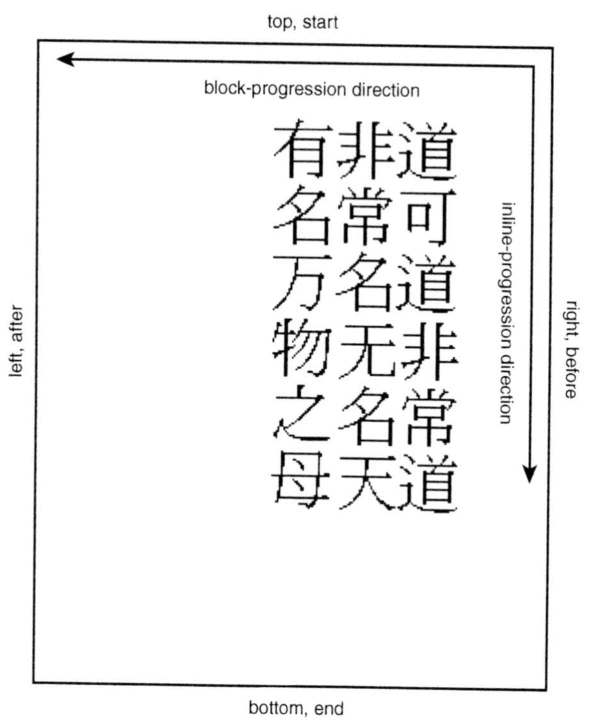

Figure 6.3

Writing directions for traditional Chinese.

The `writing-mode` property controls the direction of writing. Chapter 15, "Going Global," discusses international language features of FO and covers the `writing-mode` property in detail. Let it suffice to say here that the `writing-mode` property determines the inline-progression direction and the block-progression direction. Bidirectional properties of Unicode text may locally alter the inline-progression direction within a line. You will learn more about that detail in Chapter 15 as well. Use `writing-mode` to set the ipd and bpd.

Follow the eyes to determine the inline and block progression directions. The direction they move to read words is the inline-progression direction. The direction they move to read from one line to the next is the block-progression direction.

Let's say that another way. Text flows in a line. That is the inline-progression direction. Blocks are the paragraphs that march down the page in the block-progression direction.

The FO box model needs relative terms for the sides of boxes. Those relative terms refer to different absolute sides of the page when the writing direction changes. We cannot go on saying, "The left edge if the inline-progression direction is left-to-right or the right edge if the inline-progression direction is right-to-left." We could, but we would run out of patience in a hurry. Instead we say, "the start edge."

The *start* edge is the edge where the eye starts reading words. The *end* edge is where the eye ends to begin a new line. The *before* edge comes before the line where the eye starts reading. The *after* edge comes after the line where the eye ends reading. No matter what the direction of writing, the eye always reads from start to end, before to after.

Figures 6.1 to 6.3 have the edges labeled with their relative as well as their absolute references. The inline-progression direction is always the arrow leading from the start edge toward the end edge. The block progression direction is the arrow leading from the before edge to the after edge.

Corresponding Properties

The inline-progression direction and the block-progression direction together determine the correspondence between absolute and relative edge notations. The inline-progression direction determines the correspondence of start and end edges to the top, the bottom, the left, or the right. The block-progression direction determines the correspondence of the before and after edges.

The `border-top-color` and `border-before-color` correspond if the block-progression direction is top to bottom. To say that they correspond means that they both refer to the same edge. The first notation is the absolute notation. The second is relative. The recommendation specifies that the absolute corresponding property "wins" if a style sheet contains values for both. In this example, `border-top-color` wins over `border-before-color`. Keep it simple. Use one notation or the other.

My suggestion is that you use the relative properties exclusively. The relative properties—ones that refer to before, after, start, and end—relate clearly to the flow of text. Using the relative properties makes the style sheet immune to changes in writing direction. The only time to use an absolute property, such as the top, is when you absolutely mean the top, wherever the top may be, regardless of the direction of text flow.

Wherefore Do We Stack and Pack? Block, Inline, and Content Models

The primary reason for exposing all this detail about inline and block progression is this: Some FOs produce boxes that stack in the block progression direction. Others produce boxes that pack in the inline progression dimension. FOs that stack are `block-level` FOs. FOs that pack are `inline-level` FOs.

Block-level FOs produce boxes that stack like lines and paragraphs of text. In fact, they are the primary means for generating lines and paragraphs. The FOs classified as block level are `block` and `block-container`, `table`, `table-and-caption`, and `list-block`.

Inline-level FOs produce boxes that pack like characters into words and words into lines of text on a page. There are a few more of them than there are block-level FOs because these are the elements used to represent different sorts of marks on the page. The inline-level FOs are `basic-link`, `bidi-override`, `character`, `external-graphic`, `inline`, `inline-container`, `instream-foreign-object`, `leader`, `multi-toggle`, `page-number`, and `page-number-citation`. You will learn about all these in time. This chapter focuses on the basics—`inline` and `inline-container`.

Text, known in the XML world as PCDATA, is also inline-level content. The formatter packs text in line with inline-level FOs.

Some FOs may appear wherever block-level FOs, inline-level FOs, or text are allowed. These are `multi-switch`, `multi-properties`, `wrapper`, and `retrieve-marker`. This chapter discusses the `wrapper` only. Later chapters discuss the rest, especially Chapter 14, "Dynamic Effects."

The `content model` for ny FO is the list, or sequence, of FOs that may appear as descendants of that FO. An FO `child` is a descendant of an FO `parent` whenever the start tag of the parent comes before the child and the child comes before the end tag of the parent. The relationship looks like this:

```
<parent>
  <child>This is content of the child</child>
<parent>
```

Each FO has a content model that selects or limits the FOs that may appear within. As examples, the `block` FO may be the parent of text, inline-level, or other block-level FOs. The `list-block` FO may be only the parent of `list-item` FOs.

Border and Padding

Now let's get back to the boxes produced by FO. Every box on the page potentially has a series of frames, or rectangles, around it that form padding, border, margins, and space. Figure 6.4 illustrates.

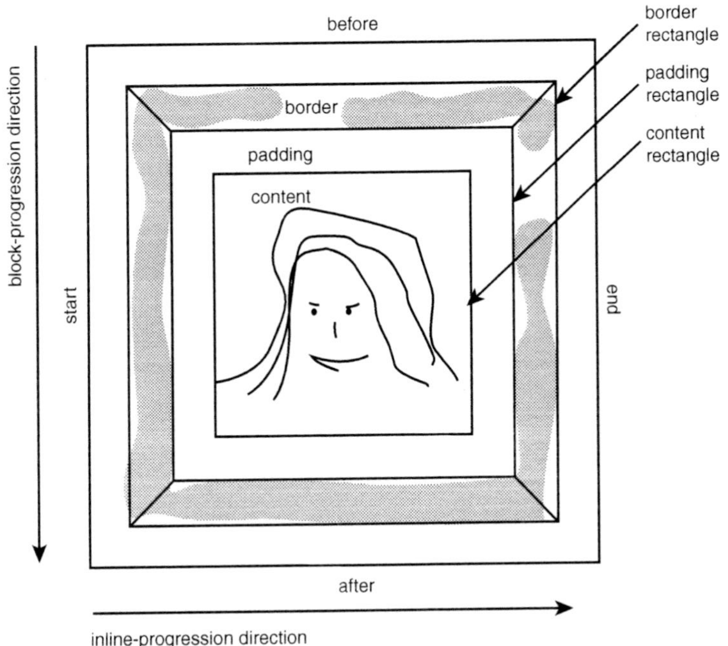

Figure 6.4
Frames around each box.

The inner rectangle encloses the content of the box. That content may be other boxes or some mark, such as a character or image. The next rectangle outside the content is the padding rectangle. The `padding-<side>-width` properties covered in Chapter 5, "Color, Fonts, and Rules," define the widths of the edges of this box, which are often zero.

Think of padding as the mat around a picture. Background colors and background images extend to the edges of the padding rectangle. The padding rectangle ends where the border begins; therefore, background color extends right to the border.

The border has width, color, and style, as discussed in Chapter 5. Think of the border as the frame of the picture. Typically it is much narrower than any padding. Usually, it is a rule or line with width equal to one or two points.

Beyond the border is a gray area called space. If you're a box that loves *Star Trek*, it's the final frontier. Space is the place that puts a little room between the border of one box and the border of another. I call it gray because it can overlap the space from another box or disappear altogether. That depends on a number of factors that we'll get to later in the chapter when we have an example to work with. For now, let's move on to some of the FOs that produce boxes.

Screenplay Example

That's entirely enough theory driven without examples. It's time to put something on the board so we can talk about it concretely. Just for fun, let's do something that produces screenplay form. Screenplay form is notoriously strict, so much so that writers of screenplays shun general-purpose word processing software for specialized screenplay writing software. Strange, but true. How does markup rise to the challenge?

We need some material. Let's mark up one of old William's plays. There's no doubt that were Shakespeare writing today, he'd write screenplays. He might write Broadway musicals; however, compare the audience size for plays with the number of people who see a Hollywood film. Old William's plays were what passed for mass entertainment in London in his day. It would have to be movies today. Listing 6.1 presents the beginning of Shakespeare's play *The Tempest* marked up as a screenplay.

Listing 6.1 *scene.xml: Screenplay Markup, Opening of* The Tempest

```
<?xml version="1.0"?>
<screenplay>
<title>The Tempest</title>
<author>William Shakespeare</author>
<scene>
  <locale type="ext">
    Ship at sea. Late afternoon.
  </locale>
  <action>
    Tempestuous <sound>noise</sound>
    of howling wind, thunder and lightning heard.
  </action>
  <shot>
    Deck of the ship, a fifteenth century sailing vessel,
    rolling and pitching.  <character>master</character>
    and <character>boatswain</character> on deck.
  </shot>
  <dialog character="master">
    Boatswain!
  </dialog>
  <dialog character="boatswain">
    Here, master: what cheer?
  </dialog>
  <shot>
```

Listing 6.1 *(continued)*

```
    Two shot of <character>master</character> and
    <character>boatswain</character>.
    Land in mid-distance.
  </shot>
  <dialog character="master">
    <direction>urgently</direction>
    Good, speak to the mariners: fall to't, yarely,
    or we run ourselves aground: bestir, bestir.
  </dialog>
  <shot>
    <character>boatswain</character> calling below decks.
    Sound of a <sound>whistle</sound>
  </shot>
  <dialog character="boatswain">
    Heigh, my hearts! cheerly, cheerly, my hearts!
    yare, yare!
  </dialog>
  <shot>
    Mariners go to work on deck, voice over
    <character>boatswain</character>
  </shot>
  <dialog character="boatswain">
    Take in the topsail. Tend to the
    master's whistle. Blow, till thou burst thy wind,
    if room enough!
  </dialog>
  <shot>
    Passengers, including
    <character>alonso</character>,
    <character>sebastian</character>,
    <character>antonio</character>,
    <character>ferdinand</character>, and
    <character>gonzalo</character>
    accost
    <character>boatswain</character>
  </shot>
  <dialog character="alonso">
    Good boatswain, have care. Where's the master?
    Play the men.
  </dialog>
  <dialog character="boatswain">
```

Listing 6.1 *(continued)*

```
    I pray now, keep below.
  </dialog>
  <dialog character="antonio">
    Where is the master, boatswain?
  </dialog>
  <dialog character="boatswain">
    Do you not hear him? You mar our labour: keep your
    cabins: you do assist the storm.
  </dialog>
  <shot>
    Two shot of
    <character>boatswain</character> and
    <character>gonzalo</character>
  </shot>
  <dialog character="gonzalo">
    Nay, good, be patient.
  </dialog>
  <dialog character="boatswain">
    When the sea is. Hence! What cares these roarers
    for the name of king? To cabin: silence! trouble us not.
  </dialog>
  <dialog character="gonzalo">
    Good, yet remember whom thou hast aboard.
  </dialog>
  <shot>
    <character>boatswain</character> as seen by
    <character>gonzalo</character>
  </shot>
  <dialog character="boatswain">
    None that I more love than myself. You are a
    counsellor; if you can command these elements to
    silence, and work the peace of the present, we will
    not hand a rope more; use your authority: if you
    cannot, give thanks you have lived so long, and make
    yourself ready in your cabin for the mischance of
    the hour, if it so hap. Cheerly, good hearts! Out
    of our way, I say.
  </dialog>
  <action>
    <character>boatswain</character> pushes past
```

Listing 6.1 *(continued)*

```
    <character>gonzalo</character>
    to assist a mariner.
  </action>
  <shot>
    Close on <character>gonzalo</character> regarding
    the storm, land looming nearby, and then
    <character>boatswain</character>.
  </shot>
  <dialog character="gonzalo">
    <direction>to himself</direction>
    I have great comfort from this fellow: methinks he
    hath no drowning mark upon him; his complexion is
    perfect gallows. Stand fast, good Fate, to his
    hanging: make the rope of his destiny our cable,
    for our own doth little advantage. If he be not
    born to be hanged, our case is miserable.
  </dialog>
</scene>
</screenplay>
```

Screenplays consist of a series of scenes. Each scene has one or more locales and a series of camera shots interspersed with actions and dialog. The bit of dialog ending the scene is precious. Shakespeare loves to close with a bang. That Gonzalo is something, isn't he? For him we coined the phrase, "gallows humor." Writing the screenplay markup by hand requires more effort on mechanics than should be asked of an author concentrating on a story. An editor designed to produce markup might help, though, and it would provide a poor-man's version of the specialized editors marketed for writing screenplays.

More likely, those specialized editors might produce markup like this to make the screenplay accessible to computer interpretation and processing for production uses or for print or online publishing. Someday, studios might require submissions not in paper form, but electronically as markup. Someday....

The style sheet to format the screenplay will contain many templates to match the various elements of the screenplay markup. The two listings that follow provide a bare-bones style sheet as a starting point. The remainder of the chapter completes them with detailed template and attribute-set definitions.

In keeping with the division of concerns that we advocate, the first Listing 6.2 provides the structural transformation from screenplay markup into FOs:

Listing 6.2 *scene.xsl: Page Layout for the Screenplay Style Sheet*

```
<?xml version='1.0'?>
<xsl:stylesheet version="1.0"
 xmlns:xsl="http://www.w3.org/1999/XSL/Transform"
 xmlns:fo="http://www.w3.org/1999/XSL/Format">

  <xsl:strip-space elements="*"/>
  <xsl:include href="scnStyle.xsl"/>

  <xsl:template match="screenplay">
    <fo:root>
      <fo:layout-master-set>
        <fo:simple-page-master
         master-name="page">
          <fo:region-body
           region-name="body"
           margin-top="0.75in"
           margin-bottom="1.0in"
           margin-left="0.5in"
           margin-right="0.5in"/>
        </fo:simple-page-master>
      </fo:layout-master-set>
      <fo:page-sequence master-reference="page">
        <fo:flow flow-name="body"
         xsl:use-attribute-sets="base">
          <xsl:apply-templates select="title"/>
          <xsl:apply-templates select="author"/>
          <xsl:apply-templates select="scene"/>
        </fo:flow>
      </fo:page-sequence>
    </fo:root>
  </xsl:template>

  <xsl:template match="title"/>
  <xsl:template match="author"/>
  <xsl:template match="scene"/>

</xsl:stylesheet>
```

The template matching the root element `screenplay` produces a page master with a three-quarter-inch top margin, a one-inch bottom margin, and half-inch margins on the left and right. The `page-sequence` contains markup for the title and author of the screenplay followed by all the scenes in the order in which they appear.

The last three templates suppress all output for `title`, `author`, and `scene` elements. These will cause the style sheet to produce an empty `flow` within the `page-sequence`. The sections that follow complete these so that the style sheet can produce some output.

The style sheet requires specific settings for a number of different elements that the following sections will elaborate. In particular, elements such as a locale, an action, or a shot require specific formatting settings. Listing 6.3 gives a skeletal beginning for these style settings. This "style file" provides properties for the different stylistic elements within the screenplay. The base style setting used by the `flow`, for example, provides font settings for the entire document:

Listing 6.3 *scnStyle.xsl: Skeletal Style Settings for the Screenplay*

```
<?xml version='1.0'?>
<xsl:stylesheet version="1.0"
 xmlns:xsl="http://www.w3.org/1999/XSL/Transform"
 xmlns:fo="http://www.w3.org/1999/XSL/Format">

  <xsl:attribute-set name="base">
    <xsl:attribute name="font-family">Courier, monospaced</xsl:attribute>
    <xsl:attribute name="font-size">12pt</xsl:attribute>
  </xsl:attribute-set>

  <xsl:attribute-set name="scene"/>
  <xsl:attribute-set name="title"/>
  <xsl:attribute-set name="author"/>
  <xsl:attribute-set name="locale"/>
  <xsl:attribute-set name="action"/>
  <xsl:attribute-set name="shot"/>
  <xsl:attribute-set name="speaker"/>
  <xsl:attribute-set name="speech"/>
  <xsl:attribute-set name="direction"/>
  <xsl:attribute-set name="character"/>
  <xsl:attribute-set name="sound"/>

</xsl:stylesheet>
```

block and block-container

Throughout this book, we have been using the `block` FO to contain paragraphs, titles, and section headings. That's just what they are for. A `block` FO groups the blocks of content that stack vertically down the page. In relative terms, it creates boxes that stack in the block-progression direction, from the before edge of the page toward the after edge.

Page breaks occur within or between blocks. If a page break occurs within a block, the block produces two boxes—one at the end of the first page and one at the beginning of the next. If that block has a border, only the edges completed on the page or column will have their border. You will get a box that looks as if it was simply chopped into two pieces at the page break.

Figure 6.5 simulates the output of a single block broken across two pages. The block has a solid border on every edge. The quote is Gonzalo's opening speech in Shakespeare's play *The Tempest*. Figure 6.6 demonstrates what you should not see. The following FO might generate the output shown in Figure 6.5:

```
<xsl:template match="dialog">
  <fo:block
   border-before-width="4pt"
   border-after-width="4pt"
   border-start-width="4pt"
   border-end-width="4pt"
   border-before-style="solid"
   border-after-style="solid"
   border-start-style="solid"
   border-end-style="solid">
    <xsl:apply-templates/>
  </fo:block>
</xsl:template>
```

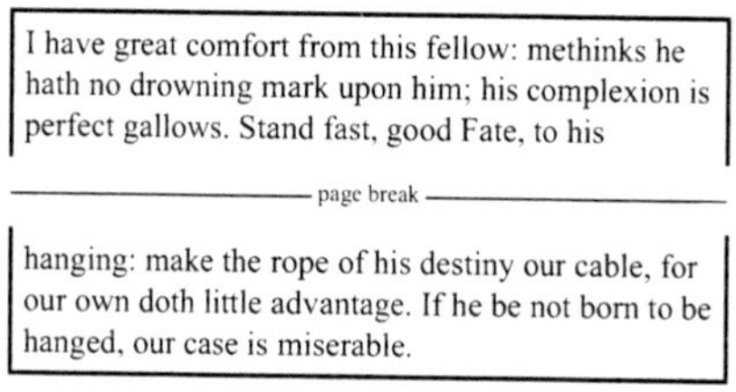

I have great comfort from this fellow: methinks he hath no drowning mark upon him; his complexion is perfect gallows. Stand fast, good Fate, to his

page break

hanging: make the rope of his destiny our cable, for our own doth little advantage. If he be not born to be hanged, our case is miserable.

Figure 6.5
Page break within a block that has borders.

I have great comfort from this fellow: methinks he hath no drowning mark upon him; his complexion is perfect gallows. Stand fast, good Fate, to his

page break

hanging: make the rope of his destiny our cable, for our own doth little advantage. If he be not born to be hanged, our case is miserable.

Figure 6.6

You will not see borders repeated like this across a break.

Use a `block-container` FO to change the `writing-mode` or `reference-orientation` property. That is, use it to rotate or change the writing direction. Use it also to absolutely position and size content. The `block-container` may not contain text or inline-level elements. It must contain a block-level FO, which is a block, a table, or a list.

One usage example of a `block-container` would be to rotate a table and place it by itself on a page. The specification would look something like the following:

```
<fo:block-container
 reference-orientation="90"
 break-before="page"
 break-after="page">
  <fo:table>
    <!– table content –>
  </fo:table>
</fo:block-container>
```

The `break-before` and `break-after` property settings cause the formatter to place the block-container alone on one or more pages. Chapter 11 covers these in detail.

Absolute Position

Another example of the use of `block-container` would be to absolutely position a logo or other graphic. Use the `absolute-position`, `top`, `left`, `right`, and `bottom` properties to place the container. The `top`, `left`, `right`, and `bottom` properties position the like-named edges of the border rectangle after accounting for space. The specification might look something like the following:

```
<fo:block-container
 absolute-position="absolute"
 top="0.5in"
 left="1in">
```

```
  <fo:block>
    <!— graphic —>
  </fo:block>
  <fo:block>
    Caption for the graphic
  </fo:block>
</fo:block-container>
```

A `block-container` may have absolute sizing, as well. The `width` and `height` properties correspond to the `inline-progression-dimension` and `block-progression-dimension` properties, all of which take a length. Use one or the other pair to specify the size of the content rectangle for the box. A `block-container` may have border, padding, and margin. Those expand the size of the box beyond the dimensions given by the absolute-sizing properties.

You can specify all four of the absolute-position properties to position all four edges of the box. If you absolutely size the box, you can specify the top or bottom and left or right. You cannot specify the left and right absolute position and then specify a width. If you do, the formatter will ignore the width in favor of the left and right margin positions. That is an example of an "over constrained" specification.

The formatter will allow you to absolutely position only a `block-container`. No other element may have the `absolute-position` property. Every other block-level or inline-level FO may have relative position.

Relative Position

Block-level FOs with the exception of `block-container` and inline-level FOs may have their `relative-position` property set equal to `relative`. Use the `top`, `left`, `right`, and `bottom` properties to position the box relative to where the formatter would otherwise place it. The formatter first places the box automatically and then moves the box relative to that location as specified.

Positive values for the left and right properties move the box in the opposite directions, which is counterintuitive. That is because the left property adds to the position of the left edge. The net effect is to move the box to the right. Positive values for the top property move the box down. Positive values for the bottom property move the box up.

The following specification will position the box slightly up and to the left relative to where the formatter would leave it:

```
<fo:block
 relative-position="relative"
 right="2pt"
```

```
bottom="2pt">
  <!— content of the block —>
</fo:block>
```

Remember that inline-level FOs may also have relative positioning properties. Let's look at a few of those inline-level FOs.

Blocks for the Screenplay Example

Now that you have the low-down on blocks, it may be evident that many of the elements in the screenplay markup must appear within blocks. The title and author will each appear within their own block. The text for a locale, shot, action, and dialog will appear stacked within blocks. Listing 6.4 fills out the three skeletal templates given earlier in Listing 6.2. Replace those three templates with the templates given here:

Listing 6.4 *Complete Templates for the Screenplay Block Elements*

```
<xsl:template match="title">
  <fo:block xsl:use-attribute-sets="title">
    <xsl:apply-templates/>
  </fo:block>
</xsl:template>

<xsl:template match="author">
  <fo:block xsl:use-attribute-sets="author">
    - by <xsl:apply-templates select="author"/>
  </fo:block>
</xsl:template>

<xsl:template match="scene">
  <xsl:apply-templates/>
  <fo:block xsl:use-attribute-sets="scene">CUT:</fo:block>
</xsl:template>

<xsl:template match="locale">
  <fo:block xsl:use-attribute-sets="locale">
    <xsl:choose>
      <xsl:when test="@type='ext'">EXT.</xsl:when>
      <xsl:when test="@type='int'">INT.</xsl:when>
    </xsl:choose>
    <xsl:apply-templates/>
  </fo:block>
</xsl:template>
```

Listing 6.4 *(continued)*

```
<xsl:template match="action">
  <fo:block xsl:use-attribute-sets="action">
    <xsl:apply-templates/>
  </fo:block>
</xsl:template>

<xsl:template match="shot">
  <fo:block xsl:use-attribute-sets="shot">
    <xsl:apply-templates/>
  </fo:block>
</xsl:template>

<xsl:template match="dialog">
  <fo:block xsl:use-attribute-sets="speaker">
    <xsl:value-of select="@character"/>
  </fo:block>
  <xsl:apply-templates select="direction"/>
  <fo:block xsl:use-attribute-sets="speech">
    <xsl:apply-templates select="text()"/>
  </fo:block>
</xsl:template>

<xsl:template match="direction">
  <fo:block xsl:use-attribute-sets="direction">
    (<xsl:apply-templates/>)
  </fo:block>
</xsl:template>
```

Most of the templates in Listing 6.4 output text content within a block. The template matching a `scene` relies on the templates matching its child elements to output a series of blocks. It follows those blocks with a single block marking the end of the scene. That is simply the text, "CUT:." The template matching `locale` uses the `type` attribute to choose the literal content INT or EXT for the result. The template matching `dialog` must format the speaker given by the `character` attribute. It then formats any stage direction followed by the actual text of the speech.

The style settings for these will appear in the attribute-set definitions given in the file scnStyle.xsl. So far, those definitions remain empty. Listings 6.6 and 6.8 developed in the remainder of the chapter will complete the attribute-set definitions called for by these templates.

Inheritance and the Wrapper

You have already seen the wrapper FO used in examples to change a font setting. That is essentially what it is for.

The `wrapper` FO specifies a property or properties that some child of the wrapper will inherit. Use the `wrapper` strictly to specify inherited properties. Most typically, use the `wrapper` to temporarily change one of the font properties, such as to change the `font-style` to `bold`.

We haven't talked about inheritance before, so let's talk about it now. If you're familiar with Cascading Style Sheets (CSS), you know that the settings of some values carry down to all the children of the element on which the setting appears. The `page-sequence` may contain a font setting, for example. Every FO in that `page-sequence` will have the same font setting, until one of them overrides the setting with a new one.

Some properties inherit by default. For the most part, the ones that make sense to inherit do, and those that don't make sense do not. All the font properties inherit. You wouldn't want to rewrite the font settings on every FO child of a `page-sequence`. A property such as `inline-progression-dimension` does not inherit. You generally do not want all the children to have the same size as the parent.

Appendix C, "A Concise Listing of Properties," indicates a default value for properties that do not inherit by default. It indicates an initial value for properties that do inherit by default. The initial value is the value applied at the root element, which has no parent from which to inherit a value. The initial value for `font-size`, for example is `medium`. Everything will have medium `font-size` until you change the value. Everything below the point of change will have the new value.

Most of the properties may also take a value equal to `inherit`. It is possible to write, `border-style="inherit"`, for example. This doesn't occur too much in practice. It's hard to think of a good example for using it, but throw it into your toolbox. The setting `border-style="inherit"` makes the `border-style` equal to the setting given on the parent—say `solid`, rather than to the default value, which is `none`.

Many properties that inherit also permit a value equal to `inherit`. There's no good reason to do this. The net effect is the same, but look at it this way. If you write `font-size="inherit"` as a reminder at some point, the formatter shouldn't complain.

Now we're ready to return to the `wrapper`. The `wrapper` is all about inheritance. It doesn't create a box. It makes no sense to specify border, padding, or background properties on a wrapper because those properties do not inherit and the wrapper itself has no border. No box, no border.

A wrapper is neither inline level nor block level. It does not interrupt block stacking or inline packing. It doesn't make any marks. It doesn't structure the output into blocks or lines. All it does is change the values of any inherited properties you specify with it. Use it wherever block-level or inline-level content may occur.

The wrapper is also the carrier of property settings relating to the multi-properties FO. Refer to Chapter 14, "Dynamic Effects," for details.

Listing 6.5 contains two more templates that you may insert directly into the style sheet started in Listing 6.2. These add special formatting to character and sound elements within the screenplay:

Listing 6.5 *Complete Templates for the Screenplay Wrapper Elements*

```
<xsl:template match="character">
  <fo:wrapper xsl:use-attribute-sets="character">
    <xsl:apply-templates/>
  </fo:wrapper>
</xsl:template>

<xsl:template match="sound">
  <fo:wrapper xsl:use-attribute-sets="sound">
    <xsl:apply-templates/>
  </fo:wrapper>
</xsl:template>
```

Listing 6.6 provides the style settings called for by the two wrappers just shown in Listing 6.5. Both of them transform any text content within the wrapper to uppercase. This has the effect of capitalizing a character name or sound effect for emphasis. It is standard practice for a screenplay. The emphasis allows production personnel to quickly scan for sound effects and characters needed in any given scene:

Listing 6.6 *Attribute-set Definitions for the Wrappers*

```
<xsl:attribute-set name="character">
  <xsl:attribute name="text-transform">uppercase</xsl:attribute>
</xsl:attribute-set>

<xsl:attribute-set name="sound">
  <xsl:attribute name="text-transform">uppercase</xsl:attribute>
</xsl:attribute-set>
```

inline and inline-container

The `inline` FO creates a box. Use it wherever inline-level content may occur when you want to decorate that content with a border or background or add space around it. The formatter will place the content of the `inline` on one or more lines, in line with any other inline content of the block. The `inline` FO may specify border, padding, and background properties. The formatter will draw any border along with the content of the inline.

When a line breaks within the content of the inline, the formatter will generate multiple boxes, one for each line needed to accommodate all the content. It will draw any start or end border once at the start, and once at the end of each line. Let's manufacture an example.

The following fragment places a border around a phrase that has fallen out of common usage. The content looks like this:

```
<?xml version="1.0"?>
<line>
  if you can command these elements to silence, and
  <phrase>work the peace of the present</phrase>,
  we will not hand a rope more;
</line>
```

Listing 6.7 provides a style sheet that will format the `line` content. The style sheet shown in the listing includes the file `rootrule.xsl` developed in Chapter 4:

Listing 6.7 *Inline Example*

```
<?xml version='1.0'?>
<xsl:stylesheet version="1.0"
 xmlns:xsl="http://www.w3.org/1999/XSL/Transform"
 xmlns:fo="http://www.w3.org/1999/XSL/Format">

  <xsl:strip-space elements="*"/>
  <xsl:include href="rootrule.xsl"/>

  <xsl:attribute-set name="phrase">
    <xsl:attribute name="border-start-style">solid</xsl:attribute>
    <xsl:attribute name="border-end-style">solid</xsl:attribute>
    <xsl:attribute name="border-before-style">solid</xsl:attribute>
    <xsl:attribute name="border-after-style">solid</xsl:attribute>
  </xsl:attribute-set>

  <xsl:template match="line">
```

Listing 6.7 *(continued)*

```
    <fo:block>
      <xsl:apply-templates/>
    </fo:block>
  </xsl:template>

  <xsl:template match="phrase">
    <fo:inline xsl:use-attribute-sets="phrase">
      <xsl:apply-templates/>
    </fo:inline>
  </xsl:template>

</xsl:stylesheet>
```

Figure 6.7 shows the rendered result, which demonstrates the condition in which the phrase breaks across a line. The inline produces no box at the end of the line or a box at the beginning of the next line. The box generated by the start of the inline has its start border. The box generated by the end of the inline has its end border.

if you can command these elements to silence, and work the peace
of the present, we will not hand a rope more;

Figure 6.7
Inline FO broken over multiple lines.

Use an `inline-container` FO whenever inline content must further contain elements stacked in the block-progression direction. That is something you will rarely do, but the XSL recommendation allows it. Following is an example to demonstrate. Given the same content as for the prior example, you alter the template of the style sheet matching `phrase` as follows:

```
<xsl:template match="phrase">
  <fo:inline-container xsl:use-attribute-set="text-box"
```

```
    inline-progression-dimension="1.5in">
     <fo:block xsl:use-attribute-sets="phrase">
       <xsl:apply-templates/>
     </fo:block>
   </fo:inline-container>
 </xsl:template>
```

You have an `inline-container` with an embedded block where you formerly placed a simple inline. Figure 6.8 shows the rendered result. The content typeset in the inline-progression direction includes a portion of content typeset in the block-progression direction.

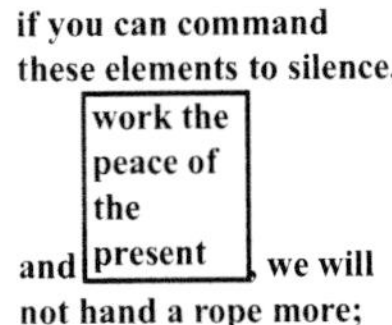

Figure 6.8
inline-container with an embedded block.

The setting for the `inline-progression-dimension` property on the `inline-container` in the preceding example prevents the formatter from typesetting the container using the entire remaining width of the line, or the width of the containing block, as it chooses. Without it, the typeset result would look something like that shown in Figure 6.9.

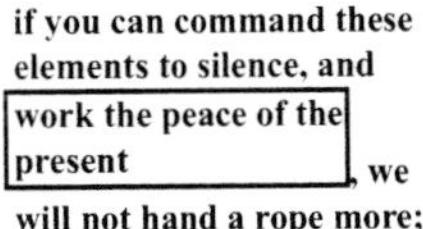

Figure 6.9
inline-container filling the remainder of the line.

Space, Margins, and Indents

Everything associated with the box outside the frame, beyond the border, is space. Space gives the box a little breathing room. It may or may not be zero. Many document styles place some space between paragraphs of text and after headings. A list or block quote may have indents on either side. The space, margin, and indent properties control that space.

The XSL recommendation has a section in its discussion about the Area Model that talks about space, conditionality, and space-resolution rules. This is a very powerful tool that has some fine points, but it is not really all that tough after you get it. Let's work with it using the screenplay example.

In the screenplay example, you have the title, shots, scene locale, and dialog. You would like lots of space before the title to place it a little above the midpoint of the page. You would like a blank line before and two blank lines after the scene locale. Description should have two lines after. The character about to speak dialog should have a line before.

The space specification for the title appears in the attribute-set for the title, as follows:

```
<xsl:attribute-set name="title">
  <xsl:attribute name="space-before.minimum">2.5in</xsl:attribute>
  <xsl:attribute name="space-before.optimum">3in</xsl:attribute>
  <xsl:attribute name="space-before.maximum">4in</xsl:attribute>
</xsl:attribute-set>
```

That provides for two and one-half inches minimum to four inches maximum between the top of the body region and the top of the first line of text for the title. The formatter starts with a value of three inches.

Conditionality

Unfortunately, when typeset, the title appears at the top of the region, with no space above it. The reason is that space is conditional. The formatter discards space that occurs at certain boundaries. It discards space before the first line on a page or in a column. It discards space after the last line on a page or column.

For the most part, this is sensible behavior. In general, you specify space to separate marks within a page—between paragraphs, for example. You don't want the space to increase the amount of margin at the top or bottom of a page, except with your title.

To get the space before the title, you need to add one more space specifier to the `title` attribute set, as follows:

```
<xsl:attribute name="space-before.conditionality">retain</xsl:attribute>
```

The default value for conditionality is `discard`. You change it to `retain`. All of a sudden, the title appears properly spaced downward on the page.

These last two attributes round out the settings for the title of the screenplay. They force the title text to appear centered within the page all in capital letters:

```
<xsl:attribute name="text-transform">uppercase</xsl:attribute>
<xsl:attribute name="text-align">center</xsl:attribute>
```

Precedence

No example is included in the screenplay style sheet, but sometimes two boxes may follow one another where one box has space after and the next has space before. The formatter does not then automatically reproduce both spaces. The effect would almost certainly be to produce too much space between the boxes. The formatter uses space precedence rules instead to determine which space it reproduces on the page.

Following are two space specifications—one for space before and one for space after:

```
<xsl:attribute name="space-after.minimum">1.5em</xsl:attribute>
<xsl:attribute name="space-after.optimum">2em</xsl:attribute>
<xsl:attribute name="space-after.maximum">4em</xsl:attribute>
<xsl:attribute name="space-after.precedence">1</xsl:attribute>

<xsl:attribute name="space-before.minimum">1em</xsl:attribute>
<xsl:attribute name="space-before.optimum">3em</xsl:attribute>
<xsl:attribute name="space-before.maximum">3.5em</xsl:attribute>
<xsl:attribute name="space-before.precedence">0</xsl:attribute>
```

The precedence value may have a number, or it may have the keyword `force`. By default, the precedence value is zero.

If any of the specifiers is `force`, the formatter will give an amount of space equal to the sum of all specifiers with the value `force`. Otherwise, it uses the space specifier with the highest numeric value precedence.

If the space specifiers have equal precedence, the formatter will give an amount of space ranging from the smallest of the two minimums to the largest of the two maximums. It will use the larger of the two optimum values.

In the preceding example, the `space-after` has higher precedence. The formatter will give a minimum of `1.5em` and a maximum of `4em`. It will start with `2em`. If the precedences were the same, the formatter would give a minimum of `1em` and a maximum of `4em`. It would start with `3em`.

There is no place for conditionality to take part, because the space is between boxes. The formatter will not discard any space here.

Margins

The `margin-top`, `margin-bottom`, `margin-left`, and `margin-right` properties are absolute properties corresponding to the relative properties—`space-before`, `space-after`, `space-start`, `space-end`, `start-indent`, and `end-indent`. The conditionality of space specified using the margin properties is always equal to `retain`.

The FO recommendation carefully describes the correspondence of margins with the various space and indent properties. Implementors have to deal with this complexity. You can make your life simple by using the relative properties in preference to the absolute margin properties. Chapter 8, "Page Styling," describes the appropriate use of margins to reserve space at the edges of the page.

The `space-start` and `space-end` properties may not be used with block-level FOs. You might be tempted to use the corresponding margin properties but `start-indent` and `end-indent` are better suited to adjust the space on either side of a block.

start-indent and end-indent

The `start-indent` and `end-indent` are very helpful properties carefully designed to manage the margins that squeeze blocks of text toward the center of the page. The length you specify extends from the content rectangle of the nearest parent `region`, `block-container`, or `inline-container` all the way into the content rectangle of the box to which it applies.

This means that the amount of the indent does not accumulate on blocks. Blocks may nest within a `block-container` or region, but their indents will always reference the edge of the `block-container` or region, not the edge of the parent block. Figure 6.10 provides a diagram to illustrate:

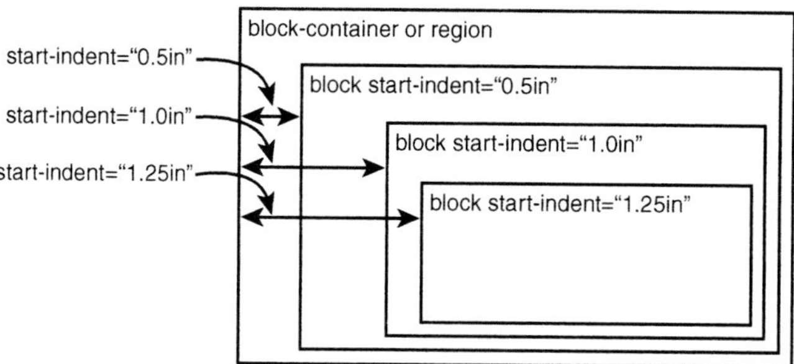

Figure 6.10
Mechanics of start and end indents.

The amount of the indent extends to the content rectangle of the box. That means that it includes any padding, border, and margin on the edge of the box that corresponds to the indent.

Listing 6.8 provides the remaining attribute set definitions not yet shown for the screenplay example. Replace the empty definitions given in Listing 6.2 with these:

Listing 6.8 *Style Sheet Fragment Completes scnStyle.xsl*

```
<xsl:attribute-set name="scene">
  <xsl:attribute name="start-indent">5in</xsl:attribute>
</xsl:attribute-set>

<xsl:attribute-set name="author">
  <xsl:attribute name="start-indent">60%</xsl:attribute>
  <xsl:attribute name="break-after">page</xsl:attribute>
</xsl:attribute-set>

<xsl:attribute-set name="locale">
  <xsl:attribute name="start-indent">1.0in</xsl:attribute>
  <xsl:attribute name="end-indent">0.5in</xsl:attribute>
  <xsl:attribute name="space-after">2em</xsl:attribute>
  <xsl:attribute name="space-after.maximum">3em</xsl:attribute>
</xsl:attribute-set>

<xsl:attribute-set name="action">
  <xsl:attribute name="start-indent">1.0in</xsl:attribute>
  <xsl:attribute name="end-indent">0.5in</xsl:attribute>
  <xsl:attribute name="space-after">2em</xsl:attribute>
  <xsl:attribute name="space-after.maximum">3em</xsl:attribute>
</xsl:attribute-set>

<xsl:attribute-set name="shot">
  <xsl:attribute name="start-indent">1.0in</xsl:attribute>
  <xsl:attribute name="end-indent">0.5in</xsl:attribute>
  <xsl:attribute name="space-after">2em</xsl:attribute>
  <xsl:attribute name="space-after.maximum">3em</xsl:attribute>
</xsl:attribute-set>

<xsl:attribute-set name="speaker">
  <xsl:attribute name="start-indent">2.5in</xsl:attribute>
  <xsl:attribute name="end-indent">1.8in</xsl:attribute>
  <xsl:attribute name="text-transform">uppercase</xsl:attribute>
  <xsl:attribute name="text-align">center</xsl:attribute>
</xsl:attribute-set>

<xsl:attribute-set name="speech">
  <xsl:attribute name="start-indent">2.5in</xsl:attribute>
  <xsl:attribute name="end-indent">1.8in</xsl:attribute>
  <xsl:attribute name="space-after">2em</xsl:attribute>
  <xsl:attribute name="space-after.maximum">3em</xsl:attribute>
```

Listing 6.8 *(continued)*

```
</xsl:attribute-set>

<xsl:attribute-set name="direction">
  <xsl:attribute name="start-indent">3.2in</xsl:attribute>
  <xsl:attribute name="end-indent">2.5in</xsl:attribute>
  <xsl:attribute name="text-align">center</xsl:attribute>
</xsl:attribute-set>
```

Many of the attribute sets shown in Listing 6.8 adjust the start and end margins using the `start-indent` and `end-indent` properties. There is no need to use any of the margin properties. The `space-before` and `space-after` settings maintain vertical spacing between elements. A block of dialog formatted using the attribute-set named speech, for example, will format with blank space after equal to 2 to 3 times the size of the font.

The screenplay format requires different indents for different elements. Dialog, for example, appears within a fairly narrow column in the center of the page. In movies, we don't make long speeches. Dialog in the narrow column eats up the page in a hurry, the same way it eats up time onscreen. This little simulation device helps the screenplay convey the pace of the film. Figure 6.11 shows a typeset sample of speech.

master
Boatswain!

boatswain
Here, master: what cheer?

master
(urgently)
Good, speak to the mariners:
fall to't, yarely, or we run
ourselves aground: bestir,
bestir.

CUT:

Figure 6.11
Typeset dialog from the screenplay.

Justification

There are four ways to justify text. It may start on the left with a ragged-right edge. That is left-justified. It may end on the right with a ragged-left edge. That is right-justified. It may fill from the left to the right edge. That is full-justified. Each line may be centered with ragged left and right edges. That is center-justified.

Use the `text-align` property to control text justification. The default alignment is `start`. That is the edge where the eye begins reading a line. XSL FO always interprets the value `left` to mean `start`, and `right` to mean `end`. Specify `center` to get center-justified text. Specify the value `justify` to get full-justified text.

Two additional values exist in FO that are slightly esoteric. The value `inside` means justify at the binding edge of the page, which may be the start or the end. The value `outside` means justify at the nonbinding edge.

The styling for the stage directions in the screenplay style sheet uses `center` alignment:

```
<xsl:attribute-set name="direction">
  <xsl:attribute name="start-indent">3.2in</xsl:attribute>
  <xsl:attribute name="end-indent">2.5in</xsl:attribute>
  <xsl:attribute name="text-align">center</xsl:attribute>
</xsl:attribute-set>
```

text-transform

One of the requirements of screenplay form is that the names of characters be printed in all capitals. The form also requires that sound effects be printed in all capitals. This allows sound-production personnel to scan quickly for needed sound effects.

Use the XSL FO `text-transform` property to alter the capitalization of text. By default, FO will leave text unmolested. With a value of `uppercase`, FO will transform any lowercase characters to uppercase. The value `lowercase` does the opposite. FO will ensure that all characters are lowercase.

The value `capitalize` causes FO to make the first character of every word an uppercase character. FO does not distinguish articles, such as "the" and "of"; therefore, this is less useful than it might seem. It won't do for capitalizing titles, for example. It might work for capitalizing section headings.

The value of `text-transform` inherits, so the style sheet places it on a wrapper. Following are the template and style sources for character. The style sheet treats the sound element similarly:

```
<xsl:attribute-set name="character">
  <xsl:attribute name="text-transform">uppercase</xsl:attribute>
</xsl:attribute-set>

  <xsl:template match="character">
  <fo:wrapper xsl:use-attribute-sets="character">
```

```
    <xsl:apply-templates/>
  </fo:wrapper>
</xsl:template>
```

Summary

What did we claim at the beginning of the chapter? Master the block and inline and the world of typesetting is at your feet. You've done it. You can ipd, bpd, start, end, before, and after with the best. You can visualize the progression of inline boxes flowing into blocks, blocks flowing into pages. Can't you? It's a well-regulated flow that you control with block-level and inline-level FOs.

If you've gotten this far, you're almost an expert on FOs. The rest is detail, how to do lists, how to do tables, and how to control lines. Congratulate yourself. This is a milestone. You can typeset your life story. Stop here and get started on your project if you like, but don't ignore the rest of the book.

The next two chapters cover more general-purpose information about controlling lines, ordering the march of page layouts, or eliminating pages altogether if scrolling is your bailiwick. Beyond that, you might skip around depending on your needs. For now, good going! Welcome to the world of XSL typesetting. Typeset something. You're a member of the club.

CHAPTER 7

White Space and Line Handling

White space. Those two words bring fear and trembling to the most knowledgeable of XML practitioners. The more they know, the greater the trepidation. Experts become weak in the knees and begin to wobble at the mere mention of those words. Their pulse and breathing rates increase, pupils dilate. They get that hunted look, avert their eyes, and excuse themselves to get a glass of water, or something stronger.

White-space handling is one of the few issues that the XSL FO subgroup has grappled with after publication of the recommendation. New problems just keep coming up, like how to preserve white space around line breaks introduced by the formatter. There seems to be no end to details regarding white space.

The reason white space is so difficult, controversial, and arcane is that we are of two minds about it. We want it, and we don't. We want to include indentation, blank lines, and line breaks to make XML sources readable in a text editor. At the same time, we don't want to have that white space affect the processing of the document. We want processors to ignore it. Sometimes. Sometimes we don't.

It's difficult to design XML and XSL so that we can see our white space and hide it too. That was a challenge to the designers of XSL that really made them sweat. Fortunately, they pretty much met the challenge. XSL has the tools we need to control white space. Most of us don't have to implement them. We didn't need to design them. We only need to understand them and use them.

The tools for managing white space in XSL are well within the reach of our understanding. For practical purposes, we can tame white space and get our work done. We'll thrive thanks to the blood, sweat, and tears given by XSL designers and implementers over white space.

Ignoring Space and Newlines

Sometimes—most of the time—we don't want any of the space from the XSL style sheet or the XML source to appear in the typeset output. Well, not quite. We do want space to separate words. The rest we'd rather have the formatter ignore.

Suppose we have the source XML shown in Listing 7.1, rife with excess white space introduced for the convenience of the human being who wrote it. There's nothing wrong with that. Human beings use computers, not the other way around. XSL should serve us by ignoring the excess white space when it typesets the document. The quote is from David Brin's excellent book, *The Transparent Society*.

Listing 7.1 *A Well-Indented Source Document*

```
<?xml version="1.0" ?>
-<quote>
  <paragraph>
    We can never learn what is flawless or unblemished with our senses alone.
    But the devastation wrought by idealists in the past shows how
    easily we can also lie to ourselves
   <emph>within</emph>
   our imaginative minds. Reason is an excellent tool for generating
   hypotheses. But it is in the world of hard, gritty practicality that honest
    folks test their favorite ideas, modify them under the heat of criticism,
    carve away errors, and join others in developing systems that work.
  </paragraph>
  <paragraph>Systems that may even be somewhat true.</paragraph>
</quote>
```

A very straightforward XSL style sheet such as the one shown in Listing 7.2 will typeset this document without unexpected line breaks or extra white space. That is as it should be. It is the normal behavior. We expect it to be the default behavior. The listing omits the root rule that outputs the `layout-master-set`, `page-sequence`, and flow. We disposed with that way back in Chapter 3, "Hello XSL World."

Listing 7.2 *A Well-Indented Style Sheet*

```
<?xml version='1.0'?>
<xsl:stylesheet version="1.0"
 xmlns:xsl="http://www.w3.org/1999/XSL/Transform"
 xmlns:fo="http://www.w3.org/1999/XSL/Format">

  <xsl:include href="rootrule.xsl"/>
```

Listing 7.2 *(continued)*

```
  <xsl:template match="paragraph">
    <fo:block space-after="6pt">
      <xsl:apply-templates/>
    </fo:block>
  </xsl:template>

  <xsl:template match="emph">
    <fo:wrapper font-style="italic">
      <xsl:apply-templates/>
    </fo:wrapper>
  </xsl:template>

</xsl:stylesheet>
```

Even the style sheet has well-indented elements with lots of extra white space and newline characters to facilitate reading and editing. Figure 7.1 shows output generated by the Antenna House formatter.

We can never learn what is flawless or unblemished with our senses alone. But the devestation wrought by idealists in the past shows how easily we can also lie to ourselves *within* our imaginative minds. Reason is an excellent tool for generating hypotheses. But it is in the world of hard, gritty practicality that honest folks test their favorite ideas, modify them under the heat of criticism, carve away errors, and join others in developing systems that work.

Systems that may even be somewhat true.

Figure 7.1
Typeset result shows expected spacing.

This is, as we said, just what you want and expect. We've also said that sometimes that is not what you want.

Honoring Newlines

Listing 7.3 shows some markup for a poem. It does not contain any markup to distinguish lines. Instead it captures the lines of each stanza more naturally, the way they would appear in print, by placing a newline character between them. You may argue that this is not optimal markup. You might prefer markup around each line. Assume this is what you have and you have to deal with it.

Listing 7.3 *A Poem Without Markup for Lines*

```
<?xml version='1.0'?>
<poem>
```

Listing 7.3 *(continued)*

```
  <title>The World Is Too Much with Us</title>
  <author>William Wordsworth</author>
  <stanza>
    The world is too much with us; late and soon,
    Getting and spending, we lay waste our powers:
    Little we see in Nature that is ours;
    We have given our hearts away, a sordid boon!
    The Sea that bares her bosom to the moon;
    The winds that will be howling at all hours,
    And are up-gathered now like sleeping flowers;
    For this, for everything, we are out of tune;
    It moves us not. --Great God! I'd rather be
    A Pagan suckled in a creed outworn;
    So might I, standing on this pleasant lea,
    Have glimpses that would make me less forlorn;
    Have sight of Proteus rising from the sea;
    Or hear old Triton blow his wreathed horn.
  </stanza>
</poem>
```

A style sheet that matches the `stanza` element and outputs the text inside of a `block` FO will produce dreadful results from the standpoint of typesetting a poem. Listing 7.4 contains such a style sheet.

Listing 7.4 *A Style Sheet to Present the Poem Markup*

```
<?xml version='1.0'?>
<xsl:stylesheet version="1.0"
 xmlns:xsl="http://www.w3.org/1999/XSL/Transform"
 xmlns:fo="http://www.w3.org/1999/XSL/Format">

  <xsl:include href="rootrule.xsl"/>
  <xsl:include href="poemstyle.xsl"/>

  <xsl:template match="title">
    <fo:block xsl:use-attribute-sets="title">
      <xsl:apply-templates/>
    </fo:block>
  </xsl:template>

  <xsl:template match="author">
    <fo:block xsl:use-attribute-sets="author">
      <xsl:text>by </xsl:text><xsl:apply-templates/>
```

Listing 7.4 *(continued)*

```
    </fo:block>
  </xsl:template>

  <xsl:template match="stanza">
    <fo:block xsl:use-attribute-sets="stanza">
      <xsl:apply-templates/>
    </fo:block>
  </xsl:template>

</xsl:stylesheet>
```

Begin with the following as the source for the style file `poemstyle.xsl` that is included in Listing 7.4. It simply holds a place for each of the different styles used by the templates:

```
<?xml version='1.0'?>
<xsl:stylesheet version="1.0"
 xmlns:xsl="http://www.w3.org/1999/XSL/Transform"
 xmlns:fo="http://www.w3.org/1999/XSL/Format">

  <xsl:attribute-set name="title"/>
  <xsl:attribute-set name="author"/>
  <xsl:attribute-set name="stanza"/>

</xsl:stylesheet>
```

Figure 7.2 demonstrates the output that will result.

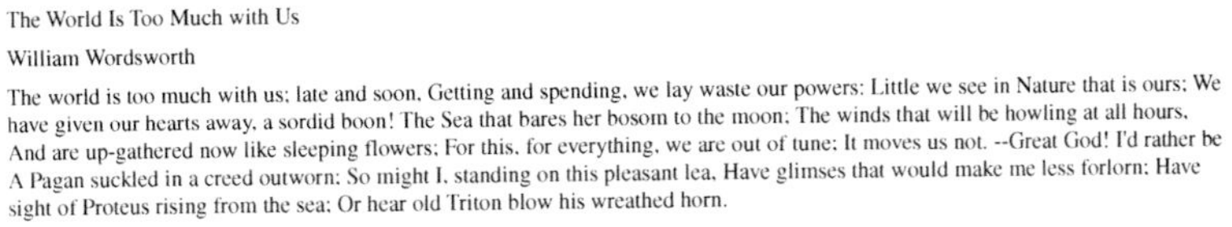

The World Is Too Much with Us

William Wordsworth

The world is too much with us; late and soon, Getting and spending, we lay waste our powers: Little we see in Nature that is ours; We have given our hearts away, a sordid boon! The Sea that bares her bosom to the moon; The winds that will be howling at all hours, And are up-gathered now like sleeping flowers; For this, for everything, we are out of tune; It moves us not. --Great God! I'd rather be A Pagan suckled in a creed outworn; So might I, standing on this pleasant lea, Have glimses that would make me less forlorn; Have sight of Proteus rising from the sea; Or hear old Triton blow his wreathed horn.

Figure 7.2
Typeset result shows lack of desired line breaks.

You see that all the lines ran together as if they belonged in a paragraph. A single change to the styling of the `stanza` element will correct this, and it's very simple. You want to preserve the newline characters from the input. You set the `linefeed-treatment` property to preserve linefeeds. Listing 7.5 completes `poemstyle.xsl` with full sets of property settings. It has added some font settings for the title and the author and left a little space between the heading and the text of the poem; note especially the settings on the attribute-set named `stanza`. It contains the setting for `linefeed-treatment` that makes all the difference:

Listing 7.5 `poemstyle.xsl` *Property Settings for the Poetry Style Sheet*

```
<?xml version='1.0'?>
<xsl:stylesheet version="1.0"
 xmlns:xsl="http://www.w3.org/1999/XSL/Transform"
 xmlns:fo="http://www.w3.org/1999/XSL/Format">

  <xsl:attribute-set name="title">
    <xsl:attribute name="font-weight">bold</xsl:attribute>
  </xsl:attribute-set>

  <xsl:attribute-set name="author">
    <xsl:attribute name="font-style">italic</xsl:attribute>
    <xsl:attribute name="space-after">3pt</xsl:attribute>
  </xsl:attribute-set>

  <xsl:attribute-set name="stanza">
    <xsl:attribute name="linefeed-treatment">preserve</xsl:attribute>
    <xsl:attribute name="space-after">3pt</xsl:attribute>
  </xsl:attribute-set>

</xsl:stylesheet>
```

Figure 7.3 shows the new result output, which looks more appropriate for a poem.

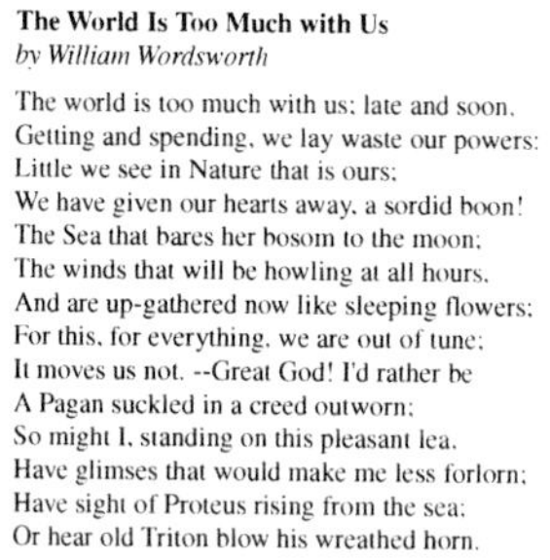

The World Is Too Much with Us
by William Wordsworth

The world is too much with us; late and soon,
Getting and spending, we lay waste our powers:
Little we see in Nature that is ours;
We have given our hearts away, a sordid boon!
The Sea that bares her bosom to the moon;
The winds that will be howling at all hours,
And are up-gathered now like sleeping flowers;
For this, for everything, we are out of tune;
It moves us not. --Great God! I'd rather be
A Pagan suckled in a creed outworn;
So might I, standing on this pleasant lea,
Have glimses that would make me less forlorn;
Have sight of Proteus rising from the sea;
Or hear old Triton blow his wreathed horn.

Figure 7.3
Typeset result honors line breaks.

Honoring Spaces

There's more to life than poetry, unfortunately. To typeset this book, for example, you have to typeset code fragments. To typeset nicely indented XML you'll have to somehow include the leading spaces following the newline. Listing 7.6 contains the full style sheet. The key is in the attribute-set applied to code:

```
<xsl:attribute-set name="code">
  <xsl:attribute name="linefeed-treatment">preserve</xsl:attribute>
  <xsl:attribute name="white-space-treatment">preserve</xsl:attribute>
  <xsl:attribute name="white-space-collapse">false</xsl:attribute>
  <xsl:attribute name="font-family">monospaced</xsl:attribute>
</xsl:attribute-set>
```

That `attribute-set` contains two lines for handling white space. The first, `white-space-treatment`, preserves white space preceding and following newlines. The second, `white-space-collapse`, prevents the formatter from collapsing multiple spaces into a single space. The monospaced font makes the result look proper for code.

Listing 7.6 places the source for the style sheet inside an XML CDATA section. That is the section that begins with the processing instruction `<![CDATA[` and ends with `]]>`:

Listing 7.6 *XML Markup of XSL Style Sheet That Honors Word Spacing*

```
<?xml version='1.0'?>
<code>
<![CDATA[<?xml version='1.0'?>
<xsl:stylesheet version="1.0"
 xmlns:xsl="http://www.w3.org/1999/XSL/Transform"
 xmlns:fo="http://www.w3.org/1999/XSL/Format">

  <xsl:include href="rootrule.xsl"/>

  <xsl:attribute-set name="code">
    <xsl:attribute name="linefeed-treatment">preserve</xsl:attribute>
    <xsl:attribute name="white-space-treatment">preserve</xsl:attribute>
    <xsl:attribute name="white-space-collapse">false</xsl:attribute>
    <xsl:attribute name="font-family">monospaced</xsl:attribute>
  </xsl:attribute-set>

  <xsl:template match="code">
    <fo:block xsl:use-attribute-sets="code">
      <xsl:apply-templates/>
    </fo:block>
  </xsl:template>

</xsl:stylesheet>]]>
```

There's nothing particularly tricky about placing literal tags within an XML document. The CDATA brackets mask the tags from interpretation by the XML parser. Without them, it would try to interpret the XSL markup within the `<code>` element.

Note that you did not place a line feed after the opening bracket, `<![CDATA[`, nor before the closing bracket, `]]>`. The style rule preserves all line feeds within the `<code>` tag. Those extra newline characters would thus appear in the typeset result. You already have one newline before. That is the newline that separates the `<code>` element from the opening CDATA bracket. You would have to place the opening CDATA bracket on the same line as the `<code>` tag to eliminate all leading lines from the typeset result. The input would then look like this:

```
<code><![CDATA[<?xml version='1.0'?>
...
</xsl:stylesheet>]]></code>
```

There's really no other way around eliminating the extra newlines at the start of the CDATA section. Sometimes the best way to eliminate line feeds from the output is to leave them out of the input.

Figure 7.4 shows the typeset result. Just for fun, it uses the style sheet to typeset the style sheet. If this book were formatted using FO, every one of the listings would have been formatted this way.

```
<?xml version='1.0'?>
<xsl:stylesheet version="1.0"
xmlns:xsl="http://www.w3.org/1999/XSL/Transform"
xmlns:fo="http://www.w3.org/1999/XSL/Format">

<xsl:include href="rootrule.xsl"/>

<xsl:attribute-set name="code">
 <xsl:attribute name="linefeed-treatment">preserve</xsl:attribute>
 <xsl:attribute name="white-space-treatment">preserve</xsl:attribute>
 <xsl:attribute name="white-space-collapse">false</xsl:attribute>
 <xsl:attribute name="font-family">monospaced</xsl:attribute>
</xsl:attribute-set>

<xsl:template match="code">
 <fo:block xsl:use-attribute-sets="code">
  <xsl:apply-templates/>
 </fo:block>
 </xsl:template>
</xsl:stylesheet>
```

Figure 7.4

Typeset style sheet that honors spaces.

Word Space

Word space is the space between words. We generally type a space character with that big long bar under our thumbs to indicate the space between words. Naturally, FO treats the space character, by default, as a word space.

We take it for granted, but the space between words was an invention. We didn't always have it. Some early language systems placedallofthecharacterstogether. That didn't last long. Others lmntdllfthvls (eliminated all of the vowels). Writing materials were precious. Folks back then didn't just borrow a sheet of paper from their classmate or rob the copy machine.

The formatter treats a character as word space by replacing the character with a fixed amount of space determined to separate words. The question arises, here in the present, just how large a word space should be. This is really a font thing. The font specifies the size of a word space. FO formatters place that amount of space between words.

None of this would be especially surprising or important, except that FO provides means to control the size of the space between words. The `word-spacing` property lets you override the size of a word space determined from the font. Its value may be a simple length, or it may be a space specifier.

Remember that a space specifier allows a range of values from a minimum to a maximum, with an optimum value for initial calculations. Let's take the Wordsworth example in Listings 7.4 and 7.5 and spread out the words a little bit. The following modification of the `stanza` attribute set of Listing 7.5 specifies `word-spacing`:

```
<xsl:attribute-set name="stanza">
  <xsl:attribute name="linefeed-treatment">preserve</xsl:attribute>
  <xsl:attribute name="space-after">3pt</xsl:attribute>
  <xsl:attribute name="word-spacing.minimum">0.15em</xsl:attribute>
  <xsl:attribute name="word-spacing.optimum">0.3em</xsl:attribute>
</xsl:attribute-set>
```

The minimum value will let the formatter squeeze spaces to as little as half their optimal amount to fit a line. By default, the maximum amount of space between words is equal to the optimum. The formatted result shown in Figure 7.5 looks just slightly different:

XSL FO formatters treat only the normal ASCII space, Unicode ``, as word space. Some spaces in the Unicode character set FO treats as characters. By default, the fixed space Unicode characters from `ߐ` to `ÈA;` and the ideographic space character, `ஸ` are not word space. The only way to make a word space with a character other than the space, `` is to place it in a character formatting object and set the `treat-as-word-space` property to `true`. The following code causes a nonbreaking space to have the amount of space specified by the word-spacing property, rather than the amount specified by the font:

```
<fo:character treat-as-word-space="true" character="&#2000;"/>
```

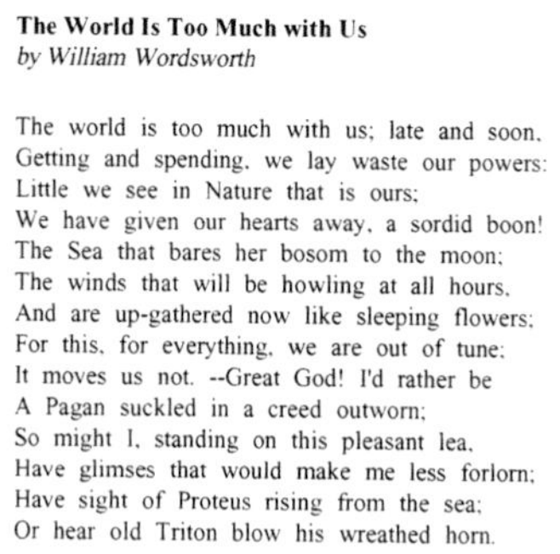

The World Is Too Much with Us
by William Wordsworth

The world is too much with us; late and soon,
Getting and spending, we lay waste our powers:
Little we see in Nature that is ours;
We have given our hearts away, a sordid boon!
The Sea that bares her bosom to the moon;
The winds that will be howling at all hours,
And are up-gathered now like sleeping flowers;
For this, for everything, we are out of tune;
It moves us not. --Great God! I'd rather be
A Pagan suckled in a creed outworn;
So might I, standing on this pleasant lea,
Have glimses that would make me less forlorn;
Have sight of Proteus rising from the sea;
Or hear old Triton blow his wreathed horn.

Figure 7.5
Spaced out words.

Line Wrapping Override

Until now, the formatter has introduced newline characters into every input we have supplied. When a word does not fit at the end of one line, the formatter places it at the start of a new line. We call this line breaking, line wrapping, or word wrapping.

The formatter carries out word wrapping or line breaking as part of the process of constructing blocks. It does so by introducing line breaks wherever a line becomes too long to fit the available space in the inline-progression dimension. Sometimes, rarely, we do not want the formatter to introduce line breaks. We do not want it to wrap words. We do not want it to mess with lines of the input.

It's difficult to think of an example when this would be desirable. Poetry certainly has a line structure that the formatter should not alter; but, given the alternative of cropping the text, you would probably prefer the wrap. It might be all right to have the long line print into the margin. You would think that the style sheet designer would prevent this through some other means, such as reducing font size or increasing the available width.

Whether or not it seems useful now, there may come a time when you might like to force the formatter to keep its paws off your lines. The `wrap-option` property provides a way to do just that. Write `wrap-option="no-wrap"` and the formatter will string lines to infinity before it dreams of introducing a line break. The default value for the `wrap-option` property is, of course, `wrap`.

Leading

Leading is not leading as in to lead or to follow, but the metal, lead, which we used to use as an additive in paint and gasoline and which the Romans used in freshwater pipes.

In the old days, when books and newspapers were printed with metal type, strips of lead separated each line of type in the galley. The next time you're frustrated in getting a typeset result the way you want it, just imagine getting your fingers black with lead and washing them before mealtime to avoid lead poisoning. Typesetting has come a long way.

To get the lead in, formatting objects provides three properties: `line-height`, `line-height-shift-adjustment`, and `line-stacking-strategy`. It turns out that in digital typesetting, it's much more convenient to adjust leading by adjusting the distance between base lines. The base line is the line along which characters march to stay in even rows across the page. Paragraphs and pages appear nicely formatted when the distance between base lines is constant throughout.

The `line-height` property determines the amount of half-leading used by the formatter in baseline placement calculations. We haven't paid any attention to leading so far, let alone half-leading, and everything has come out just fine. Thank goodness for good default values.

The default value for `line-height` is `normal`. Formatters interpret this as equal to 1 to 1.2 times the height of the font. For the most part, that is a pretty good number. We don't need to mess with it.

If you want more distance between lines, you can increase the `line-height`. An integer setting, such as `line-height="1.8"`, will provide a multiple of the font height. That is handy because if you change the font, the line height automatically adjusts for the height of the new font. You can also specify `line-height` as an absolute length, such as `line-height="24pt"`.

The `line-height` property takes a value of type `space`. That means it has minimum, optimum, and maximum components. Specifying a range of space for the `line-height` may allow the formatter to adjust the space between blocks to get a better fit within a page.

Unfortunately, the world is sometimes more complex. Sometimes lines of text may have figures or small images embedded within them. They may sometimes have mixed fonts. This is not usual, but the formatter must allow for it.

The old saying goes that there's more than one way to skin a cat. That's rather graphic, but in this case appropriate. Accounting for mixed content in a line is like skinning a cat. The cat, naturally, does not want to cooperate. FO defines three ways to get the job done.

The line-stacking-strategy property determines which of the three methods the formatter should use to calculate the position of each base line and account for mixed content in each line. The three values are line-height, font-height, and max-height. The last is the default. You will learn about each in turn.

Figure 7.6 illustrates two lines that will form the basis for our comparison of the three line-stacking strategies. The first line contains text in Times Roman, which will be the base font, or the font specified for the block within which the formatter stacks these lines. It also contains a character from a symbol font and three characters from the Monotype Corsiva font. The second line contains two words typeset in somewhat smaller Monotype Corsiva.

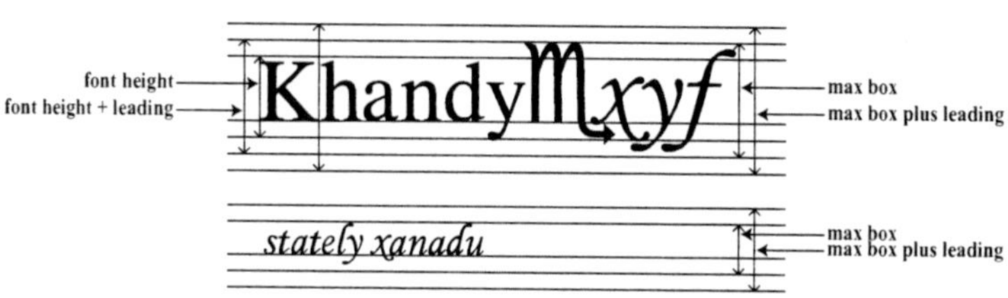

Figure 7.6

Lines illustrating font-height and varying max-height.

The first line of the figure illustrates the base font metrics for the block in a line that also contains larger elements. The second line of the figure illustrates content that has no elements equal to the height of the base font. The significance of these two cases will become evident in the following three figures as we illustrate the line-stacking strategies.

Figure 7.7 illustrates the max-height line-stacking strategy. This is the default strategy used by the formatter to space lines. The formatter determines the smallest box height required to enclose all the boxes in the line. This accounts for the maximum of the ascents above the base line and the maximum of the descents below the base line.

The formatter enlarges that box by the amount of leading. It distributes that leading half above and half below the boxes in the line. The formatter now has a box that contains the largest boxes in the line, plus a little above, plus a little below. It butts that box against the top of the block, and then repeats the process with each succeeding line, butting one up against the other.

The max-height strategy uses the maximum box size in each line, together with the leading, without reference to the height of the base font for the block. Its main characteristic is to provide a constant amount of space between each line. That amount is roughly equal to the amount of leading.

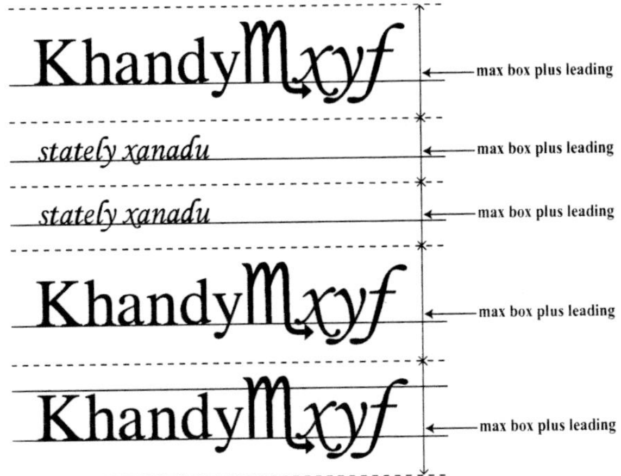

Figure 7.7
Lines stacked with strategy, max-height.

Figure 7.8 illustrates the `font-height` strategy. The formatter makes no reference whatsoever to the height of boxes within the lines. Instead, it positions base lines at equal distances through the block. It fixes the distance between base lines equal to the height of the base font plus the amount of leading. It places the first base line at a distance below the top of the box equal to the font ascent plus half of the leading. It places the bottom of the box below the last baseline at a distance equal to the font descent plus half of the leading.

Characters or inline elements may overlap between lines if they extend higher or lower above or below the base line than the font ascent or descent. The amount of leading is the only space that separates inline elements that are larger than the base font.

The main characteristic of the `font-height` strategy is equal spacing between base lines. The visible white space between lines increases when the content of the line is smaller than the height of the base font and decreases when the content of the line is larger than the height of the base font.

Figure 7.9 illustrates the `line-height` strategy. This strategy effectively combines the `max-height` and `font-height` strategies. It could be called the `max-max` strategy, because it uses the maximum of the two and produces the most space between lines. The formatter determines the maximum box as with the `max-height` strategy. If the height is smaller than the font height, the formatter increases the height of the box to equal the `font-height`.

The main characteristic of the `line-height` strategy is that it produces results that best match those produced by the line-stacking strategy employed by CSS.

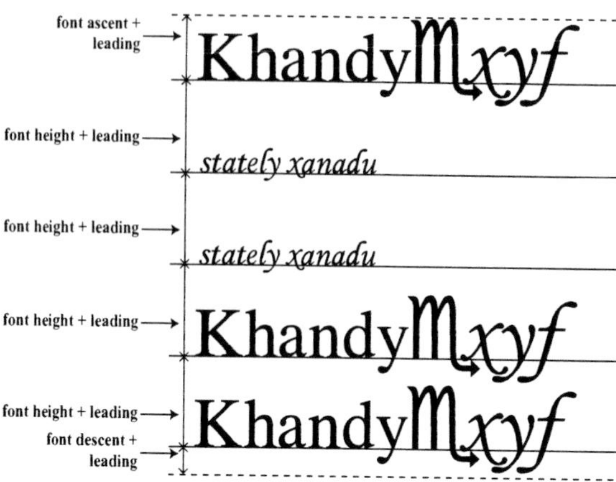

Figure 7.8

Lines stacked with strategy, font-height.

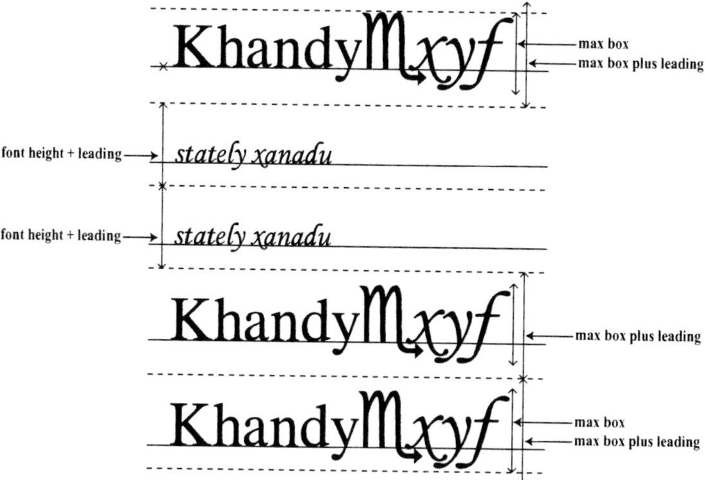

Figure 7.9

Lines stacked with strategy, line-height.

Subscripts and Superscripts

Once in a while, you might like to shift characters off the base line a little bit. The formatting property that enables this is aptly called `baseline-shift`. Values include `sub` and `super`, which correspond to subscript and superscript. You may also specify a length. A positive length moves the baseline in the shift direction. For most cases with Latin scripts, the shift direction is toward the before edge. That is up.

There really isn't much to it. It provides another useful purpose for the `wrapper` formatting object. Here is a rule for superscript as an example:

```
<xsl:template match="sup">
  <fo:wrapper
   font-size="0.7"
   baseline-shift="super">
    <xsl:apply-templates/>
  </fo:wrapper>
</xsl:template>
```

Note the font size reduction as well, to seven-tenths the size of the normal font.

Paragraph Separation

In Chapter 6, "Block and Inline," you learned about the `text-align` property, which specifies the alignment of the left and right edges of lines of text in blocks. Recall that text alignment values are `left`, `right`, `justified`, `inside`, or `outside`. You also reviewed `start-indent`, which added space between the start edge of the page and the beginning of lines of text.

Some texts separate paragraphs with extra space. Others separate paragraphs by giving an extra amount of indentation to the first line of each paragraph. The `text-indent` property adds to the amount of indentation of the first line of text in a block.

The default value for `text-indent` is zero. When it is positive, first lines will have some extra space before the first character. They will be indented. When `text-indent` is negative, first lines stick out into the margin toward the start edge. That is unusual, but the formatter allows it.

Not to be left out, the end of the last line may also have an indent. A designer may want to separate paragraphs by reducing or enlarging the available width for the last lines. The `last-line-end-indent` property removes available width from the end edge of the last line of each paragraph, if positive. If negative, the last line of each paragraph may be longer.

Figure 7.10 demonstrates paragraphs formatted with positive values for `text-indent` and `last-line-end-indent`. Figure 7.11 demonstrates negative values. The text excerpts are from Frank McCourt's bestseller, *Angela's Ashes*. First, here is the template which generated the paragraph shown in Figure 7.10:

```
<xsl:template match="p">
  <fo:block
    text-indent="0.5in"
    last-line-end-indent="0.5in"
    text-align="justify"
    text-align-last="justify">
    <xsl:apply-templates/>
  </fo:block>
</xsl:template>
```

And I suppose they'll be wanting sugar and milk on top of everything or they might be banging on my door looking for an egg if you don't mind. I don't know why we have to pay for Angela's mistakes.

Jesus, says Grandma. 'tis a good thing you didn't own that stable in Bethlehem or the Holy Family would still be wanderin' the world crumblin' with the hunger.

Figure 7.10

Text and last-line indents given positive amounts.

The template used to produce the output shown in Figure 7.11 differs only in the value for the `last-line-indent` property:

```
<xsl:template match="p">
  <fo:block
    text-indent="-0.5in"
    last-line-end-indent="-0.5in"
    text-align="justify"
    text-align-last="justify">
    <xsl:apply-templates/>
  </fo:block>
</xsl:template>
```

Look at what he did. Thrun up his First Communion breakfast. Thrun up the body and blood of Jesus. I have God in me backyard. What am I goin' to do? I'll take him to the Jesuits for they know the sins of the Pope himself.

She dragged me through the streets of Limerick. She told the neighbors and passing strangers about God in her backyard. She pushed me into the confession box.

Figure 7.11

Text and last-line indents given negative amounts.

Both examples force justification of the last line to show the full extent of the line from start to end. The last line typically has less than the required amount of text to fill the line. That is why full justification looks strange on the last line.

You'll recall that we used a value of `justify` for the `text-align` property in Chapter 5. The last lines of those paragraphs looked fine; the justify value does not apply to the last line.

The `text-align-last` property determines the alignment of the last line of each block. The formatter treats the default value, relative, relative to the value of the text-align property. The `relative` value is the same as the value for `text-align` except when that value is `justify`. When the value for the `text-align` property is `justify`, the formatter uses start alignment, not justification on the last line. This default behavior provides what you normally expect. You may change it for special effects, such as in Figures 7.10 and 7.11. The same values that apply to the text-align property also apply to the `text-align-last` property. Those values are `start`, `end`, `justify`, `center`, `inside`, and `outside`.

Summary

White space and newline handling is critical to effective presentation of XML content. XSL provides excellent tools for managing white space. You explored the use of block- and line-related properties to control line breaks and sequences of multiple spaces. That enabled you to typeset examples of code and of verse.

You found that white space is not only about the amount of space between words and where you choose to break lines. White space also occurs between and around paragraphs and at the ends of lines. The first and last lines of a paragraph may have additional indentation. You learned how to control all these features through use of block- and line-related properties provided by XSL FO.

CHAPTER 8
Page Styling

The designers of XSL Version 1.0 provided a simple page model consisting of five regions. They left a door open to expand this model in a later version should there be demand. This simple model provides sufficient power to express the most common page layouts. XSL also provides means to define multiple layouts and switch between them from one page to the next in the sequence of pages.

This design of this book provides one example of a page sequence. The first page of a chapter differs in layout from all subsequent pages of the chapter. We will try several examples, contrived and otherwise, to demonstrate the range of page layout combinations that you can express with XSL.

Simple Page Model

Use the `simple-page-master` FO to define a layout for typesetting pages. The layout may use one or more of five regions. The five regions have predefined locations, one at each edge of the page and one in the middle. They are called the `before`, `end`, `after`, `start`, and `body` regions. Figure 8.1 illustrates.

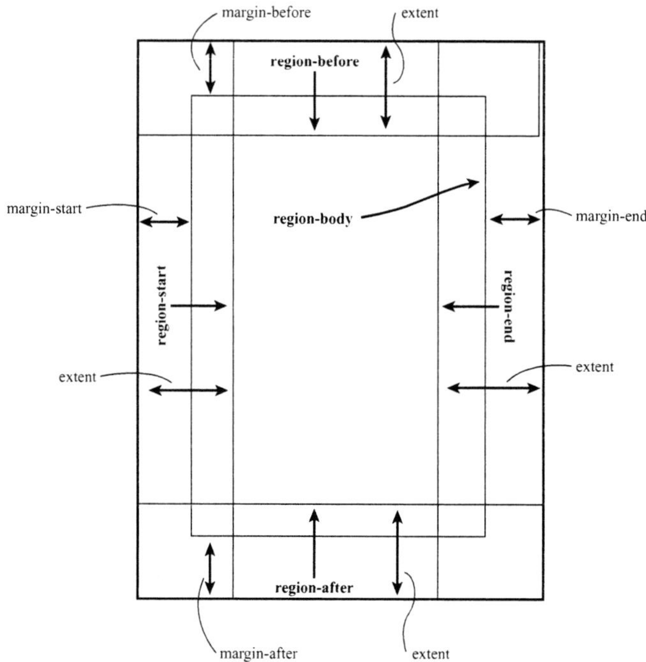

Figure 8.1
Regions of the simple-page-master.

The `region-body` FO defines the region in the center of the page. The other four regions have names according to the edge of the page on which they occur. The `region-start` occurs on the start edge, and so forth. We will refer to these as the *side regions*.

The side regions and the body region are very different creatures. The side regions stick to the edges of the page. Their *extent* is the distance to which they extend into the page. The side regions interact with each other at the corners.

The body region floats in the middle of the page without any interaction whatsoever with the side regions. Margin amounts position the edges of the `region-body`.

Figure 8.2 shows the body region overlapping all the side regions. That is to emphasize that the size of the body region has no relationship to the sizes of the side regions. You will usually make the body region float inside the side regions, as in Figure 8.1, but you are not required to do so. There may be a reason you would like to have overlap. If so, you can.

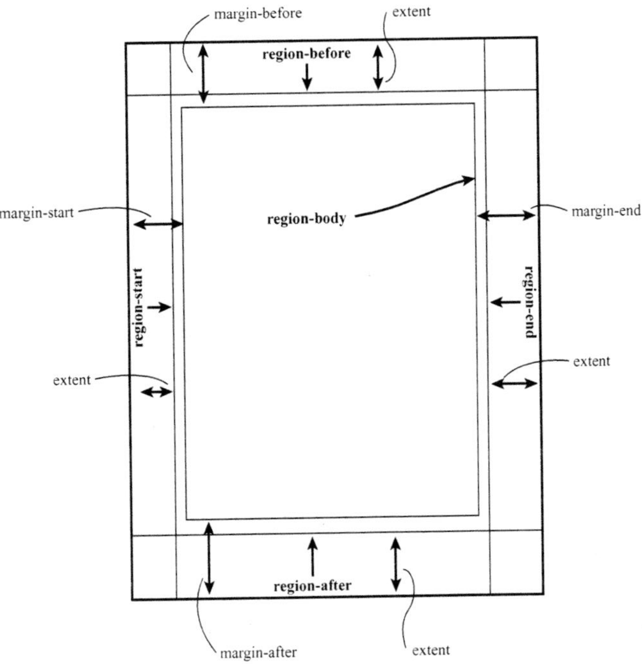

Figure 8.2
The region-body *floats in the center of the page.*

The only difference between Figure 8.1 and Figure 8.2 is the relationship of the extents to the margins. In Figure 8.2 the extents of the side regions exceed the margins of the body region. In Figure 8.1 the margins of the body region exceed the extents of the side regions.

Control the extent of the side regions using the `extent` property. The `extent` property accepts a length value, such as `0.5in`. The extent is the distance of the inner edge of the region from the edge of the page. Figures 8.1 and 8.2 mark the extents of each of the side regions.

Control the size and location of the body region using the margin properties. The `margin-top` property accepts a length and gives the distance from the top edge of the page to the top edge of the body region. Treat the other margins of the body region using the `margin-left`, `margin-right`, and `margin-bottom` properties.

You may have noticed that you switched from relative edges to absolute edges when you moved from region locations to margin amounts. This is a tricky spot. To get this right we have to slow down a bit, back up, and return to the `simple-page-master`.

Page Dimensions, reference-orientation, and writing-mode

The properties on the simple-page-master describe the dimensions of the page, how to orient the content of the page, and how to flow the content. Let's begin with the page size and orientation.

The output media has intrinsic properties. Before we even think of arranging content on the media, we think of the media coming out of some device with four edges—top, bottom, left, and right. We also think of the media as having a default size—8 1/2 by 11 inches, A4, legal, and so on.

Use the page-width and page-height properties of the simple-page-master to fix the width and height of the page. Omit the page-width and page-height properties to get a default page size configured in the formatter.

You cannot change the starting orientation of the media. If the width of the media is 8.5 inches and the height is 11 inches, the short edge is on top. This is the universe you inherit. You can specify the size of media you would like, but you always start with a top edge implied by the media itself.

Use the margin properties on the simple-page-master to carve away blank space around the edges of the page. The margin properties are absolute. They refer to the top or left edges of the universe implied by the media.

The reference-orientation property on the simple-page-master changes the worldview within the universe of the page. It defines a new edge as the top edge. A reference-orientation of 90 rotates the top edge to the left. It does this for all content of the page, not for the page itself. Let's work an example to make this clear.

Set page-width equal to 8.5 inches, page-height equal to 11 inches, margin-top and margin-bottom equal to 1 inch, and reference-orientation to 90, as follows:

```
<fo:simple-page-master
 master-name="landscape"
 page-width="8.5in" page-height="11in"
 margin-top="1in" margin-bottom="1in"
 reference-orientation="90">
  <!— region definitions —>
</fo:simple-page-master>
```

Figure 8.3 illustrates the settings. The question now is this: What are the working dimensions of the page and what is the length of the top edge?

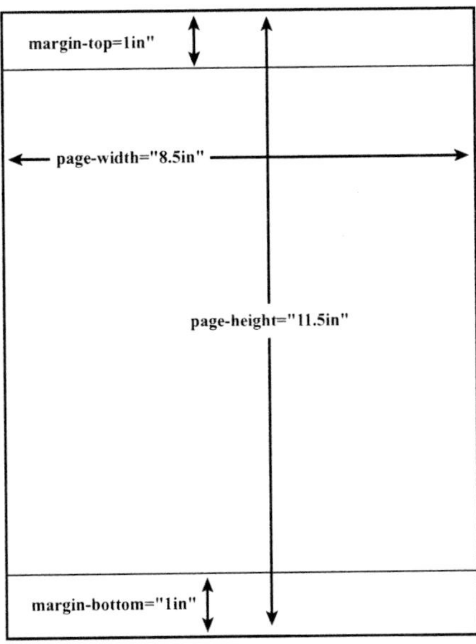

Figure 8.3
Page dimensions and margin on the simple-page-master.

The `page-width`, `page-height`, and `margin properties` refer to the page as it is before applying any `reference-orientation`. They refer to the raw media. The `margin-top` and `margin-bottom` therefore reduce the height of the working area from 11 inches to 9 inches. The `reference-orientation` applies to the area inside the margins. The setting of 90 reorients the world so that the 9-inch left edge is now the top.

It may help you to think of two rectangles. The outer rectangle is the universe we have to begin with. It is the given. The margin properties refer to that universe. They carve out a new rectangle inside that universe, a new world. The `reference-orientation` defines the worldview for the inner rectangle. Call the outer rectangle the *viewport rectangle*. Call the inner rectangle the *reference rectangle*. Figure 8.4 illustrates a reference rectangle reoriented 90 degrees relative to a viewport rectangle. It would be coded as follows:

```
<fo:simple-page-master
 master-name="landscape"
 page-width="8.5in" page-height="11in"
 margin-top="1in" margin-bottom="1in"
 margin-left="1in" margin-right="1in"
 reference-orientation="90">
  <!— region definitions —>
</fo:simple-page-master>
```

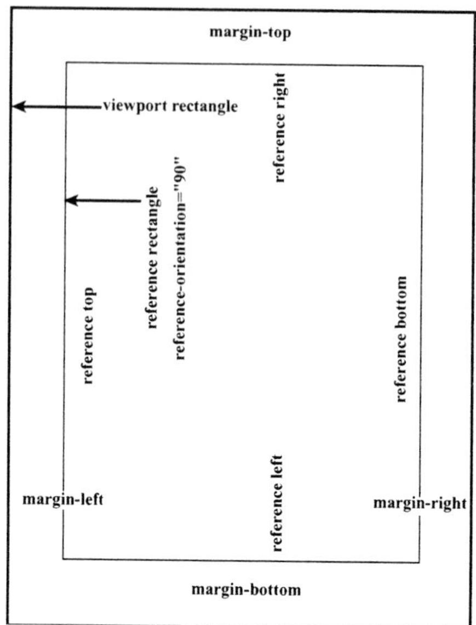

Figure 8.4
Viewport and reference rectangles.

All the labels of the viewport rectangle in Figure 8.4 correspond to the worldview defined by the page. All the labels of the reference rectangle in Figure 8.4 correspond to the new worldview set by the `reference-orientation`. The `block-container` and `inline-container` FOs, and all of the region FOs, also define viewport and reference rectangles. Those work the same way the viewport and reference rectangles in the page do.

Just like `reference-orientation`, the `writing-mode` defines a new direction for the inner rectangle. Chapter 6, "Block and Inline," detailed the relationship between the `reference-orientation` and the `writing-mode`. The `reference-orientation` determines which edge is the top. The `writing-mode` determines which is the before edge and which is the start edge.

Regions Revisited

When we started this chapter, life was simple. We had regions around the edges of the page and a body region within. Then we noticed that the margins referred to absolute edges and the regions referred to relative edges. That got us to think about the page margins, `reference-orientation`, and `writing-mode` set on the `simple-page-master`.

The outside edges of the side regions correspond to the edges of the page reference rectangle. That is the inner rectangle formed after subtracting `margin-top`, `margin-left`, and so on—settings given on the `simple-page-master`.

The before, after, start, and end regions correspond to the before, after, start, and end edges of the page reference rectangle. Those are the edges formed after allowing for the `reference-orientation` and `writing-mode` settings on the `simple-page-master`.

Figure 8.5 places the content of Figure 8.2 within the reference rectangle of Figure 8.4 to illustrate the relationship of the region rectangles to the page reference rectangle. It illustrates a complete page-master definition as follows:

```
<fo:simple-page-master
 master-name="landscape"
 page-width="8.5in" page-height="11in"
 margin-top="1in" margin-bottom="1in"
 margin-left="1in" margin-right="1in"
 reference-orientation="90">
  <region-body
   margin-top="1.25in" margin-bottom="1.25in"
   margin-left="1.25in" margin-right="1.25in"/>
  <region-before extent="1in"/>
  <region-after extent="1in"/>
  <region-start extent="1in"/>
  <region-end extent="1in"/>
</fo:simple-page-master>
```

The figure illustrates several relationships worth noting. The margins specified for the page on the `simple-page-master` and the margins specified for the `region-body` accumulate. The side regions align with the page reference rectangle, not strictly to the edges of the page. The margins on the `region-body` serve to keep the content of the body clear of content of the side regions. Finally, note that the `region-before` and the `margin-top` of the `region-body` are both on the left side of the page. They refer to the page-reference rectangle reoriented by the `reference-orientation` property of the `simple-page-master`.

Precedence

The figures demonstrating the side regions have so far played fast and loose with the corners. We have drawn them so that they overlap. Let's have a look at another property of regions that explains how the formatter handles the corners where the side regions overlap.

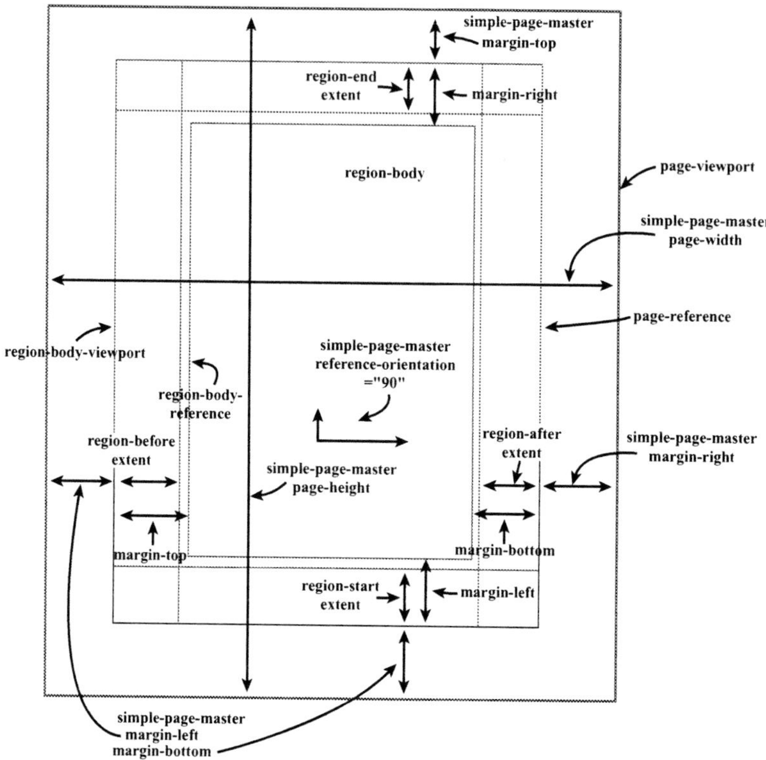

Figure 8.5

The complete page model with page reference rotated 90 degrees.

The `region-before` and `region-after` FOs have a property called `precedence`. The other regions do not have this property. The `precedence` property has two values, `true` and `false`. When the value of the precedence property is `true`, the region extends to the corners. Any regions on the adjacent edges will extend to abut the region with precedence. When the value is `false`, the region extends as far into the corner as it can without overlapping any region on an adjacent edge. The default value is `false`.

Figure 8.6 illustrates precedence. The `region-before` has the default precedence, `false`. The regions at the start and end edges extend to the before edge. The `region-after` has precedence `true`. It extends to the start and end edges.

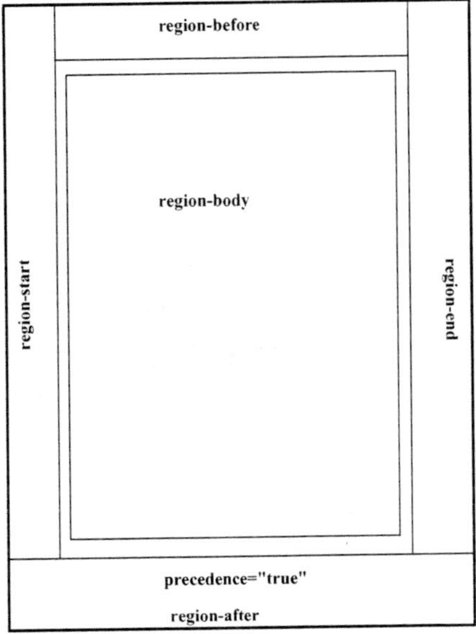

Figure 8.6
Precedence of side regions at the corners.

Background Properties

You may use the background properties on each region. Background colors and image properties apply. The border, padding, and margin properties do not apply to the regions. You may specify them, but they should be ignored. The recommendation specifies that, for now, the border and padding widths of the regions must remain zero.

The following page master places a background image in the start-edge region and a background color on the body region. The start region overlaps the body by one-quarter inch:

```
<fo:simple-page-master
 master-name="page"
 page-width="8.5in" page-height="11in"
 margin-top="0.5in" margin-bottom="0.5in"
 margin-left="0.5in" margin-right="0.25in">
  <region-body
   margin-left="1in"
   background-color="teal"/>
  <region-start extent="1.25in"
   background-image="tealBinder"
   background-repeat="repeat-y"/>
</fo:simple-page-master>
```

Flow and Static Content

It's time to talk about how to place content in the regions of the page. If we define a region on a page, it makes sense to consider that we may want to place something in it. The `flow` and `static-content` FOs define content to place into regions of the page.

In Chapter 4, "Hello XSL World," you saw that the page sequence contains the textual content of a page. All the examples up to now have placed that content in a `flow` FO. The flow contains content that flows from page to page. When the formatter finishes outputting all the elements of the flow, it finishes the page sequence.

Some content of a page may be content that the formatter should repeat on every page. The XSL recommendation provides the `static-content` FO for that content. It is static in the sense that it does not flow. It remains the same from page to page.

Both the `flow` and `static-content` FOs specify a region of the page master using the `flow-name` property. The `flow-name` property refers to the `region-name` property of some region in the `simple-page-master`. You may also use the generic names, `xsl-region-body`, `xsl-region-start`, `xsl-region-end`, `xsl-region-before`, and `xsl-region-after` to refer to regions in a page master by position rather than by name.

When the value of the `flow-name` property for a `static-content` FO does not match any region on the current page master, the formatter will not typeset that content anywhere on the page. This does not mean that it will not typeset the content on any page. Another page may have a different page master, as you will see in the following section. This enables you to specify content that appears on some pages, but not on others.

Both `flow` and `static-content` FOs contain one or more block FOs that make up the material to format within their selected region. The major difference is that the formatter will repeat all the `static-content` on every page. It will place as much of the content of the flow as it can fit within the selected region and start a new page for anything that does not.

Listing 8.1 contains a style sheet that uses static-content to format a chapter title in the region-before of every page. It flows the text of the chapter into the region-body.

Listing 8.1 *Style Sheet Demonstrates the Use of* static-content

```
<?xml version='1.0'?>
<xsl:stylesheet version="1.0"
 xmlns:xsl="http://www.w3.org/1999/XSL/Transform"
 xmlns:fo="http://www.w3.org/1999/XSL/Format">

  <xsl:template match="/">
```

Listing 8.1 *(continued)*

```
    <fo:root>
      <fo:layout-master-set>
        <fo:simple-page-master
         master-name="page">
          <fo:region-before extent="0.5in">
          <fo:region-body
           region-name="body"
           margin-top="0.75in"
           margin-bottom="1in"
           margin-left="0.5in"
           margin-right="0.5in"/>
        </fo:simple-page-master>
      </fo:layout-master-set>
      <fo:page-sequence master-name="page">
        <xsl:apply-templates/>
      </fo:page-sequence>
    </fo:root>
  </xsl:template>

  <xsl:template match="chapter">
    <fo:static-content flow-name="xsl-region-before">
      <fo:block text-align="end">
        <xsl:value-of select="title"/>
      </fo:block>
    </fo:static-content>
    <fo:flow flow-name="body">
      <fo:block>
        <xsl:apply-templates/>
      </fo:block>
    </fo:flow>
  </xsl:template>

</xsl:stylesheet>
```

The following section regarding sequences provides specific examples of `static-content` and `flow` mappings to regions and the formatted output that results.

Sequences

The first part of this chapter discussed the definition of individual page layouts using the simple-page-master and region FOs. One of the properties of a simple-page-master was a master-name. That implies that we may have multiple masters. This section demonstrates how to make use of multiple page masters and alternate page layouts and sequence them within a document.

One of the things we do with kindergarten children for math readiness is teach them patterns and sequences. The simplest is the alternating sequence, abab. Then we learn to recognize abbabb, and then we throw in a third element, abcabc, at which time we can get very fancy, abbacbbc. The same patterns apply to sequences of pages, only we'll start with the simplest of all: abbbb... Don't worry. It gets tougher in first grade.

Simple Sequence

XSL provides the page-sequence-master FO to specify sequences of layouts. The page-sequence-master must contain references to other masters. Let's look at an example to make this clear.

```
<simple-page-master master-name="a">
  ...
</simple-page-master>

<simple-page-master master-name="b">
  ...
</simple-page-master>

<page-sequence-master master-name="abbb">
  <single-page-master-reference master-reference="a"/>
  <repeatable-page-master-reference master-reference="b"/>
</page-sequence-master>
```

A page-sequence that references the page-sequence-master abbb will flow content into the first page according to the layout specified by the simple-page-master with master-name "a." It will flow all subsequent content onto pages according to the layout specified by the simple-page-master with master-name "b." This is the abbb pattern; thus, the name.

Combining Sequences

Now let's do the kindergarten basic sequence, abab. This requires some cleverness with page-sequence-master and master references. Assume the layout-master-set contains simple-page-masters with master-name properties equal to "a" and "b." We start with a page-sequence-master that refers first to "a" and then to "b," as follows:

```
<fo:page-sequence-master master-name="ab">
```

```
  <fo:single-page-master-reference master-reference="a"/>
  <fo:single-page-master-reference master-reference="b"/>
</fo:page-sequence-master>
```

You would never want to refer to this master from a `page-sequence`, however. It defines two pages and then runs dry. It quits after two. It goes no further, and we can all count past two.

The `abab` master repeats the `ab` master over and over again using a `repeatable-page-master-reference`, like this:

```
<fo:page-sequence-master master-name="abab">
  <fo:repeatable-page-master-reference master-reference="ab"/>
</fo:page-sequence-master>
```

That's all there is to it. We define a `page-sequence` with the value of its `master-reference property` equal to "abab" to refer to this alternating pages sequence. The `repeatable-page-master-reference` causes the formatter to use the `ab` pair over and over again.

This is not quite the same as defining a master for odd and even pages, but it does demonstrate the power of having one `page-sequence-master` refer to another.

Odd and Even

Another common layout sequence is the odd-page, even-page alternating sequence. Odd pages may have the name of the chapter in the heading. Even pages may have the name of the book in the heading. The right margin may be larger on even pages and the left margin larger on odd pages to accommodate the binding of the book. The place where the pages meet at the binding is known in typesetting circles as the *gutter*. Things are really bad in typesetting when content falls into the gutter.

To start with, here are two `simple-page-master` FOs that define regions for odd and even page headers:

```
<fo:simple-page-master master-name="oddLayout">
  <fo:region-before region-name="oddHead"
   extent="0.5in"/>
  <fo:region-after region-name="folio"
   extent="0.5in"/>
  <fo:region-body region-name="text"
   margin-top="0.75in"
   margin-bottom="0.8in"
   margin-left="0.75in"
```

```
    margin-right="0.5in"
    extent="0.5in"/>
</fo:simple-page-master>

<fo:simple-page-master master-name="evenLayout">
  <fo:region-before region-name="evenHead"
   extent="0.5in"/>
  <fo:region-after region-name="folio"
   extent="0.5in"/>
  <fo:region-body region-name="text"
   margin-top="0.75in"
   margin-bottom="0.8in"
   margin-left="0.5in"
   margin-right="0.75in"/>
</fo:simple-page-master>
```

The first `simple-page-master` defines the layout for the odd page. It contains a `region-before` FO with the name "oddHead." The `region-body` FO has a left margin greater than the right. The extra 1/4 inch on the left margin keeps the text out of the gutter. The second `simple-page-master` has extra margin on the right. It defines a `region-before` FO with the name "evenHead."

The next required piece is a master that uses the odd layout on odd pages and the even layout on even pages. You need two new FOs for that. They are `repeatable-page-master-alternatives` and `conditional-page-master-reference`.

The `repeatable-page-master-alternatives` FO encloses one or more `conditional-page-master-reference` FOs. It selects the first `conditional-page-master-reference` that applies to the current page. Have a look at the definition for the odd and even page usage:

```
<fo:page-sequence-master master-name="oddEven">
  <fo:repeatable-page-master-alternatives>
    <fo:conditional-page-master-reference
     odd-or-even="odd"
     master-reference="oddLayout"/>
    <fo:conditional-page-master-reference
     odd-or-even="even"
     master-reference="evenLayout"/>
  </fo:repeatable-page-master-alternatives>
</fo:page-sequence-master>
```

The first `conditional-page-master-reference` in the example refers through its master-reference property to the page master with the name "oddLayout." The second conditional-page-master-reference refers to the page master with the name "evenLayout." Both have a property, odd-or-even. That property selects whether the conditional-page-master-reference applies to an odd page or to an even page. This is all it takes to get separate layouts for the odd and even pages in a book.

The static-content and flow FOs within the page-sequence must use the regions defined by the simple-page-master selected for each page. The following demonstrates:

```
<fo:page-sequence master-reference="oddEven">
  <fo:static-content flow-name="oddHead">
    <fo:block>Chapter 8.  Page Styling</fo:block>
  </fo:static-content>
  <fo:static-content flow-name="evenHead">
    <fo:block>XSL: Formatting Object</fo:block>
  </fo:static-content>
  <fo:static-content flow-name="folio">
    <fo:block>- <fo:page-number/> -</fo:block>
  </fo:static-content>
  <fo:flow flow-name="text">
    <fo:block>Flow deep river.</fo:block>
  </fo:flow>
</fo:page-sequence>
```

First note that the page-sequence refers to the repeatable-page-master-alternatives named "oddEven." After that come three blocks of static content. One refers to the region named "oddHead." The next refers to the region named "evenHead." The third refers to the region named "folio."

On an odd page, the formatter will select the simple-page-master named "oddLayout." That layout defines a region named "oddHead." It does not define a region named "evenHead." The formatter will not render the static-content FO with flow-name="evenHead" because the layout master defines no region with that name.

The page-sequence defines all the content that may appear on pages. That does not mean that all the content will appear on all the pages. The formatter includes only content for which it can find a matching region within which to render that content.

Blank Pages

Often when formatting a document, we would like all pages that begin a chapter or a section to begin on the right-side page. That is an odd-numbered page.

The way to get each chapter to start on an odd-numbered page is to specify the property `break-before="odd-page"` on the first FO generated into the flow. That requires that the break that comes before the FO place the FO on an odd-numbered page. If the break that comes before will place the FO on an even-numbered page, the formatter must produce a blank page as the even page and start the FO on the odd-numbered page that follows.

Now suppose you would like to use a different layout for the blank page. Suppose the blank page should omit the running header and/or folio. Another possibility is that the blank page must have a reassuring message indicating that it was intentionally left blank. Either way, you will need a special layout for the blank page. You will also need a method for selecting it.

Here is `static-content` for the body of a blank page:

```
<fo:static-content flow-name="blank">
  <fo:block>This page intentionally left blank.</fo:block>
</fo:static-content>
```

There must be a page master that defines a region named "blank." Here is one that builds on the even page master. It has a body region with the same margins that will contain the reassuring message. It contains no regions for the running header or footer:

```
<fo:simple-page-master master-name="blankLayout">
  <fo:region-body region-name="blank"
   margin-top="0.75in"
   margin-bottom="0.8in"
   margin-left="0.5in"
   margin-right="0.75in"/>
</fo:simple-page-master>
```

Add one more `conditional-page-master-reference` to the `repeatable-page-master-alternatives`. The conditional reference selects the blank page layout. It uses the `blank-or-not-blank` property to select only a blank page:

```
<fo:page-sequence-master master-name="oddEven">
  <fo:repeatable-page-master-alternatives>
    <fo:conditional-page-master-reference
     blank-or-not-blank="blank"
     master-reference="blankLayout"/>
    <fo:conditional-page-master-reference
     odd-or-even="odd"
     master-reference="oddLayout"/>
    <fo:conditional-page-master-reference
     odd-or-even="even"
     master-reference="evenLayout"/>
  </fo:repeatable-page-master-alternatives>
</fo:page-sequence-master>
```

In this case, the order of the conditional-page-master-reference FOs is critical. The repeatable-page-master-alternatives FO matches the first condition that holds true. If the condition on the blank page followed the condition on the even page, the formatter would use the master for the even page. The symptom would be that the folio and header appear on the page. The page would be blank, without the message indicating that it was intentionally blank.

It is an error to specify a repeatable-page-master-alternatives FO with no conditional-page-master that selects for a condition. The formatter can quit right there. A page is always odd or even; therefore, you are safe if you have a condition for the odd and for the even pages.

Back to the First Page

Let's now re-examine the first page scenario. The simple sequence section earlier in the chapter handled the first page scenario using a single-page-master-reference followed by a repeatable-page-master-reference. That worked just fine and was perfectly valid.

Now suppose you want to do that, but you also want odd, even, and blank page masters. FOs come to the rescue with one more condition you can set on a conditional-page-master-reference. The page-position property specifies a condition based on the location of the page in the page sequence. The value first passes the test if the page is first in the sequence. Here, finally, is a complete master sequence specification for the chapters of a book:

```
<fo:page-sequence-master master-name="oddEven">
  <fo:repeatable-page-master-alternatives>
    <fo:conditional-page-master-reference
     page-position="first"
     master-reference="chapter"/>
    <fo:conditional-page-master-reference
     blank-or-not-blank="blank"
     master-reference="blankLayout"/>
    <fo:conditional-page-master-reference
     odd-or-even="odd"
     master-reference="oddLayout"/>
    <fo:conditional-page-master-reference
     odd-or-even="even"
     master-reference="evenLayout"/>
  </fo:repeatable-page-master-alternatives>
</fo:page-sequence-master>
```

Infinite Pages

The `layout-master-set` provides enough power of expression for you to shoot yourself in the foot. It is possible to define the page masters and sequences in such a way that the formatter can never finish processing all the input. A formatter may detect this at runtime, or it may not. It might go about happily producing pages until you give up and bring it to a halt.

The easiest way to make an infinite specification is to specify a page master without a region name to match the flow name. Here is an example:

```
<fo:root xmlns:fo="http://www.w3.org/1999/XSL/Format">
  <fo:layout-master-set>
    <fo:simple-page-master master-name="a">
      <fo:region-after region-name="folio"
       extent="0.5in"/>
      <fo:region-body region-name="body"
       margin-top="0.75in"
       margin-bottom="0.8in"
       margin-left="0.5in"
       margin-right="0.75in"/>
    </fo:simple-page-master>
  </fo:layout-master-set>

  <fo:page-sequence master-reference="a">
    <fo:flow flow-name="text">
      <fo:block>Flow deep river.</fo:block>
    </fo:flow>
  </fo:page-sequence>
</fo:root>
```

Three formatters each behaved differently given this specification. One formatter halted. Another wrote a message indicating that it is an error to specify a master with no matching region for the flow. A third started processing and never finished. The second was the only one which behaved incorrectly. The third merely behaved badly.

The following equivalent specification gave the same result. The recommendation specifies that referring to a `simple-page-master` is equivalent to referring to a `page-sequence-master` with a `repeatable-page-master-reference`, like this:

```
<fo:root xmlns:fo="http://www.w3.org/1999/XSL/Format">
  <fo:layout-master-set>
    <fo:simple-page-master master-name="a">
      <fo:region-before region-name="oddHead"
       extent="0.5in"/>
```

```
      <fo:region-body region-name="body"
       margin-top="0.75in"
       margin-bottom="0.8in"
       margin-left="0.5in"
       margin-right="0.75in"/>
    </fo:simple-page-master>
    <fo:page-sequence-master master-name="b">
      <fo:repeatable-page-master-reference master-reference="a"/>
    </fo:page-sequence-master>
  </fo:layout-master-set>

  <fo:page-sequence master-reference="b">
    <fo:flow flow-name="text">
      <fo:block>Flow deep river.</fo:block>
    </fo:flow>
  </fo:page-sequence>
</fo:root>
```

The `repeatable-page-master-alternatives` FO offers the most opportunity for error. One error is to specify the conditions such that the formatter cannot find one that is true for a page. One of the conditions must always be true. If you follow the models given in this chapter, you should be able to steer clear of most problems.

Summary

Formatting objects provides a rich capability for specifying sequences of page layouts. The region model for each layout is very simple, but rich enough for the majority of applications. You have seen how to specify `simple-page-masters` and `page-sequence-masters` that handle most common situations, including those encountered in typesetting a journal or a book. It is magic to see the content of the flow distributed over multiple pages with alternating layouts. Try it with a longer content document. You'll find it very rewarding.

CHAPTER 9
Tables and Alignments

This chapter describes the tabular layout elements and the attributes that control them. It begins with simple tabular alignment of enumerated data. From there it moves on to data that has a very record-oriented structure. Phone calls, account transactions, sales records, and shipping bills all represent record-oriented data that is usually presented in tabular form. This will demonstrate markup that produces tables from record-oriented data.

Tabular Alignment

Data that is not record oriented, but merely needs enumeration in tabular form, can be presented with the simplest form of table. Consider a list of XSL properties, like that shown in Listing 9.1. The XML markup records the names of properties within `<property>` elements. The number attribute contains a section reference to the XSL FO recommendation.

You could list the table properties as `border-after-precedence`, `border-before-precedence`, `border-collapse`, `border-end-precedence`, `border-separation`, `border-start-precedence`, and so forth. You could also align the list on tab stops to make it easier to read. Here is the source listing for the XML input:

Listing 9.1 *XSL Table Properties*

```
<?xml version='1.0'?>
<property-list>
  <group name="Table Properties">
    <property number="7.26.1">border-after-precedence</property>
    <property number="7.26.2">border-before-precedence</property>
    <property number="7.26.3">border-collapse</property>
    <property number="7.26.4">border-end-precedence</property>
    <property number="7.26.5">border-separation</property>
    <property number="7.26.6">border-start-precedence</property>
    <property number="7.26.7">caption-side</property>
    <property number="7.26.8">column-number</property>
    <property number="7.26.9">column-width</property>
    <property number="7.26.10">empty-cells</property>
    <property number="7.26.11">ends-row</property>
    <property number="7.26.12">number-columns-repeated</property>
    <property number="7.26.13">number-columns-spanned</property>
    <property number="7.26.14">number-rows-spanned</property>
    <property number="7.26.15">starts-row</property>
    <property number="7.26.16">table-layout</property>
    <property number="7.26.17">table-omit-footer-at-break</property>
    <property number="7.26.18">table-omit-header-at-break</property>
  </group>
</property-list>
```

The XML content markup supplies some tabular data about table properties. Suppose you want to simply enumerate the content of the property entries, as in the paragraph preceding the listing. Suppose you want to enumerate them in a form that's somewhat easier to scan. Suppose you would like to align the entries on tab stops so that you get three or four of them on a line and they all align vertically.

Begin with this usual boilerplate for a stylesheet that includes the basic page layout, `rootrule.xsl` introduced in Chapter 4, "Hello XSL World":

```
<?xml version='1.0'?>
<xsl:stylesheet version="1.0"
 xmlns:xsl="http://www.w3.org/1999/XSL/Transform"
 xmlns:fo="http://www.w3.org/1999/XSL/Format">

  <xsl:strip-space elements="*"/>
  <xsl:include href="rootrule.xsl"/>

</xsl:stylesheet>
```

The simplest form of tabular alignment requires only table cells inside a table body. The templates that follow create the necessary structure. First, insert into the style sheet a template that matches the group and outputs the table body:

```
<xsl:template match="group">
  <fo:table>
    <fo:table-body>
      <xsl:apply-templates/>
    </fo:table-body>
  </fo:table>
</xsl:template>
```

That template simply outputs a `table` with a `table-body` inside. All tables in XSL must at minimum contain a `table-body`. You'll get to the other things a table may contain later. The XSL `apply-templates` directive inside the `table-body` will process all the property elements. You need a template to match property elements and output table cells. Add the following:

```
<xsl:template match="property">
  <fo:table-cell>
    <xsl:if test="position() mod 3 = 0">
      <xsl:attribute name="ends-row">true</xsl:attribute>
    </xsl:if>
    <fo:block>
      <xsl:apply-templates/>
    </fo:block>
  </fo:table-cell>
</xsl:template>
```

The magic of this template occurs within the `table-cell` FO. The test written within the `xsl:if` element adds an attribute to every third cell. That attribute sets the `ends-row` property of the cell to `true`. This causes a row break, and the resulting output is nicely aligned in three columns.

The template could just as easily have used the `starts-row` property on each table cell that starts a row. The `xsl:if` statement would then have appeared as follows. The revised test selects the first of three rather than the last of three. The revised attribute sets the `starts-row` property on the `table-cell`. Both forms work and there is little difference whether you use the `starts-row` or the `ends-row` form. The point is that one or the other, but not both, are required to make a row break.

```
<xsl:if test="position() mod 3 = 1">
  <xsl:attribute name="starts-row">true</xsl:attribute>
</xsl:if>
```

The `xsl:if` construction slightly hides the fact that the content of the `table-cell` is a block. Every table cell in XSL must contain a block-level FO. This style sheet outputs a block enclosing the text content of the property element. Figure 9.1 demonstrates the output from the style sheet as given so far.

border-after-precedence	border-before-precedence	border-collapse
border-end-precedence	border-separation	border-start-precedence
caption-side	column-number	column-width
empty-cells	ends-row	number-columns-repeated
number-columns-spanned	number-rows-spanned	starts-row
table-layout	table-omit-footer-at-break	table-omit-header-at-break

Figure 9.1

Tabular listing of table properties.

Figure 9.1 and the style sheet you've developed to this point demonstrate that you can use only the `table`, `table-body`, and `table-cell` FOs to achieve tabular alignment. You use the `starts-row` or `ends-row` property on the first or last `table-cell` in each row to start or end the row.

The only difficulty with the output in Figure 9.1 is that the columns have no space between them. The end of the widest entry in each column runs right into the beginning of the entry in the next column. The output needs a little bit of space between cells, and you can accomplish this in two ways.

The first way is to setup the table so that it has separate borders and some amount of space between borders in the inline-progression dimension. Change the line that outputs the table FO so that it adds two properties to the table, as follows:

```
<fo:table
 border-collapse="separate"
 border-separation.inline-progression-direction="6pt">
```

The first property requires that borders be separate. The second requires that the amount of separation between borders in the (horizontal) inline-progression dimension be 6 points. The "Separate and Collapsed Borders" section later in this chapter discusses these properties in more detail. For now, enjoy the improved result shown in Figure 9.2.

border-after-precedence	border-before-precedence	border-collapse
border-end-precedence	border-separation	border-start-precedence
caption-side	column-number	column-width
empty-cells	ends-row	number-columns-repeated
number-columns-spanned	number-rows-spanned	starts-row
table-layout	table-omit-footer-at-break	table-omit-header-at-break

Figure 9.2

Tabular listing with space between cells.

The other way to add space between the cells is to pad the cells. Remove the border-collapse and border-separation properties from the table and change the line that outputs the table-cell FO so that it adds the padding-end property as follows:

```
<fo:table-cell padding-end="6pt">
```

That change will produce a result that appears identical to the result shown in Figure 9.2. It is not quite identical because the last cell in each row has some padding after it. If there was a border on the table, that padding would produce extra space on the right side between the table content and its border. That brings us to borders and tables.

Separate and Collapsed Borders

With separate borders, only the table and table-cell produce a border. With collapsed borders, every element of a table may have border and padding. The table-and-caption, table, table-row, table-column, table-cell, table-body, table-header, and table-footer may each have their own border specification. This provides many levels at which to apply borders in a table. The borders often coincide. The top and bottom borders of a cell coincide with the borders of the row. The left and right borders of a column may coincide with those of another column or with those of the table.

The border-collapse property sets the type of border. The "Border Collapse" section following this one describes that in detail. Let's finish with the separate borders first. Listing 9.2 adds border specifications to both the table and table-cell elements used in the tabular alignment example:

Listing 9.2 *Tabular Layout with Borders*

```
<?xml version='1.0'?>
<xsl:stylesheet version="1.0"
 xmlns:xsl="http://www.w3.org/1999/XSL/Transform"
 xmlns:fo="http://www.w3.org/1999/XSL/Format">

  <xsl:strip-space elements="*"/>
  <xsl:include href="rootrule.xsl"/>

  <xsl:attribute-set name="borders">
    <xsl:attribute name="border-before-width">2pt</xsl:attribute>
    <xsl:attribute name="border-after-width">2pt</xsl:attribute>
    <xsl:attribute name="border-start-width">2pt</xsl:attribute>
    <xsl:attribute name="border-end-width">2pt</xsl:attribute>
```

Listing 9.2 *(continued)*

```
    <xsl:attribute name="padding-before">3pt</xsl:attribute>
    <xsl:attribute name="padding-after">3pt</xsl:attribute>
    <xsl:attribute name="padding-start">3pt</xsl:attribute>
    <xsl:attribute name="padding-end">3pt</xsl:attribute>
  </xsl:attribute-set>

  <xsl:attribute-set name="solid">
    <xsl:attribute name="border-before-style">solid</xsl:attribute>
    <xsl:attribute name="border-after-style">solid</xsl:attribute>
    <xsl:attribute name="border-start-style">solid</xsl:attribute>
    <xsl:attribute name="border-end-style">solid</xsl:attribute>
  </xsl:attribute-set>

  <xsl:attribute-set name="dashed">
    <xsl:attribute name="border-before-style">dashed</xsl:attribute>
    <xsl:attribute name="border-after-style">dashed</xsl:attribute>
    <xsl:attribute name="border-start-style">dashed</xsl:attribute>
    <xsl:attribute name="border-end-style">dashed</xsl:attribute>
  </xsl:attribute-set>

  <xsl:template match="group">
    <fo:table
     xsl:use-attribute-sets="borders solid"
     border-collapse="separate"
     border-separation.inline-progression-direction="6pt"
     border-separation.block-progression-direction="2pt">
      <fo:table-body>
        <xsl:apply-templates/>
      </fo:table-body>
    </fo:table>
  </xsl:template>

  <xsl:template match="property">
    <fo:table-cell
     xsl:use-attribute-sets="borders dashed">
      <xsl:if test="position() mod 3 = 0">
        <xsl:attribute name="ends-row">true</xsl:attribute>
      </xsl:if>
      <fo:block>
        <xsl:apply-templates/>
      </fo:block>
```

Listing 9.2 *(continued)*

```
    </fo:table-cell>
  </xsl:template>

</xsl:stylesheet>
```

Listing 9.2 adds three attribute sets. The templates are pretty much the same as developed in the "Tabular Alignment" section, with three exceptions. The `table` and `table-cell` FOs now use the attribute sets to add borders. This is the first time we have combined attribute sets in an example. The value of the `xsl:use-attribute-sets` attribute simply lists the attribute sets with space between each name.

The `table` FO now has `border-separation` given for the block-progression dimension. That provides some space between the top and bottom borders of the cells. Figure 9.3 shows the rendered result.

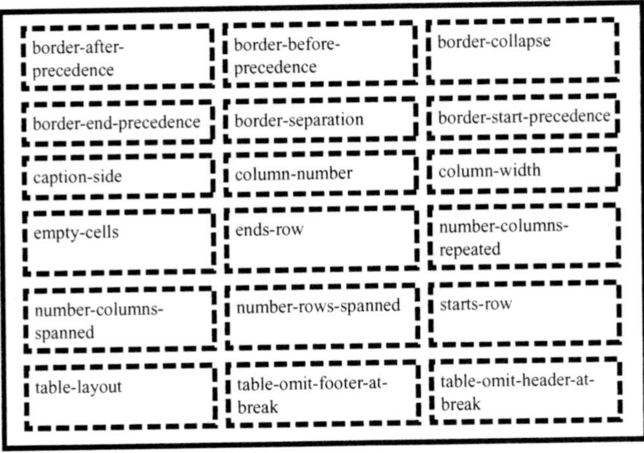

Figure 9.3
Tabular layout with borders.

There are a number of things to note about the rendering in Figure 9.3. First is that some of the cells wrapped. There was no longer enough horizontal space to accommodate the full width of the property names. The wrapping occurs in the block within the cell. Some of the blocks, given limited width, wrapped the property name on a hyphen.

Wherever one cell wrapped, the entire row grew in height. Cells remain aligned in rows and columns. The content of each cell is aligned at the upper-left corner.

The space within each cell, between the text and the dotted border, comes from the padding on the cell. The style sheet provides equal padding around the content of each cell. Padding always appears between the content and border of the FO that specifies it. Without the padding, the cell border would touch the first letter of each entry and the tops and bottoms of the lines.

There is more horizontal space between cells than vertical space. The space between the dotted lines comes from the `border-separation` property on the `table`. The `border-separation` property is a complex property with two components. It has an `inline-progression-direction` and a `block-progression-direction` component. The style sheet specifies 6 points of space between borders in the `inline-progression-direction`. It specifies only 2 points in the `block-progression-direction`. Without this space, the dotted borders would touch each other.

There is also more space between the borders of the table and the borders of the cells at the left and right than at the top and bottom. The `border-separation` property of the table sets that space as well.

Finally, note that there is more space between the cell borders and the table borders than between cell borders. That is because of the padding on the table. The padding on the table accumulates with the amount of border separation.

Collapsed Borders

The separated border behavior results from one single setting on the table. That setting is the value of the `border-collapse` property. If we change one single line of the style sheet, the resulting output will be radically different. Figure 9.4 demonstrates the result of changing the value of `border-collapse` from `separate` to `collapse`. We could just as well have deleted the property setting. The value `collapse` is the default value for the `border-collapse` property.

border-after-precedence	border-before-precedence	border-collapse
border-end-precedence	border-separation	border-start-precedence
caption-side	column-number	column-width
empty-cells	ends-row	number-columns-repeated
number-columns-spanned	number-rows-spanned	starts-row
table-layout	table-omit-footer-at-break	table-omit-header-at-break

Figure 9.4

Tabular layout with collapsed borders.

Figure 9.4 uses what we call the collapsed border model. In this model, the formatter looks at all the coincident borders and selects one to render. The method for selection is complex, but for the most part it gives you what you expect. In this case, the table border runs all the way around the cells, and dotted borders run between them.

That the rules for selecting a border are complex doesn't mean we can't understand them. If any of the borders has a border style setting of `hidden`, the formatter will not render a border. After that, the formatter selects the widest border. If all the borders are the same width, it selects the border with style `double`, `solid`, `dashed`, `dotted`, `ridge`, `outset`, `groove`, or `inset`—in that order of precedence. A `solid` border covers a `dashed` border that covers a `dotted` border, and so forth.

If the borders are the same style but differ only in color, the formatter chooses the color of the cell border over the color of the row border, the row border over the column, and the column over the table. FO inherits all this behavior from the CSS collapsing border model. The shared behavior makes FO collapsing borders entirely compatible with CSS.

XSL Collapsed Borders with Precedence

XSL supplies an additional border resolution model that CSS does not. The third value for the `border-collapse` property after `separate` and `collapsed` is `collapsed-with-precedence`. With `border-collapse` set to `collapsed-with-precedence`, the formatter will resolve the borders first using the value of the border precedence property for each table element. The border precedence properties are `border-after-precedence`, `border-before-precedence`, `border-end-precedence`, and `border-start-precedence`.

The default values for these border precedence properties are different on each table element. Table 9.1 shows the defaults. A higher number wins over a lower number. That gives the table precedence over rows, columns, and cells, which is the opposite of the CSS precedence. The `collapsed-with-precedence` setting gives you the collapsed look with explicit control over the border selected.

Table 9.1 *Default Border Precedence for Collapsed Borders with Precedence*

FO	Precedence	FO	Precedence
table	6	table-cell	5
table-column	4	table-row	3
table-body	2	table-header	1
table-footer	0		

Explicit Rows

So far we have been able to explore a great deal about the properties of tables using only two table FOs—`table` and `table-cell`. We used the `ends-row` property on some of the `table-cell` FOs to create the row structure of the table. It's time to add another table FO to the picture. The `table-row` FO explicitly designates each row of the table. That is an alternative to the implicit assignment of rows using the `ends-row` attribute on a `table-cell`.

That we now have explicit rows in the tables suggests that we now have record-oriented data to format. This will sometimes be data resulting from a database query. Call data for a cellular phone account provides one example of record-oriented data. Each phone call is a record. Each record will be a row of the table.

Listing 9.3 shows a sample data set. All the phone data is fabricated. It's the dull sort of detail that is meaningless to most, but which sometimes kindles memories—where you went last month, whom you talked to, or that phone call with Aunt Sally.

Listing 9.3 *Record-Oriented Data*

```
<?xml version='1.0'?>
<phone-usage>
  <account id="267627104">
    <date>June 12, 2002</date>
    <name>Peter Priceless</name>
    <address>153 Sunrise Highway</address>
    <city>Bronx</city>
    <state>NY</state>
    <zip>10246</zip>
  </account>
  <call-data number="(838)288-0001">
    <detail>
      <date>05/16</date>
      <time t="pm">04:35</time>
      <minutes rate="O">2</minutes>
      <origin>Home Area</origin>
      <number>(000)000-2143</number>
      <destination>Voice Mail</destination>
      <airtime-charge>prepaid</airtime-charge>
      <total-charge>0.00</total-charge>
    </detail>
    <detail>
      <date>05/16</date>
```

Listing 9.3 *(continued)*

```
      <time t="pm">10:10</time>
      <minutes rate="O">77</minutes>
      <origin>Home Area</origin>
      <number>(999)000-3268</number>
      <destination>Ocala,FL</destination>
      <airtime-charge>prepaid</airtime-charge>
      <total-charge>0.00</total-charge>
    </detail>
    <detail>
      <date>05/17</date>
      <time t="pm">06:47</time>
      <minutes rate="O">2</minutes>
      <origin>Home Area</origin>
      <number>(000)000-0411</number>
      <destination>411 Connect</destination>
      <airtime-charge>prepaid</airtime-charge>
      <other-charge type="DA">0.99</other-charge>
      <total-charge>0.99</total-charge>
    </detail>
    <detail>
      <date>05/22</date>
      <time t="am">08:02</time>
      <minutes rate="P">5</minutes>
      <origin>Home Area</origin>
      <number>(000)999-8384</number>
      <destination>incoming</destination>
      <airtime-charge>prepaid</airtime-charge>
      <total-charge>0.00</total-charge>
    </detail>
  </call-data>
</phone-usage>
```

The listing contains usage data for a single account with call detail for a single phone number. The call detail contains four records corresponding to four cellular phone calls. Each call will be a row in the table. The detail element contains the data for each call. A template matching the detail element outputs the row:

```
<xsl:template match="detail">
  <fo:table-row>
    <xsl:apply-templates/>
  </fo:table-row>
</xsl:template>
```

A template matching the call-data element outputs the table. The other templates output cells of the table. Each uses a different alignment on the block within the cell. Listing 9.4 contains the full source:

Listing 9.4 *First Cut at a Style Sheet for the Call Data*

```
<?xml version='1.0'?>
<xsl:stylesheet version="1.0"
 xmlns:xsl="http://www.w3.org/1999/XSL/Transform"
 xmlns:fo="http://www.w3.org/1999/XSL/Format">

  <xsl:strip-space elements="*"/>
  <xsl:include href="rootrule.xsl"/>
  <xsl:include href="phonestyle.xsl"/>

  <xsl:template match="account"/>

  <xsl:template match="call-data">
    <fo:table>
      <fo:table-body>
        <xsl:apply-templates/>
      </fo:table-body>
    </fo:table>
  </xsl:template>

  <xsl:template match="detail">
    <fo:table-row>
      <xsl:apply-templates/>
    </fo:table-row>
  </xsl:template>

  <xsl:template
   match="date|number|airtime-charge|total-charge">
    <fo:table-cell
     xsl:use-attribute-sets="cell-padding">
      <fo:block text-align="end">
        <xsl:value-of select="."/>
      </fo:block>
    </fo:table-cell>
  </xsl:template>

  <xsl:template match="origin|destination">
    <fo:table-cell
```

Listing 9.4 *(continued)*

```
      xsl:use-attribute-sets="cell-padding">
      <fo:block text-align="center">
        <xsl:value-of select="."/>
      </fo:block>
    </fo:table-cell>
  </xsl:template>

  <xsl:template match="time">
    <fo:table-cell
     xsl:use-attribute-sets="cell-padding">
      <fo:block text-align="end">
        <xsl:value-of select="."/>
        <xsl:value-of select="@t"/>
      </fo:block>
    </fo:table-cell>
  </xsl:template>

  <xsl:template match="minutes|other-charge">
    <fo:table-cell
     xsl:use-attribute-sets="cell-padding">
      <fo:block text-align="end">
        <xsl:value-of select="@rate|@type"/>
      </fo:block>
    </fo:table-cell>
    <fo:table-cell
     xsl:use-attribute-sets="cell-padding">
      <fo:block text-align="end">
        <xsl:value-of select="."/>
      </fo:block>
    </fo:table-cell>
  </xsl:template>

</xsl:stylesheet>
```

The first template, the one that matches the `account` element, suppresses all processing of that element and its children. The last template, the one that matches the `minutes` or `other-charge` element, outputs two cells. The first contains the value of the `rate` or `type` attribute. The second calls out the content of the element in an end-aligned block.

The style sheet named `phonestyle.xsl` imported by the code in Listing 9.4 contains a single attribute set for the cell padding, as follows:

```
<xsl:attribute-set name="cell-padding">
  <xsl:attribute name="padding-start">2pt</xsl:attribute>
  <xsl:attribute name="padding-end">2pt</xsl:attribute>
</xsl:attribute-set>
```

The section, "Placing Headers and Footers on a Table" later in this chapter will place additional attribute sets in `phonestyle.xsl`.

Figure 9.5 shows the result output.

05/16	04:35pm	O	2	Home Area	(000)000-2143	Voice Mail	prepaid	0.00	
05/16	10:10pm	O	77	Home Area	(999)000-3268	Ocala,FL	prepaid	0.00	
05/17	06:47pm	O	2	Home Area	(000)000-0411	411 Connect	prepaid	DA 0.99	0.99
05/22	08:02am	P	5	Home Area	(000)999-8384	incoming	prepaid	0.00	

Figure 9.5
The typeset result from the style sheet shown in Listing 9.4.

This is not a bad start. Everything is nicely aligned in columns and justified as we expect. The main problem appears in the last column. The third entry contains two extra fields. The style sheet does not output empty cells to fill columns that have no data value.

One way to solve this is with lots of XSLT gymnastics involving `xsl:if` commands to test for the presence of each cell. Another is to require the input to supply empty elements for the empty data. The solution is simpler than this. XSL allows us to place a cell in a particular column based on a column number. This solution requires only three additional lines of the style sheet. Replace the template that matches `total-charge` as follows:

```
<xsl:template
 match="date|number|airtime-charge|tostal-charge">
  <fo:table-cell
   xsl:use-attribute-sets="cell-padding">
    <xsl:if test="name()='total-charge'">
      <xsl:attribute name="column-number">11</xsl:attribute>
    </xsl:if>
    <fo:block text-align="end">
      <xsl:value-of select="."/>
    </fo:block>
  </fo:table-cell>
</xsl:template>
```

The three new lines introduce an `xsl:if` test for the `total-charge` element. The `table-cell` output for that element contains a `column-number` property set to the value 11. That fixes the `total-charge` in the eleventh column, no matter how many columns come before. The new output shown in Figure 9.7 results from this minor change:

05/16 04:35pm	O	2	Home Area (000)000-2143	Voice Mail	prepaid		0.00
05/16 10:10pm	O	77	Home Area (999)000-3268	Ocala,FL	prepaid		0.00
05/17 06:47pm	O	2	Home Area (000)000-0411	411 Connect	prepaid	DA 0.99	0.99
05/22 08:02am	P	5	Home Area (000)999-8384	incoming	prepaid		0.00

Figure 9.6

Typeset result shows properly aligned total-charge.

Table Column Definitions

The formatter composed the table in the preceding section using natural widths for each of the columns. The natural width is roughly the amount of width needed to format the widest cell in the column. This is a simplification, but it serves well enough within this context.

Statements like this cell phone call detail usually require fixed column widths for consistent appearance from one statement to the next. Use the XSL `table-column` element to specify fixed widths for one or more of the columns in a table. The following modification of the template matching `call-data` in Listing 9.4 demonstrates a set of `column-width` definitions:

```
<xsl:template match="call-data">
  <fo:table table-layout="fixed">
    <fo:table-column column-number="1"
     column-width="0.5in" text-align="end"/>
    <fo:table-column column-number="2"
     column-width="0.75in" text-align="end"/>
    <fo:table-column column-number="3"
     column-width="0.25in" text-align="end"/>
    <fo:table-column column-number="4"
     column-width="0.25in" text-align="end"/>
    <fo:table-column column-number="5"
     column-width="1.0in" text-align="center"/>
    <fo:table-column column-number="6"
     column-width="1.0in" text-align="end"/>
    <fo:table-column column-number="7"
     column-width="1.0in" text-align="center"/>
    <fo:table-column column-number="8"
     column-width="0.75in" text-align="end"/>
    <fo:table-column column-number="9"
     column-width="0.25in" text-align="end"/>
    <fo:table-column column-number="10"
     column-width="0.5in" text-align="end"/>
    <fo:table-column column-number="11"
```

```
        column-width="0.5in" text-align="end"/>
      <fo:table-body>
        <xsl:apply-templates/>
      </fo:table-body>
    </fo:table>
  </xsl:template>
```

Use the `table-column` FO as an initial child of the table FO, before any `table-header` or `table-footer` and before the `table-body`. The `table-column` FO is always empty. Use it only to specify column properties.

The modified template also adds a property setting to the table FO. The `table-layout` property defaults to automatic layout, which requires the formatter to compute the width of every column. With all the column widths fixed explicitly, you can set the value of `table-layout` to `fixed`. The `fixed` setting allows the formatter to use a much faster algorithm for placing cells of the table. It also requires explicit column widths given by a `table-column` FO for every column in the table. Some formatters will format only tables that have the value `table-layout` set to `fixed`. Figure 9.7 shows the typeset result from the modified style sheet.

05/16	04:35pm	O	2	Home Area	(000)000-2143	Voice Mail	prepaid		0.00
05/16	10:10pm	O	77	Home Area	(999)000-3268	Ocala,FL	prepaid		0.00
05/17	06:47pm	O	2	Home Area	(000)000-0411	411 Connect	prepaid DA	0.99	0.99
05/22	08:02am	P	5	Home Area	(000)999-8384	incoming	prepaid		0.00

Figure 9.7

Typeset result shows fixed-width columns.

The other thing you did in the `table-column` definitions was set the `text-align` property for each column. The `text-align` property is an inherited property, but the block children of the `table-cell` FOs are not descendents of the `table-column` elements. The special value `from-table-column()` given to the `text-align` property on the block FOs will copy a property value from the `table-column` to the like-named property within that column. Look at the value for the `text-align` property in this reworked template:

```
<xsl:template
 match="date|number|airtime-charge|total-charge|origin|destination">
  <fo:table-cell
   xsl:use-attribute-sets="cell-padding">
    <xsl:if test="name()='total-charge'">
      <xsl:attribute name="column-number">11</xsl:attribute>
    </xsl:if>
    <fo:block text-align="from-table-column()">
      <xsl:value-of select="."/>
```

```
      </fo:block>
    </fo:table-cell>
  </xsl:template>
```

This template now matches the `origin` and `destination` elements as well. The special template that matched those elements is now unnecessary. The two original templates were identical except for the value of the `text-align` property. Now they are entirely identical and can be merged. Listing 9.5 shows the entire style sheet as a checkpoint:

Listing 9.5 *Completed Style Sheet for the Body of the Call Data*

```
<?xml version='1.0'?>
<xsl:stylesheet version="1.0"
 xmlns:xsl="http://www.w3.org/1999/XSL/Transform"
 xmlns:fo="http://www.w3.org/1999/XSL/Format">

  <xsl:strip-space elements="*"/>
  <xsl:include href="rootrule.xsl"/>
  <xsl:include href="phonestyle.xsl"/>

  <xsl:template match="account"/>

  <xsl:template match="call-data">
    <fo:table table-layout="fixed">
      <fo:table-column column-number="1"
       column-width="30pt" text-align="end"/>
      <fo:table-column column-number="2"
       column-width="40pt" text-align="end"/>
      <fo:table-column column-number="3"
       column-width="36pt" text-align="center"/>
      <fo:table-column column-number="4"
       column-width="36pt" text-align="end"/>
      <fo:table-column column-number="5"
       column-width="72pt" text-align="center"/>
      <fo:table-column column-number="6"
       column-width="72pt" text-align="end"/>
      <fo:table-column column-number="7"
       column-width="72pt" text-align="center"/>
      <fo:table-column column-number="8"
       column-width="36pt" text-align="end"/>
      <fo:table-column column-number="9"
       column-width="30pt" text-align="end"/>
      <fo:table-column column-number="10"
```

Listing 9.5 *(continued)*

```
      column-width="40pt" text-align="end"/>
     <fo:table-column column-number="11"
      column-width="40pt" text-align="end"/>
     <fo:table-body>
       <xsl:apply-templates/>
     </fo:table-body>
   </fo:table>
 </xsl:template>

 <xsl:template match="detail">
   <fo:table-row>
     <xsl:apply-templates/>
   </fo:table-row>
 </xsl:template>

 <xsl:template
  match="date|number|airtime-charge|total-charge|origin|destination">
   <fo:table-cell
    xsl:use-attribute-sets="cell-padding">
     <xsl:if test="name()='total-charge'">
       <xsl:attribute name="column-number">11</xsl:attribute>
     </xsl:if>
     <fo:block text-align="from-table-column()">
       <xsl:value-of select="."/>
     </fo:block>
   </fo:table-cell>
 </xsl:template>

 <xsl:template match="time">
   <fo:table-cell
    xsl:use-attribute-sets="cell-padding">
     <fo:block text-align="from-table-column()">
       <xsl:value-of select="."/>
       <xsl:value-of select="@t"/>
     </fo:block>
   </fo:table-cell>
 </xsl:template>

 <xsl:template match="minutes|other-charge">
   <fo:table-cell
    xsl:use-attribute-sets="cell-padding">
```

Listing 9.5 *(continued)*

```
      <fo:block text-align="from-table-column()">
        <xsl:value-of select="@rate|@type"/>
      </fo:block>
    </fo:table-cell>
    <fo:table-cell
     xsl:use-attribute-sets="cell-padding">
      <fo:block text-align="from-table-column()">
        <xsl:value-of select="."/>
      </fo:block>
    </fo:table-cell>
  </xsl:template>

</xsl:stylesheet>
```

Placing Headers and Footers on a Table

Use the `table-header` and `table-footer` FOs to specify content that appears in columns at the before or after edge of the table body. These FOs must appear in fixed order—header and then footer—within the `table` FO after any `table-column` definitions and before the `table-body` FO.

The content model for the `table-header` and `table-footer` FOs is the same as the content model for the `table-body`. The header and footer may contain multiple rows delimited by properties of the cells or by `table-row` FOs just as shown for the table body. Specify a series of `table-cell` FOs or a series of `table-row` FOs within the `table-header` and `table-footer`.

The `table-header` and `table-footer` are the two FOs that very often have literal content written into the style sheet. They have very little extracted from the XML source data or document. Listing 9.6 provides an XSL fragment containing a simple header for the call data example of Listing 9.5. Insert it after the last `table-column` FO and before the `table-body`:

Listing 9.6 *Style Sheet Fragment for Table Header*

```
    <fo:table-header>
      <fo:table-cell xsl:use-attribute-sets="header-cell">
        <fo:block xsl:use-attribute-sets="header">
          Date
        </fo:block>
```

Listing 9.6 *(continued)*

```
        </fo:table-cell>
        <fo:table-cell xsl:use-attribute-sets="header-cell">
          <fo:block xsl:use-attribute-sets="header">
            Time
          </fo:block>
        </fo:table-cell>
        <fo:table-cell xsl:use-attribute-sets="header-cell">
          <fo:block xsl:use-attribute-sets="header">
            Rate
          </fo:block>
        </fo:table-cell>
        <fo:table-cell xsl:use-attribute-sets="header-cell">
          <fo:block xsl:use-attribute-sets="header">
            Minutes
          </fo:block>
        </fo:table-cell>
        <fo:table-cell xsl:use-attribute-sets="header-cell">
          <fo:block xsl:use-attribute-sets="header">
            Origin
          </fo:block>
        </fo:table-cell>
        <fo:table-cell xsl:use-attribute-sets="header-cell">
          <fo:block xsl:use-attribute-sets="header">
            Number
          </fo:block>
        </fo:table-cell>
        <fo:table-cell xsl:use-attribute-sets="header-cell">
          <fo:block xsl:use-attribute-sets="header">
            Destination
          </fo:block>
        </fo:table-cell>
        <fo:table-cell xsl:use-attribute-sets="header-cell">
          <fo:block xsl:use-attribute-sets="header">
            Charge
          </fo:block>
        </fo:table-cell>
        <fo:table-cell xsl:use-attribute-sets="header-cell">
          <fo:block xsl:use-attribute-sets="header">
            Other Type
          </fo:block>
        </fo:table-cell>
        <fo:table-cell xsl:use-attribute-sets="header-cell">
```

Listing 9.6 *(continued)*

```
        <fo:block xsl:use-attribute-sets="header">
          Other Charges
        </fo:block>
      </fo:table-cell>
      <fo:table-cell xsl:use-attribute-sets="header-cell">
        <fo:block xsl:use-attribute-sets="header">
          Total Charges
        </fo:block>
      </fo:table-cell>
    </fo:table-header>
```

These are the header and header-cell attribute sets to use in phonestyle.xsl:

```
<xsl:attribute-set name="header-cell">
  <xsl:attribute name="display-align">after</xsl:attribute>
</xsl:attribute-set>

<xsl:attribute-set name="header">
  <xsl:attribute name="text-align">center</xsl:attribute>
  <xsl:attribute name="font-weight">bold</xsl:attribute>
</xsl:attribute-set>
```

A very long table with many entries might require more than one page in the output. The formatter automatically repeats the table header and footer whenever a table breaks across a page. You can use two properties to change that behavior. The first is the table-omit-header-at-break property. Set it to true to omit the header everywhere but at the very beginning, before the first row of the table. The second is the table-omit-footer-at-break property. Set it to true to omit the footer everywhere but at the very end, after the last row of the table. Specify both properties on the table FO like this:

```
<fo:table
 table-omit-header-at-break="true"
 table-omit-footer-at-break="true">
```

Figure 9.8 shows the finished table, complete with the header.

Date	Time	Rate	Minutes	Origin	Number	Destination	Charge	Other Type	Other Charges	Total Charges
05/16	04:35pm	O	2	Home Area	(000)000-2143	Voice Mail	prepaid			0.00
05/16	10:10pm	O	77	Home Area	(999)000-3268	Ocala,FL	prepaid			0.00
05/17	06:47pm	O	2	Home Area	(000)000-0411	411 Connect	prepaid	DA	0.99	0.99
05/22	08:02am	P	5	Home Area	(000)999-8384	incoming	prepaid			0.00

Figure 9.8
Finished table with header.

Column and Row Spanning

Column and row spanning occurs when you want some content to take the space of more than one column or more than one row. It is especially useful in building headers or footers in a table, but it is not restricted to the `table-header` or `table-footer`. Elements of the `table-body` may span rows or columns as well.

Figure 9.9 demonstrates a table header with spanned rows and columns. It is from a log used for flight planning and progress tracking. It takes 150 lines of code to generate this header and much of the structure repeats, so the following will develop enough of the source to demonstrate the spanning:

To	Mag'	Distance		Est'	Est' Time		Actual Time		Actual
	Hdg	Leg	Total	GS	Leg	Total	Leg	Total	GS

Figure 9.9
A flight log demonstrates column and row spanning.

Listing 9.7 shows the content of the file `flightlog.xsl` to be included by the flight log style sheet. It provides the full collection of attribute sets for the style sheet. Those attribute sets define border styles for major and minor divisions, with major divisions getting a double line and thicker total width. The `number-columns-spanned` property appears in the attribute set named `major-head`. The attribute set named `header-cell` uses the `number-rows-spanned` property.

Listing 9.7 *flightlog.xsl: Attribute Set Definitions for the Flight Log Style Sheet*

```
<?xml version='1.0'?>
<xsl:stylesheet version="1.0"
 xmlns:xsl="http://www.w3.org/1999/XSL/Transform"
 xmlns:fo="http://www.w3.org/1999/XSL/Format">

  <xsl:attribute-set name="major-div">
    <xsl:attribute name="border-start-style">double</xsl:attribute>
    <xsl:attribute name="border-start-width">1.5pt</xsl:attribute>
  </xsl:attribute-set>
```

Listing 9.7 *(continued)*

```
  <xsl:attribute-set name="minor-div">
    <xsl:attribute name="border-start-style">solid</xsl:attribute>
    <xsl:attribute name="border-start-width">0.5pt</xsl:attribute>
  </xsl:attribute-set>

  <xsl:attribute-set name="col">
    <xsl:attribute name="column-width">40pt</xsl:attribute>
  </xsl:attribute-set>

  <xsl:attribute-set name="major-head">
    <xsl:attribute name="number-columns-spanned">2</xsl:attribute>
    <xsl:attribute name="border-after-style">solid</xsl:attribute>
    <xsl:attribute name="border-after-width">0.5pt</xsl:attribute>
  </xsl:attribute-set>

  <xsl:attribute-set name="header-cell">
    <xsl:attribute name="number-rows-spanned">2</xsl:attribute>
    <xsl:attribute name="display-align">after</xsl:attribute>
  </xsl:attribute-set>

  <xsl:attribute-set name="header">
    <xsl:attribute name="text-align">center</xsl:attribute>
    <xsl:attribute name="font-weight">bold</xsl:attribute>
  </xsl:attribute-set>

  <xsl:attribute-set name="cell-padding">
    <xsl:attribute name="padding-start">2pt</xsl:attribute>
    <xsl:attribute name="padding-end">2pt</xsl:attribute>
  </xsl:attribute-set>

</xsl:stylesheet>
```

The `col` attribute set defines the constant width used by all columns except the first. Placing this setting in an attribute set enables you to write the setting only once. That facilitates change should you choose to increase or decrease the column width. All but the first of the `table-column` elements in the table call on the `col` attribute set.

The single-column cells use the `header-cell` attribute set to align the text content with the bottom of the cell. The `number-rows-spanned` property setting gives those cells two rows of height, the entire height of the header.

The `major-head` attribute set defines an alternative to the `header-cell` attribute set. The `number-columns-spanned` property setting gives cells two columns of width. All three of the headings that span two columns call on the `major-head` attribute set. Those cells contain the headings for "Distance," "Est' Time," and "Actual Time." This attribute set also adds the single-line bottom border that separates each major heading from the two minor headings below it.

The `block` FO within each cell uses the `header` attribute set to center the text horizontally and make it bold. All the cells use `cell-padding` to keep a little bit of space between their text and their borders.

Listing 9.8 contains enough of the style sheet to typeset the first four columns of the header shown in Figure 9.10. The rest of the columns use the same techniques shown in this source. Start with a quick look at the listing. The prose that follows explains the important details:

Listing 9.8 *Header for the Flight Log*

```
<?xml version='1.0'?>
<xsl:stylesheet version="1.0"
 xmlns:xsl="http://www.w3.org/1999/XSL/Transform"
 xmlns:fo="http://www.w3.org/1999/XSL/Format">

  <xsl:strip-space elements="*"/>
  <xsl:include href="rootrule.xsl"/>
  <xsl:include href="logstyle.xsl"/>

  <xsl:template match="flight-log">
    <fo:table
     font-size="11pt"
     border-start-style="solid"
     border-start-width="2.0pt"
     border-end-style="solid"
     border-end-width="2.0pt"
     border-before-style="solid"
     border-before-width="2.0pt"
     border-after-style="solid"
     border-after-width="2.0pt"
     table-layout="fixed">
      <fo:table-column column-number="1" column-width="72pt"/>
      <fo:table-column column-number="2"
       xsl:use-attribute-sets="col major-div"/>
      <fo:table-column column-number="3"
       xsl:use-attribute-sets="col major-div"/>
```

Listing 9.8 *(continued)*

```
<fo:table-column column-number="4"
 xsl:use-attribute-sets="col minor-div"/>
<!— column definitions omitted here —>
<fo:table-header>
  <fo:table-row>
    <fo:table-cell
     xsl:use-attribute-sets="header-cell cell-padding">
      <fo:block xsl:use-attribute-sets="header"
       text-align="start">
        To
      </fo:block>
    </fo:table-cell>
    <fo:table-cell
     xsl:use-attribute-sets="header-cell cell-padding">
      <fo:block xsl:use-attribute-sets="header">
        Mag' Hdg
      </fo:block>
    </fo:table-cell>
    <fo:table-cell
     xsl:use-attribute-sets="major-head cell-padding">
      <fo:block xsl:use-attribute-sets="header">
        Distance
      </fo:block>
    </fo:table-cell>
    <!— cell definitions omitted here —>
  </fo:table-row>
  <fo:table-row
   border-after-style="double"
   border-after-width="1.5pt">
    <fo:table-cell
     column-number="3"
     xsl:use-attribute-sets="cell-padding">
      <fo:block xsl:use-attribute-sets="header">
        Leg
      </fo:block>
    </fo:table-cell>
    <fo:table-cell
     xsl:use-attribute-sets="cell-padding">
      <fo:block xsl:use-attribute-sets="header">
        Total
      </fo:block>
    </fo:table-cell>
```

Listing 9.8 *(continued)*

```
          <!— cell definitions omitted here —>
        </fo:table-row>
      </fo:table-header>
      <fo:table-body>
        <xsl:apply-templates/>
      </fo:table-body>
    </fo:table>
  </xsl:template>

</xsl:stylesheet>
```

The single template of the style sheet matches the flight-log element. An XML source as simple as the following will suffice to display the result:

```
<?xml version='1.0'?>
<flight-log/>
```

The `table` FO supplies a solid, 2-point border on all sides and defines the font size equal to 11 points. It gives the formatter a clue about fixed table layout because it supplies a width for every column.

The `table-column` definitions begin with a borderless first column that has almost double the width of all the other columns. This is the column in which the pilot enters the waypoint, or check point, in the log. Airline pilots use a log like this, by the way, to track fuel usage and update estimated arrival time.

The next three columns use a `major-div` or `minor-div` attribute set to get a double- or single-ruled border. The formatter would automatically assign column numbers equal to the settings given, but there's no harm in providing them explicitly.

The `table-header` begins after the `table-column` definitions and contains two rows. The first row defines all the single-column headers and the first line of the double-column headers. The single-column headers span two rows because they refer to the `header-cell` attribute set. The double-column headers span two columns because they refer to the `major-head` attribute set.

The second row of the header has a `border-after-style` setting of `double` to separate the header from the rest of the table. It contains no cell definitions for the single-column headers. Those were defined in the first row and spanned into this row. It defines only the minor headings that appear under the two-column headings.

There is no need for the `column-number` attribute on the first cell of the second row. The formatter should compute the positions of columns left unoccupied by the spanned rows and fill those with the given cells. Indicating the beginning column number 3 serves to make the intent explicit for a reader of the style sheet.

That is the whole of the header example with spanned rows and columns. You now know how to accomplish some pretty sophisticated results using table cells. Remember that the cell spanning properties apply equally well to cells in the `table-body` or `table-footer` as they do to cells in the `table-header`.

Content of a Cell

It seems strange to get this far into tables without discussing the content of a cell, but here we are. So far, you've used a simple block with text as the content of every cell. The `table-cell` FO actually allows a few different FOs as content.

The content of a table cell must be one or more block-level FOs. Recall that the block-level FOs are `block`, `block-container`, `table-and-caption`, `table`, and `list-block`. You can put a word, a number, or a paragraph into a `table-cell`, but you must enclose it in a block. You can put a `block-container` in a cell and change the reference orientation. You can put a list in a cell. You can put another table in a cell.

Table Within a Table

Suppose you would like a table that formats a brief description of an FO together with a list of applicable properties. You can return to the example that began this chapter for the inner table, which lists properties. The outer table will have three cells in two columns. The left column will have the name of the formatting object in a cell above the list of properties. The right column will have the description.

Listing 9.9 contains the source for one such item. The markup describes the `table-body` FO and lists applicable properties. It contains three elements—`tag`, `description`, and `properties`—to format in three cells of a table:

Listing 9.9 *Sample Data for Table Formatting*

```
fo-list>
  <fo>
    <tag>table-body</tag>
    <description>
      Enclose the data rows of a table within
```

Listing 9.9 *(continued)*

```
        the table-body formatting object.
        Enclose each data row in a table-row
        formatting object.
        The table-body FO may also directly include
        table-cell formatting objects.
        It may not, however contain a mix of table-row
        and table-cell FOs as direct descendents.
      </description>
      <properties>
        <property-group>
          Common Accessibility Properties
        </property-group>
        <property-group>
          Common Aural Properties
        </property-group>
        <property-group>
          Common Border, Padding, and Background Properties
        </property-group>
        <property-group>
          Common Relative Position Properties
        </property-group>
        <property>border-after-precedence</property>
        <property>border-before-precedence</property>
        <property>border-end-precedence</property>
        <property>border-start-precedence</property>
        <property>id</property>
        <property>visibility</property>
      </properties>
  </fo>
</fo-list>
```

Listing 9.10 contains the source for the style sheet. The template that matches the `fo` tag outputs a complete table, including table rows and table cells. The `xsl:apply-templates` operation in each cell uses the `select` attribute to carefully select its content:

Listing 9.10 *Style Sheet Formats a Table Within a* table-cell

```
<?xml version='1.0'?>
<xsl:stylesheet version="1.0"
 xmlns:xsl="http://www.w3.org/1999/XSL/Transform"
 xmlns:fo="http://www.w3.org/1999/XSL/Format">
```

Listing 9.10 *(continued)*

```
<xsl:strip-space elements="*"/>
<xsl:include href="rootrule.xsl"/>

<xsl:attribute-set name="borders">
  <xsl:attribute name="border-before-style">solid</xsl:attribute>
  <xsl:attribute name="border-after-style">solid</xsl:attribute>
  <xsl:attribute name="border-start-style">solid</xsl:attribute>
  <xsl:attribute name="border-end-style">solid</xsl:attribute>
  <xsl:attribute name="border-before-width">1pt</xsl:attribute>
  <xsl:attribute name="border-after-width">1pt</xsl:attribute>
  <xsl:attribute name="border-start-width">1pt</xsl:attribute>
  <xsl:attribute name="border-end-width">1pt</xsl:attribute>
  <xsl:attribute name="padding-before">3pt</xsl:attribute>
  <xsl:attribute name="padding-after">3pt</xsl:attribute>
  <xsl:attribute name="padding-start">3pt</xsl:attribute>
  <xsl:attribute name="padding-end">3pt</xsl:attribute>
</xsl:attribute-set>

<xsl:template match="fo">
  <fo:table>
    <fo:table-body>
      <fo:table-row>
        <fo:table-cell
         xsl:use-attribute-sets="borders">
          <xsl:apply-templates select="tag"/>
        </fo:table-cell>
        <fo:table-cell
         number-rows-spanned="2"
         xsl:use-attribute-sets="borders">
          <xsl:apply-templates select="description"/>
        </fo:table-cell>
      </fo:table-row>
      <fo:table-row>
        <fo:table-cell
         xsl:use-attribute-sets="borders">
          <xsl:apply-templates select="properties"/>
        </fo:table-cell>
      </fo:table-row>
    </fo:table-body>
  </fo:table>
</xsl:template>
```

Listing 9.10 *(continued)*

```
  <xsl:template match="tag">
    <fo:block
     font-weight="bold">
      <xsl:apply-templates/>
    </fo:block>
  </xsl:template>

  <xsl:template match="description">
    <fo:block>
      <xsl:apply-templates/>
    </fo:block>
  </xsl:template>

  <xsl:template match="properties">
    <fo:table
     border-collapse="separate"
     border-separation.inline-progression-direction="6pt"
     border-separation.block-progression-direction="2pt">
      <fo:table-body>
        <xsl:apply-templates/>
      </fo:table-body>
    </fo:table>
  </xsl:template>

  <xsl:template match="property|property-group">
    <fo:table-cell>
      <xsl:if test="position() mod 3 = 0">
        <xsl:attribute name="ends-row">true</xsl:attribute>
      </xsl:if>
      <fo:block>
        <xsl:apply-templates/>
      </fo:block>
    </fo:table-cell>
  </xsl:template>

</xsl:stylesheet>
```

The last two templates of the style sheet are nearly verbatim, if not exact, duplicates of the templates used in Listing 9.2 to format the first table example of this chapter. They format the property list into three columns. The template that matches `properties` formats a new table within the cell opened by the template that matches the `fo` element.

The result shown in Figure 9.10 is not perfect, but it conveys the idea. The lower-left cell contains the table-formatted list of properties. It is not perfect, because the line wrapping within each cell of the property listing makes the listing difficult to read in a left-to-right scan. The white space in the columns makes it difficult to read in a column-oriented scan. You might be grateful that we did not use this format for Appendix B, "A Concise Listing of Formatting Objects."

table-body			Enclose the data rows of a table within the table-body formatting object. Enclose each data row in a table-row formatting object. The table-body FO may also directly include table-cell formatting objects. It may not, however contain a mix of table-row and table-cell FO's as direct descendents.
Common Accessibility Properties	Common Aural Properties	Common Border, Padding, and Background Properties	
Common Relative Position Properties	border-after-precedence	border-before-precedence	
border-end-precedence	border-start-precedence	id	
visibility			

Figure 9.10

Table formatted within a table-cell.

Cell Alignments

Whether the content is another table, a list, or merely a block, you will sometimes want to adjust the location of that content horizontally or vertically within the cell. Positioning in the block-progression dimension is fairly straightforward. Positioning in the inline-progression dimension somewhat depends on the content of the cell.

Use the `display-align` property to accomplish positioning in the block-progression dimension. The value `before` sets the before edge of the first contained block flush with the before edge of the cell. The value `after` sets the after edge of the last contained block flush with the after edge of the cell. The value `center` places equal amounts of space before and after the contained blocks.

Figure 9.11 demonstrates the three values for cell alignment. Each cell contains the start element of the source used to generate it.

<table-cell display-align="before">	<table-cell display-align="center">	<table-cell display-align="after">	This table cell works to make all of the cells in this row taller.

Figure 9.11

Display alignments in a cell.

Inline-Progression Alignment

Alignment within a cell in the inline-progression direction occurs from the block contained in the cell. Use the `text-align` property on the block FO to align the content of the block as discussed in Chapter 6, "Block and Inline," in the section titled "Justification." The `table-cell` does not itself allow the `text-align` property. Set the property on the blocks within the `table-cell`.

If the content of the cell is a table or a list, you might want to enclose that within a block FO so that you can align it using the `text-align` property on the block. Remember that you can place padding on the `table-cell` to increase the amount of white space between the cell border and the content of the cell.

Captioning a Table

Very often, a table shown in a book, an article, a paper, or a report has a caption describing the content of the table. There remain two table-related FOs not yet described. Those are the FOs for captions—`table-and-caption` and `table-caption`.

The `table-and-caption` FO contains first a `table-caption` and then a `table`. The `table-caption` FO contains one or more block-level FOs just like a `table-cell` does. The `table` is a normal table like any of the tables described so far in this chapter.

Revive the very simple table example of Listing 9.2. Add two empty attribute sets and modify the template that matches the group element as shown here. The content of the table remains unchanged:

```
<xsl:attribute-set name="caption-side"/>

<xsl:attribute-set name="caption"/>

<xsl:template match="group">
  <fo:table-and-caption
   xsl:use-attribute-sets="caption-side">
    <fo:table-caption
     xsl:use-attribute-sets="caption">
      <fo:block><xsl:value-of select="@name"/></fo:block>
    </fo:table-caption>
    <fo:table
      <!— Content of the table as in Listing 9.2 —>
    </fo:table>
  </fo:table-and-caption>
</xsl:template>
```

Formatting this new example causes the words "Table Properties" to print above the table beginning at its start edge. Figure 9.12 demonstrates the result:

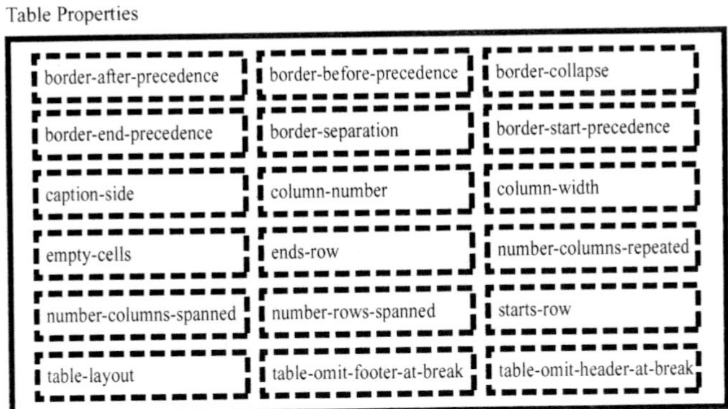
Table Properties

border-after-precedence	border-before-precedence	border-collapse
border-end-precedence	border-separation	border-start-precedence
caption-side	column-number	column-width
empty-cells	ends-row	number-columns-repeated
number-columns-spanned	number-rows-spanned	starts-row
table-layout	table-omit-footer-at-break	table-omit-header-at-break

Figure 9.12
Table with a caption.

The caption on the table need not appear above the table. You may just as often want it below the table. Use the `caption-side` property on the `table-and-caption` FO to specify the edge of the table at which the formatter should place the caption. A value of `after` will place the caption `after` the table. The caption will move to the bottom in this example. Try setting the `caption-side` property as follows:

```
<xsl:attribute-set name="caption-side">
  <xsl:attribute name="caption-side">after</xsl:attribute>
</xsl:attribute-set>
```

A value of `start` will place the caption on the left in this example. Some formatters may not support captions on the start or end edges of the table.

The formatter may try to determine a reasonable width for a side caption, but will more likely give satisfactory results if you specify the width. Do this by giving the `inline-progression-dimension` on the `table-caption`, as follows:

```
<xsl:attribute-set name="caption-side">
  <xsl:attribute name="caption-side">start</xsl:attribute>
</xsl:attribute-set>

<xsl:attribute-set name="caption">
  <xsl:attribute name="inline-progression-dimension">1in</xsl:attribute>
</xsl:attribute-set>
```

Align the content of a table caption using the `text-align` property. The following settings center the caption beneath the table:

```
<xsl:attribute-set name="caption-side">
  <xsl:attribute name="caption-side">after</xsl:attribute>
  <xsl:attribute name="text-align">center</xsl:attribute>
</xsl:attribute-set>
```

Full Table Structure

The `table-and-caption` FO completes the full complement of table-related FOs. The complete table structure includes a table caption, table, headers, footers, body, rows, and cells. XSL supplies a formatting object for each. Some of them are optional, as you have seen. Figure 9.13 shows the full structure of an XSL table. Required elements are shown with bold type. The ellipses mean there may be more than one:

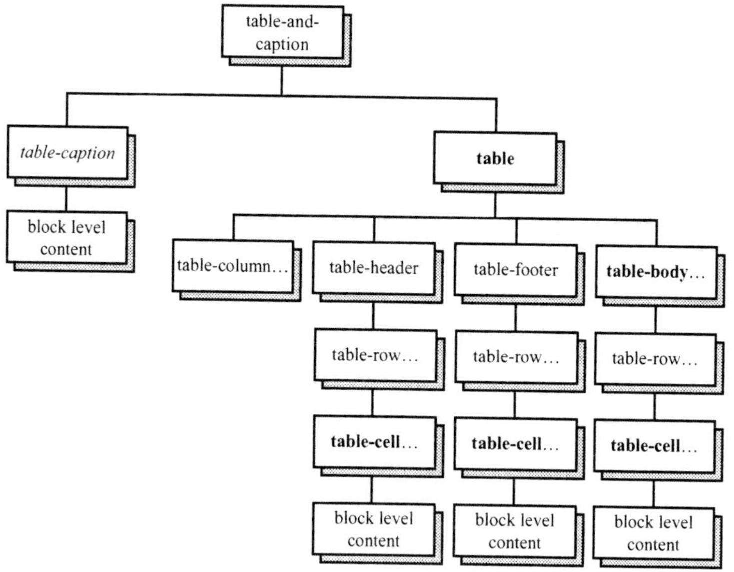

Figure 9.13
The full table structure.

Only three of the table formatting objects, the `table`, `table-body`, and `table-cell`, are mandatory. The rest are optional. It makes sense to supply a `table-caption` if there is a `table-and-caption`, but even that is not required. Figure 9.13 shows the FOs left to right in the order in which they must appear.

Summary

Table support in XSL is extensive and very powerful. XSL supports separated and collapsed border models. It allows you to alter the precedence for the collapsed border model. It supports two methods for breaking data into rows—one using attributes of the cells and the other explicitly grouping cells in `table-row` FOs. Cells may have their column position explicitly assigned or determined by their position relative to other cells.

The content of a table cell may be one or more blocks, lists, or even other tables. This makes tables a very powerful layout tool.

The next chapter covers lists and leaders. After tables, lists and leaders will be a walk in the park.

CHAPTER 10

Lists and Leaders

One of the most fascinating things about lists in XSL is that they allow overlapping content without absolute positioning. The list-related formatting objects enable you to produce parallel overlapping output streams. The introduction to list geometry will describe how the overlap occurs. The sections that follow describe the more usual applications to bulleted items and checklists, enumerated lists, and descriptive lists.

The chapter ends with a discussion of leaders, which are useful in lists, such as a table of contents. The discussion of leaders also describes using them to place blanks in the text, such as with legal forms.

Structure of a List

XSL provides four FOs for producing lists. They are the `list-block`, `list-item`, `list-item-label`, and `list-item-body`. The `list-block` contains one or more `list-item` FOs. Each `list-item` FO must contain first a `list-item-label` and then a `list-item-body`. The `list-item-label` and `list-item-body` both contain block-level FOs. The nested structure of a list looks like this:

```
<fo:list-block>
  <fo:list-item>
    <fo:list-item-label>
      <fo:block>
        ...
      </fo:block>
    </fo:list-item-label>
    <fo:list-item-body>
      <fo:block>
        ...
      </fo:block>
    </fo:list-item-body>
  </fo:list-item>
</fo:list-block>
```

List Geometry

Lists allow horizontal synchronization of two columns of flowed content. That is the most general description possible of the way the list FOs behave in XSL. Each `list-item` begins a new pair of columns that align at the before edge (their tops). The `list-item-label` places content in a column adjacent to the start edge. It is the FO that normally contains a bullet, number, or term. The `list-item-body` places content in a column adjacent to the end edge. It is the FO that normally contains the content of a list item. Figure 10.1 illustrates list geometry for the discussion that follows.

Each `list-item` in Figure 10.1 has size in the block-progression dimension great enough to contain the largest of the `list-item-label` or `list-item-body`. The `list-item` aligns both the label and the body at its before edge.

The value of the `end-indent` property on the `list-item-label` limits its size in the inline-progression dimension. The value of the `start-indent` property on the `list-item-body` begins the body somewhere clear of the label.

The `provisional-distance-between-starts` and `provisional-label-separation` properties will help set the `end-indent` for the label and the `start-indent` for the body under very specific circumstances. Those circumstances follow shortly. For now, note that the label and body will overlap if you specify a setting for `end-indent` on the label that leaves greater label size (in the inline progression dimension) than the size of the `start-indent` on the body. If you omit the indent properties, the label and body will entirely overlap (see Figure 10.2).

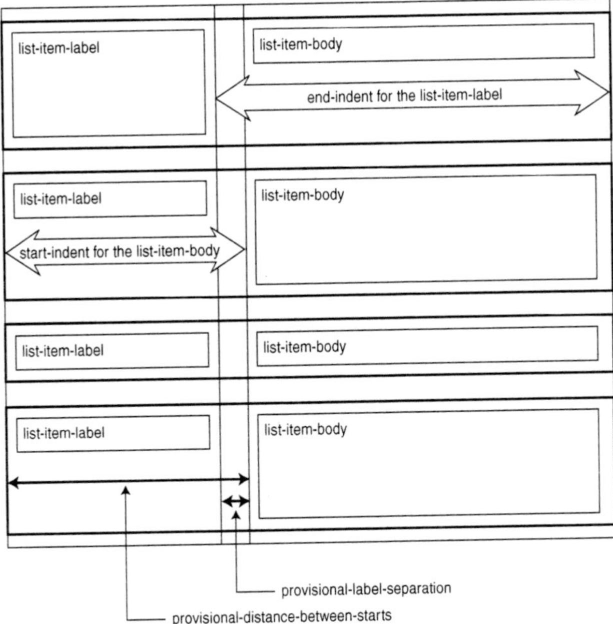

Figure 10.1
Geometry of the list FOs.

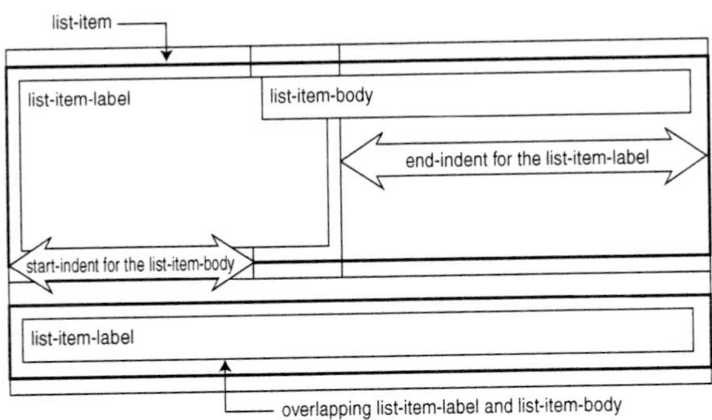

Figure 10.2
Overlapping list item label and body.

Figure 10.2 shows two list items. In the first item, the end indent for the label is smaller than the width of the body. The start indent for the body is smaller than the width of the label. The small start and end indents allow the label and the body to overlap in a column just left of center.

The second item in the list illustrated by Figure 10.2 has no end indent setting for the label and no start indent for the body. That item illustrates the extreme case in which the label and the body entirely overlap.

By now you get the picture. The usual case, the normal usage of lists requires setting at least the two properties—`end-indent` on the `list-item-label` and `start-indent` on the `list-item-body`. XSL provides two functions that assist in setting those two properties. They are `body-start()` and `label-end()`. The last item in Figure 10.1 illustrates. Use the `body-start()` function as the value for the `start-indent` property on the `list-item-body`. Use the `label-end()` function as the value of the `end-indent` for the `list-item-label`. The section that follows, "Bullets and Checklists," illustrates this usage.

The `body-start()` function calculates the width of the containing block and then subtracts the value of the `provisional-distance-between-starts`. The `label-end()` function subtracts the `provisional-label-separation` from the `provisional-distance-between-starts`.

The value for the `provisional-distance-between-starts` property defaults to `24pt`. The value for `provisional-label-separation` defaults to `6pt`. That yields an 18-point column width for the labels with at least 6 points of space between the label and the body of each list item.

Use the `provisional-distance-between-starts` and `provisional-label-separation` properties on the `list-block` FO. If this description of the general geometry of XSL lists seems at all confusing, never worry. The following sections illustrate with concrete examples. They cover the most usual cases you will encounter in practice.

Bullets and Checklists

Bulleted lists have a series of items marked with some symbol at the start edge followed by the text of the item. A checklist uses an open box or circle in the place of a bullet. Here is a partial list of items to bring on a camping trip:

```
<?xml version="1.0"?>
  <checklist>
  <item>tent</item>
  <item>sleeping bag</item>
  <item>change of clothes</item>
  <item>food</item>
  <item>camp stove</item>
  <item>mess kit</item>
  <item>matches</item>
  <item>first aid kit</item>
  <item>marshmallows</item>
  <item>chocolate bars</item>
  <item>graham crackers</item>
</checklist>
```

The kids won't go without the last items—the marshmallows, at minimum. Listing 10.1 provides an XSL style sheet for formatting the checklist:

Listing 10.1 *Style Sheet Formats a Checklist*

```
<?xml version='1.0'?>
<xsl:stylesheet version="1.0"
 xmlns:xsl="http://www.w3.org/1999/XSL/Transform"
 xmlns:fo="http://www.w3.org/1999/XSL/Format">

  <xsl:strip-space elements="*"/>
  <xsl:include href="rootrule.xsl"/>

  <xsl:attribute-set name="list-geometry">
    <xsl:attribute name="provisional-distance-between-starts">
      12pt</xsl:attribute>
    <xsl:attribute name="provisional-label-separation">4pt</xsl:attribute>
  </xsl:attribute-set>

  <xsl:template match="checklist">
    <fo:list-block xsl:use-attribute-sets="list-geometry">
      <xsl:apply-templates/>
    </fo:list-block>
  </xsl:template>
```

Listing 10.1 *(continued)*

```
  <xsl:template match="item">
    <fo:list-item>
      <fo:list-item-label end-indent="label-end()">
        <fo:block font-weight="bold">
          <fo:character character="&#x25A1;"/>
        </fo:block>
      </fo:list-item-label>
      <fo:list-item-body start-indent="body-start()">
        <fo:block>
          <xsl:apply-templates/>
        </fo:block>
      </fo:list-item-body>
    </fo:list-item>
  </xsl:template>

</xsl:stylesheet>
```

The template that matches the checklist outputs the `list-block`. The template that matches each item outputs the `list-item`, `list-item-label`, and `list-item-body`. There are five lines to note in particular. These five lines define the geometry of the list. They align the check boxes and the checklist items.

First note the two lines in the attribute set named `list-geometry`. The line that begins the `list-block` uses the `list-geometry` attribute set. The `provisional-distance-between starts` provides 12 points from the start of the check bullet to the start of the checklist item. The `provisional-label-separation` provides at least 4 points between the check bullet and the start of the checklist item.

The line that begins a `list-item-label` contains the setting for the `end-indent` property. The value for `end-indent` equal to `label-end()` restricts the width of the label according to the values for `provisional-distance between starts` and `provisional-label-separation` specified in the `list-geometry` attribute set. The line that begins a `list-item-body` contains the setting for the `start-indent` property. The value for `start-indent` equal to `body-start()` starts the checklist item text 4 points clear of the checklist item bullet.

Figure 10.3 shows the output of the checklist style sheet of Listing 10.2:

- ☐ tent
- ☐ sleeping bag
- ☐ change of clothes
- ☐ food
- ☐ camp stove
- ☐ mess kit
- ☐ first aid kit
- ☐ marshmallows
- ☐ chocolate bars
- ☐ graham crackers

Figure 10.3
A checklist rendered by the style sheet.

Content of a List Item

Both the `list-item-label` and `list-item-body` contain block-level FOs. The may contain a `block`, a `block-container`, a `table`, or another `list-block`. Use a `list-block` within a `list-item-body` to create an outline format. The outer list contains major headings. The inner list contains minor headings. The next section, "Enumerated Lists" provides an example of an outline format.

The list items in the checklist example use a single block in both the label and the body. The body places the text of the checklist item inside of the block. The list uses an inline FO, `character`, to select a Unicode symbol corresponding to the open circle. The entity, `○` selects the character formatted in the label. Figure 10.4 shows a number of useful values for the `character` property of a `character` FO within a `list-item-label`.

Enumerated List

The enumerated list looks pretty much the same as the bulleted list, except it contains a number at the start edge in the place of the bullet. Most of the work to produce the number occurs in the style sheet. The FOs have little to do with numbering list items.

The style sheet would, in fact, look pretty much like the one shown in Listing 10.1. In place of a bullet, it would produce a number. The example for this section will add a second level of list so that you can see something really new.

Figure 10.5 demonstrates an outline formatted using the style sheet you will develop in this section. The outline shows a very small portion of the federal laws that regulate aviation. This gives a hint of the thorough and extensive oversight, regulation, and certification that the United States Government provides within its territory for aircraft, airspace, air-traffic control, flight schools, pilots, flight controllers, aircraft technicians, and other aviation professionals.

Symbol	Entity	Description
†	†	dagger
‡	‡	double dagger
•	•	round bullet
‣	‣	tringular bullet
●	●	black circle
○	○	white circle
■	■	black square
□	□	white square
◆	◆	black diamond
◇	◇	white diamond
★	★	black star
☆	☆	white star

Symbol	Entity	Description
◊	◊	lozenge or total mark
☐	☐	ballot box
☑	☑	ballot box with check
☒	☒	ballot box with x
✓	✓	tick, check mark
✗	✗	ballot cross
♀	♀	female symbol
♂	♂	male symbol
☎	☎	telephone symbol
☞	☞	right pointing index
✶	✶	six-pointed star
➤	➤	black rightwards arrowhead

Figure 10.4
Some Unicode constants for bullets.

The list item labels in Figure 10.5 use a legal-outline numbering scheme. Each label contains the number of the current item and all items that contain it in outline. The formatter calculated these from the position of the item within the source document.

The list item bodies format all subordinate items as a nested list after the title of the current item. The codes after each item title indicate the explicit designation given in the Code of Federal Regulations (CFR) for the section named. They demonstrate a second method of generating numbers for outline content.

The following shows a fragment of the source input used to generate Figure 10.5. It shows enough to demonstrate the entire structure of the input. The rest is repetition:

```
<?xml version="1.0"?>
<cfr title="14" index="I">
  <title>Federal Aviation Regulations.</title>
  <subchapter index="D">
    <title>Airmen.</title>
    <part index="61">
      <title>
```

```
        Certification: pilots, flight instructors, and ground instructors.
      </title>
      <subpart index="1">
        <title>Applicability and definitions.</title>
      </subpart>
    </part>
  </subchapter>
</cfr>
```

I Federal Aviation Regulations. 14 CFR I
- *I.A* Airmen. 14 CFR I (D)
  - *I.A.1* Certification: pilots, flight instructors, and ground instructors. 14 CFR I (D) 61
    - *I.A.1.a* Applicability and definitions. 14 CFR I (D) 61.1
    - *I.A.1.b* Requirement for certificates, ratings, and authorizations. 14 CFR I (D) 61.3
    - *I.A.1.c* Qualification and approval of flight simulators and flight training devices. 14 CFR I (D) 61.4
    - *I.A.1.d* Certificates and ratings issued under this part. 14 CFR I (D) 61.5
  - *I.A.2* Medical standards and certification. 14 CFR I (D) 67
    - *I.A.2.a* Applicability. 14 CFR I (D) 67.1
    - *I.A.2.b* Issue. 14 CFR I (D) 67.3
    - *I.A.2.c* Access to national driver register. 14 CFR I (D) 67.7
    - *I.A.2.d* Eligibility. 14 CFR I (D) 67.101
    - *I.A.2.e* Eye. 14 CFR I (D) 67.103
    - *I.A.2.f* Ear, nose, throat, and equalibrium. 14 CFR I (D) 67.105
    - *I.A.2.g* Mental. 14 CFR I (D) 67.107
- *I.B* Air traffic and general operating rules. 14 CFR I (F)
  - *I.B.1* General Operating and Flight Rules. 14 CFR I (F) 91
    - *I.B.1.a* Applicability. 14 CFR I (F) 91.1
    - *I.B.1.b* Responsibility and authority of the pilot in command. 14 CFR I (F) 91.
    - *I.B.1.c* Pilot in command of aircraft requiring more than one required pilot. 14 CFR I (F) 91.5
    - *I.B.1.d* Civil aircraft airworthiness. 14 CFR I (F) 91.7
    - *I.B.1.e* Civil aircraft flight manual, marking, and placard requirements. 14 CFR I (F) 91.9
    - *I.B.1.f* Prohibition on interference with crewmembers. 14 CFR I (F) 91.11
  - *I.B.2* Security control of air traffic. 14 CFR I (F) 99
    - *I.B.2.a* Applicability. 14 CFR I (F) 99.1
    - *I.B.2.b* Definitions. 14 CFR I (F) 99.3
    - *I.B.2.c* Emergency situations. 14 CFR I (F) 99.5
    - *I.B.2.d* Special security instructions. 14 CFR I (F) 99.7

Figure 10.5
An outline demonstrating nested lists and numbering.

The outer element encodes the title number and index for this aviation portion of the CFR as attributes. The `title` element encodes the description. All the elements shown fall under Chapter I of Title 14.

Subchapters, parts, and subparts all appear as subordinate elements nested within their containing parts. Each has an `index` attribute that gives their index designation from the CFR. Each contains a `title` element that gives their description.

The style sheet used to format the output shown in Figure 10.5 uses a number of advanced features to generate numbers. It also contains some recursive structure to generate lists within lists. Listing 10.2 shows the beginning elements of the complete source. Two templates matching the `title` element mask the `title` from processing by `apply-templates`. One of the item templates will call for the `title` explicitly. The `list-geometry` attribute set provides the properties required on the `list-block` FO. The text following the listing discusses in detail the additional templates needed to produce the outline:

Listing 10.2 *Beginning of a Style Sheet to Format an Outline*

```
<?xml version='1.0'?>
<xsl:stylesheet version="1.0"
 xmlns:xsl="http://www.w3.org/1999/XSL/Transform"
 xmlns:fo="http://www.w3.org/1999/XSL/Format">

  <xsl:strip-space elements="*"/>
  <xsl:include href="rootrule.xsl"/>

  <xsl:template match="title"/>
  <xsl:template match="title" mode="cfrnum"/>

  <xsl:attribute-set name="list-geometry">
    <xsl:attribute name="provisional-distance-between-starts">
      3pc
    </xsl:attribute>
    <xsl:attribute name="provisional-label-separation">
      4pt
    </xsl:attribute>
  </xsl:attribute-set>

</xsl:stylesheet>
```

One way to read a style sheet is to begin with the template that matches the top-level element and follow the processing with the input document structure in mind. The template that matches the top level `cfr` element outputs a list block. It calls on the template named `item` to produce the content of the block. Add this and the remaining templates described in this section to the style sheet begun in Listing 10.2:

```
<xsl:template match="cfr">
  <fo:list-block xsl:use-attribute-sets="list-geometry">
    <xsl:call-template name="item"/>
  </fo:list-block>
</xsl:template>
```

The template named `item` outputs a complete list item, including the item label and the item body. It calls on yet another template named `item-label` to generate the label of the item:

```
<xsl:template name="item">
  <fo:list-item>
    <xsl:call-template name="item-label"/>
    <fo:list-item-body start-indent="body-start()">
      <xsl:call-template name="index-title"/>
      <fo:list-block
       xsl:use-attribute-sets="list-geometry">
        <xsl:apply-templates/>
      </fo:list-block>
    </fo:list-item-body>
  </fo:list-item>
</xsl:template>
```

The `item-label` template outputs a `list-item-label`. It contains the XSL mechanism for automatically generating a number. All the details about generating numbers in a style sheet are beyond the scope of this book about FO, but an explanation of the example shown here follows:

```
<xsl:template name="item-label">
  <fo:list-item-label end-indent="label-end()">
    <fo:block
     text-align="end"
     font-style="italic">
      <xsl:number
       level="multiple"
       from="/"
       count="cfr|subchapter|part|subpart"
       format="I.A.1.a.i"/>
    </fo:block>
  </fo:list-item-label>
</xsl:template>
```

The XSL number element counts from the cfr element down each level of the input to the current element. The setting of multiple for the level attribute causes it to generate a number at every level along the way. The setting of the count attribute has it count only the structural elements—cfr, subchapter, part, and subpart. It does not count the title elements.

The value of the format attribute for XSL number generates Roman numerals for the first level. The transform numbers the level represented by subchapter elements with capital letters A, B, C, and so forth. The level represented by part elements gets the usual ordinal numbers 1, 2, 3, and so forth.

The list item label for every one of the lists at every level contains this same content. That is why it is coded as a named template. Two of the templates in the style sheet make use of this template to generate a label.

After calling the item-label template, the template named item generates a body for the item. The list-item-body outputs the title and the index for the current input element. It calls a template named index-title to do so. The item body generated by the item template goes further than generating a title. It also anticipates a nested list. Just like the template matching cfr that started us off, the body of the item template starts a list block and then processes the child elements from the input.

At this point, the processor has generated all the direct output from the top-level element, cfr. The apply-templates directive inside the list-block of the item template will process the subordinate elements, subchapter, part, and subpart. The subchapter and part elements are both items of a higher-level list and both contain a nested list. The template matching them matches these and calls the list item template just discussed. These recursive calls to the item template cause the output of nested lists:

```
<xsl:template match="subchapter|part">
  <xsl:call-template name="item"/>
</xsl:template>
```

At some level, the processing must stop generating nested lists. The template that matches the subpart element outputs the same item label as the rest of the items, but the item body it produces does not contain a nested list block:

```
<xsl:template match="subpart">
  <fo:list-item>
    <xsl:call-template name="item-label"/>
    <fo:list-item-body start-indent="body-start()">
      <xsl:call-template name="index-title"/>
    </fo:list-item-body>
```

```
    </fo:list-item>
  </xsl:template>
```

The body of the item contains the title and index only. Like the `item` template, it calls the template named `index-title` to output the title and index. Write the `index-title` template like this:

```
<xsl:template name="index-title">
  <fo:block>
    <xsl:value-of select="title"/>
    <xsl:text> </xsl:text>
    <xsl:apply-templates mode="cfrnum" select="."/>
  </fo:block>
</xsl:template>
```

The `index-title` template outputs the block within a `list-item-body` that contains the title. It follows the title with a space and then begins a formula for generating the full CFR index reference for the current section. The call to `apply-templates` selects the current element and begins a new mode named `cfrnum`. Listing 10.3 shows the templates that process elements of the input in the `cfrnum` mode:

Listing 10.3 *Templates to Generate the CFR Index References*

```
<xsl:template match="cfr" mode="cfrnum">
   <xsl:value-of select="@title"/>
   <xsl:text> CFR </xsl:text>
   <xsl:value-of select="@index"/>
</xsl:template>

<xsl:template match="subchapter" mode="cfrnum">
   <xsl:apply-templates
    select="ancestor::*[1]" mode="cfrnum"/>
   <xsl:text> (</xsl:text>
   <xsl:value-of select="@index"/>
   <xsl:text>) </xsl:text>
</xsl:template>

<xsl:template match="part" mode="cfrnum">
   <xsl:apply-templates
    select="ancestor::*[1]" mode="cfrnum"/>
   <xsl:value-of select="@index"/>
</xsl:template>
```

Listing 10.3 *(continued)*

```
<xsl:template match="subpart" mode="cfrnum">
   <xsl:apply-templates
    select="ancestor::*[1]" mode="cfrnum"/>
   <xsl:text>.</xsl:text>
   <xsl:value-of select="@index"/>
</xsl:template>
```

Add the templates of Listing 10.3 to your style sheet as well. Each of these templates begins by formatting the reference for its immediate ancestor. Each template follows the ancestor reference with the formatted index for the matched input element. The recursive pattern repeated in each template causes the formatter to walk up the input tree from the current node through leading calls to `apply-templates`. The formatter then winds back out of those calls, down the tree, generating a part of the index before exiting each template.

That covers all the dozen or so templates used to create the output shown in Figure 10.5 at the beginning of this section. The example in this section demonstrated nesting of FO `list-block` elements within the FO `list-item-body`. It also demonstrated two very different methods for generating numbers within an enumerated list.

Descriptive List

Descriptive lists have a short item in the column at the starting edge with descriptive material following. This section presents an example of a descriptive list using a short glossary of aerobatics terms.

The source for the glossary contains records of terms and their definitions. These aren't official definitions, just mine. The following XML source contains two records by way of example. You can easily reproduce the rest by referring to the output:

```
<?xml version="1.0"?>
<glossary>
  <term>Loop</term>
  <def>Flight transitioning through 360 degrees of
  rotation around the lateral axis, describing a
  circle in the vertical plane.</def>
  <term>Aileron Roll</term>
  <def>One of two types of rolls in which the
  wing tips describe an arc around the longitudinal
```

```
  axis of the airplane.  An aileron roll may be
  either a slow roll or a hesitation roll.</def>
</glossary>
```

Listing 10.4 demonstrates a style sheet for typesetting the glossary. It looks just like Listing 10.1, which produced a checklist. The main differences are the values for the `provisional-label-separation` and `provisional-distance-between starts` and in the content of the `list-item-label`.

Listing 10.4 *Style Sheet Formats a Descriptive List*

```
<?xml version='1.0'?>
<xsl:stylesheet version="1.0"
 xmlns:xsl="http://www.w3.org/1999/XSL/Transform"
 xmlns:fo="http://www.w3.org/1999/XSL/Format">

  <xsl:strip-space elements="*"/>
  <xsl:include href="rootrule.xsl"/>

  <xsl:attribute-set name="list-geometry">
    <xsl:attribute name="provisional-distance-between-starts">
      8pc
    </xsl:attribute>
    <xsl:attribute name="provisional-label-separation">12pt</xsl:attribute>
  </xsl:attribute-set>

  <xsl:template match="glossary">
    <fo:list-block xsl:use-attribute-sets="list-geometry">
      <xsl:apply-templates select="term">
        <xsl:sort/>
      </xsl:apply-templates>
    </fo:list-block>
  </xsl:template>

  <xsl:template match="term">
    <fo:list-item>
      <fo:list-item-label end-indent="label-end()">
        <fo:block font-weight="bold">
          <xsl:apply-templates/>
        </fo:block>
      </fo:list-item-label>
      <fo:list-item-body start-indent="body-start()">
```

Listing 10.4 *(continued)*

```
        <fo:block>
          <xsl:apply-templates select="following-sibling::def[1]"/>
        </fo:block>
      </fo:list-item-body>
    </fo:list-item>
  </xsl:template>

</xsl:stylesheet>
```

The template that matches the glossary element contains an XSL `apply-templates` to process the terms within the `list-block`. That `apply-templates` element is not empty, as usual, but contains an XSL `sort`. The `sort` causes the transform engine to process the terms in alphabetical order, rather than in the order that they are written. The result shown in Figure 10.6 has sorted glossary items in a descriptive list.

List Within a Table

The previous chapter promised to demonstrate a list within a table but held off because you hadn't yet been introduced to lists. This section makes good on the promise.

The source for this example is the one presented in Listing 9.9 of the previous chapter, in the section titled, "Table Within a Table." Revise the style sheet shown in Listing 9.10 of the same section using list FOs. Replace the two templates that match the `<properties>`, `<property>`, and `<property-group>` elements with the following two templates:

```
<xsl:template match="properties">
  <fo:list-block>
    <xsl:apply-templates/>
  </fo:list-block>
</xsl:template>

<xsl:template match="property|property-group">
  <fo:list-item>
    <fo:list-item-label end-indent="label-end()">
      <fo:character character="&#x2020;"/>
    </fo:list-item-label>
    <fo:list-item-body start-indent="body-start()">
      <fo:block>
```

```
        <xsl:apply-templates/>
      </fo:block>
    </fo:list-item-body>
  </fo:list-item>
</xsl:template>
```

Aileron Roll One of two types of rolls in which the wing tips describe an arc around the longitudinal axis of the airplane. An aileron roll may be either a slow roll or a hesitation roll.

Avalanche A full loop with a snap roll integrated at the 180 degree point in the loop.

Cross-Over Spin An upright spin entered from inverted flight or an inverted spin entered from upright flight.

Half Cuban Eight A 5/8th loop followed by a half roll on the 45 degree line.

Hammerhead A vertical up followed by a 180 rotation around the yaw axis at near zero airspeed followed by vertical down and return to horizontal flight.

Hesitation Roll An aileron roll of 90 to 720 degrees of rotation with equal length pauses at every 45, 90, or 180 degrees of rotation.

Humpty Bump A vertical up followed by a half loop followed by vertical down and return to horizontal flight.

Immelmann An inside half loop up with a half roll to upright integrated at the top of the loop.

Loop Flight transitioning through 360 degrees of rotation around the lateral axis, describing a circle in the vertical plane.

Slow Roll An aileron roll with continuous rotation through 90 to 720 degrees of arc. The term, "slow" distinguishes the roll from a snap roll or hesitation roll. The rate of rotation may be very rapid.

Snap Roll A positive or negative accelerated stall in horizontal flight with 180 to 720 degrees of rotation around the longitudinal axis.

Spin A positive or negative stall in horizontal flight transitioning to rotation around the longitudinal and yaw axis in the vertical, recovery in the vertical after 180 to 720 degrees of rotation followed by return to horizontal flight.

Figure 10.6

A glossary rendered as a descriptive list.

These format each property or property-group element as an item in a list. The template that matches the `<properties>` element outputs the list itself. Figure 10.7 demonstrates the formatted result. The revised templates also swapped the `apply-templates` that match `properties` and `description` within the template matching the `fo` element so that the properties appear in a longer, narrower column on the right side.

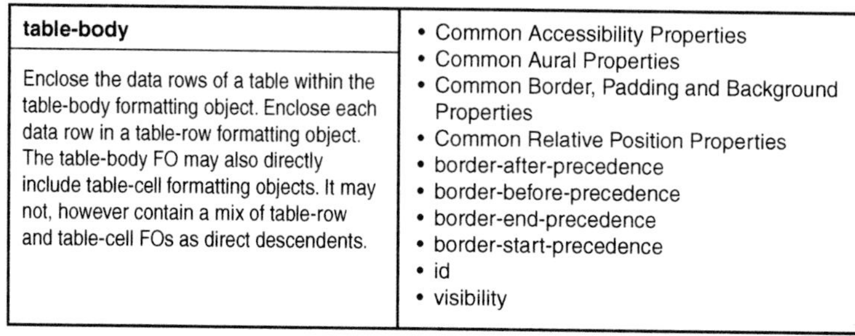

table-body	
Enclose the data rows of a table within the table-body formatting object. Enclose each data row in a table-row formatting object. The table-body FO may also directly include table-cell formatting objects. It may not, however contain a mix of table-row and table-cell FOs as direct descendents.	• Common Accessibility Properties • Common Aural Properties • Common Border, Padding and Background Properties • Common Relative Position Properties • border-after-precedence • border-before-precedence • border-end-precedence • border-start-precedence • id • visibility

Figure 10.7
List formatted within a table-cell.

This new list layout is an improvement over the tabular layout shown in the previous chapter. The main problem with it is that it will look awkward, given a short description and a long list of properties. There will be too much white space in the description box.

The list within a table ends the direct discussion of list FOs. The sections so far in this chapter have shown lists used for generating checklist items, enumerated items in an outline, and a descriptive list or glossary. The last section discusses leaders, which may sometimes, but not always, be used within lists.

Lead Me On

The `leader` FO is an `inline` FO. The typical use for a leader is in a table of contents or list of figures. More generally, you might use it to place horizontal decorations within a line. Place it anywhere within a block along with other inline content. Use it all by itself within a block to create a horizontal rule as a separator. Here is the basic form of the `leader` FO. The following will demonstrate several examples of its use:

```
<fo:leader leader-pattern="rule"/>
```

Table of Contents

One use of the leader .is as a line leading across the page to connect elements justified at the start edge with elements justified at the end edge. The leader format is typical of a table of contents (TOC). This section will show this most conventional use of the leader FO. It will also introduce the `page-number-citation` FO that automatically generates the page number at which cited content appears.

Begin with some contents to format in the TOC. It may be called a table of contents, but we won't use a table to format it. We'll format the contents as stacked blocks using leaders. Following are some entries for a book of poetry:

```
<?xml version="1.0"?>
<poetry>
  <poet>
    <given-name>Wystan Hugh</given-name>
    <surname>Auden</surname>
    <born>1907</born>
    <died>1973</died>
    <poem>
      <title>September 1, 1939</title>
      <stanza/>
    </poem>
  </poet>
  <poet>
    <given-name>William</given-name>
    <surname>Blake</surname>
    <born>1757</born>
    <died>1827</died>
    <poem>
      <title>The Tiger</title>
      <stanza/>
    </poem>
  </poet>
</poetry>
```

The poet elements repeat for each poet represented in the book of poetry. The poem elements repeat for each poem authored by a given poet. The TOC will not list every poem. It will list every poet, giving the page number where the book reproduces poems written by that poet.

Figure 10.8 shows the result table of contents:

Shakespeare, William (1564 - 1616)..5
Donne, John (1573 - 1631)..8
Milton, John (1608 - 1674)..11
Blake, William (1757 - 1827)..23
Burns, Robert (1759 - 1796)..24
Wordsworth, William (1770 - 1850)..25
Coleridge, Samuel Taylor (1772 - 1839)..27
Byron, Lord George Gordon (1788 - 1824)..29
Shelley, Percy Bysshe (1792 - 1822)..29
Keats, John (1795 - 1821)..32
Tennyson, Lord Alfred (1809 - 1892)..37
Browning, Robert (1812 - 1889)..40
Whitman, Walt (1819 - 1892)..41
Dickinson, Emily (1830 - 1886)..44
Yeats, William Butler (1865 - 1939)..49
Frost, Robert (1875 - 1963)..53
Eliot, Thomas Stearns (1888 - 1965)..53
Auden, Wystan Hugh (1907 - 1973)..58

Figure 10.8
A table of contents for a book of poetry.

The content of Listing 10.5 generates the table of contents as shown:

Listing 10.5 *Style Sheet Formats a Table of Contents*

```
<?xml version='1.0'?>
<xsl:stylesheet version="1.0"
 xmlns:xsl="http://www.w3.org/1999/XSL/Transform"
 xmlns:fo="http://www.w3.org/1999/XSL/Format">

  <xsl:strip-space elements="*"/>
  <xsl:include href="rootrule.xsl"/>

  <xsl:template match="poetry">
    <xsl:apply-templates>
      <xsl:sort select="born" data-type="number"/>
    </xsl:apply-templates>
  </xsl:template>

  <xsl:template match="poet">
    <fo:block text-align-last="justify">
      <xsl:value-of select="surname"/>
      <xsl:text>, </xsl:text>
      <xsl:value-of select="given-name"/>
      <xsl:text> (</xsl:text>
```

Listing 10.5 *(continued)*

```
      <xsl:value-of select="born"/>
      <xsl:text> - </xsl:text>
      <xsl:value-of select="died"/>
      <xsl:text>)</xsl:text>
      <fo:leader leader-pattern="dots"
       leader-alignment="reference-area"/>
      <fo:page-number-citation>
        <xsl:attribute name="ref-id">
          <xsl:value-of select="surname"/>
        </xsl:attribute>
      </fo:page-number-citation>
    </fo:block>
  </xsl:template>

</xsl:stylesheet>
```

The `poetry` template outputs the poets sorted by date of birth, the same order that their work appears in the book. The `poet` template outputs a fully justified block containing the name and years of life of the poet followed by the leaders, followed by the reference to the page where the poems begin.

The reason this works. is that the leader length contains stretch and shrink. Recall that lengths are compound types with minimum, optimum, and maximum values. The default for the `leader-length` property is at minimum zero, optimally 12 points at the maximum 100% of the width of the containing block. The setting of `justify` for `text-align-last` ensures that the one and only line of the block stretches from the start edge to the end edge. The formatter applies the stretch to the size of the leader. The leader stretches to connect the name of the poet with the page number.

The `leader-alignment` property specifies that the leader must place its repeated content as if that content began at the start edge of the reference rectangle. In this case, the `region-body` sets the reference rectangle. The effect is to align all the dots vertically. This gives a more pleasing and regular appearance to the leaders in the TOC.

The `page-number-citation` is new. The effect of the `page-number-citation` is to print the number of the page on which some other FO generates its first mark. The `ref-id` property on the `page-number-citation` must match the `id` property of some other FO. XML requires that the `id` property be unique for every element in a document.

The style sheet templates that typeset the pages of the book will output one FO at the beginning of the section for a given poet. The section header FO will have its `id` property set to the surname of the poet. This works because we have no two poets with the same last name. Here is an example demonstrating what the template formatting poems in the pages of the book might look like:

```
<xsl:template match="poet">
  <fo:block
   text-align="center"
   font-weight="bold">
    <xsl:attribute name="id">
      <xsl:value-of select="surname"/>
    </xsl:attribute>
    <xsl:value-of select="surname"/>
    <xsl:text>, </xsl:text>
    <xsl:value-of select="given-name"/>
  </fo:block>
  <xsl:apply-templates/>
</xsl:template>
```

The block that contains .the poet's name as a center-aligned bold header also contains an `id` property equal to the poet's surname. If the formatter typesets this block on page 40, a `page-number-citation` with `ref-id` matching the `id` of this block will typeset the number 40.

Fill in the Blanks

Leaders are also. useful for making blanks in a form. Anywhere that you need some underlined blank space inline with some text, you can use a leader. The output shown in Figure 10.9 demonstrates a form that is familiar to many of us:

DATE ________

PAY TO THE
ORDER OF ______________________________ $ ________

____ DOLLARS

Figure 10.9

Check out this form using the leader FO.

Each of the three lines of the check is different, and each demonstrates a different trick to using leaders. The content of Listing 10.6 generates the form:

Listing 10.6 *Style Sheet Formats a Check Form*

```
<?xml version='1.0'?>
<xsl:stylesheet version="1.0"
 xmlns:xsl="http://www.w3.org/1999/XSL/Transform"
 xmlns:fo="http://www.w3.org/1999/XSL/Format">

  <xsl:strip-space elements="*"/>
  <xsl:include href="rootrule.xsl"/>

  <xsl:template match="check">
    <fo:block line-height="3pc" text-align="end">
      <xsl:text>DATE</xsl:text>
      <fo:leader
       leader-pattern="rule"
       leader-length="1in"/>
    </fo:block>
    <fo:block line-height="3pc" text-align-last="justify">
      <fo:inline-container inline-progression-dimension="6.5pc">
        <fo:block line-height="1.0" text-align-last="start">
          <xsl:text>PAY TO THE ORDER OF</xsl:text>
        </fo:block>
      </fo:inline-container>
      <fo:leader leader-pattern="rule"/>.
      <fo:inline space-start="1pc">
        <xsl:text>$</xsl:text>
        <fo:leader
         leader-pattern="rule"
         leader-length="1in"/>
      </fo:inline>
    </fo:block>
    <fo:block line-height="3pc" text-align-last="justify">
      <fo:leader leader-pattern="rule"/>
      <xsl:text>DOLLARS</xsl:text>
    </fo:block>
  </xsl:template>

</xsl:stylesheet>
```

The template in Listing 10.6 contains three blocks, each of which produces one line. Each has a line height of 3 picas to ensure space for writing in the form. The first block places the text labeling the blank before a leader fixed at a 1-inch length. The `rule` leader pattern draws a 1-inch rule for the blank. The end alignment on the block keeps the whole thing at the end edge, to the right.

The second block is the most sophisticated of the three. It has an `inline-container` to format a block with "PAY TO THE ORDER OF" written within it. The width of the `inline-container` was adjusted by trial and error to produce the line break after the word "TO." A `leader` FO follows the `inline-container` with full default minimum and maximum flexibility from zero to 100% of the width of the block. It fills the center of the page out to the third element on the line.

The third element on the second line is the dollar amount for the check. The `inline` FO places 1 pica of space between the preceding leader and the dollar sign. It includes its own leader of 1-inch width after the dollar sign.

The block surrounding the. three elements of the second line gives justification to the line using the `text-align-last` property. The leader in the center leaves space for writing the payee by taking all the stretch of the line between the fixed width `inline-container` at the start and the fixed width `inline` FO at the end.

The last block, like the second one, uses the `text-align-last` property to stretch the line to the full width of the form. In this case, the leader starts the line and the text ends it.

Here is the simple XML input required to process the example for yourself:

```
<?xml version="1.0"?>
<check/>
```

Horizontal Rules

The example of forms. demonstrated that a leader will draw a horizontal rule. A leader all by itself in a block may serve to separate sections of a document. The rules used to offset listings in this book are an example. Draw them using a construction like this:

```
<fo:block>
  <fo:leader leader-pattern="rule" leader-length="100%"/>
</fo:block>
```

Use the `rule-style` and `rule-thickness` properties to adjust the appearance of the horizontal rule drawn by the leader. The `rule-style` property takes many of the same values as the border style properties. Valid values are `dotted`, `dashed`, `solid`, `double`, groove, or ridge. The default is solid. The rule-thickness .property accepts a length. The default is 1 point. The following creates a thicker, ridged rule the full width of the page:

```
<fo:block>
  <fo:leader leader-pattern="rule" leader-length="100%"
   rule-style="ridge" rule-thickness="2pt"/>
</fo:block>
```

The examples so far have demonstrated use of the leader with the leader-pattern property set to produce dots or set to produce a rule. There are two ways to get a dotted leader, both shown here:

```
<fo:leader leader-pattern="rule" rule-style="dotted"/>

<fo:leader leader-pattern="dots"/>
```

There are two major differences between a leader-pattern set to dots and a leader-pattern set to rule with rule-style set to dotted. The dots leader pattern may work with the leader-alignment property to align the dots vertically with other leaders that use the same pattern. The dotted rule style may adjust the size of the dots using the rule-thickness property.

Leaders are not limited to dashed, solid, or dotted rules or to dots. The FO recommendation allows a leader to create space by the default setting for leader-pattern. It also provides a use-content setting for the leader-pattern property. That setting requires text or inline content within the leader that the formatter will repeat to fill the space of the leader.

Here is a complete style. sheet with an example of a leader that uses an image as content. Process the style sheet with the same simple XML input used for the check example of the previous section. Figure 10.10 shows the result:

```
<?xml version='1.0'?>
<xsl:stylesheet version="1.0"
 xmlns:xsl="http://www.w3.org/1999/XSL/Transform"
 xmlns:fo="http://www.w3.org/1999/XSL/Format">

  <xsl:strip-space elements="*"/>
  <xsl:include href="rootrule.xsl"/>

  <xsl:template match="check">
    <fo:block>
```

```
      <fo:leader leader-pattern="use-content"
       leader-length="100%">
        <fo:external-graphic src="scroll.bmp"/>
      </fo:leader>
    </fo:block>
  </xsl:template>

</xsl:stylesheet>.
```

Figure 10.10

Graphical content repeated within a leader.

Summary

Lists allow horizontal synchronization of two columns of flowed content. An XSL list functions for bullet, enumerated, or descriptive list types. Lists may be nested within lists, and style sheet templates provide numbers for list items.

The leader FO is a highly versatile tool for generating rules or leading lines. You used them in a table of contents as true leaders, to output horizontal rules as blanks in forms, and to place separating marks across the page. Along the way, we visited the `page-number-citation` FO that formats the page number at which some formatted content first appears.

The next chapter introduces keeps, which keep content together, and breaks, which force content into a new column or page. It also introduces columnar layout and controls for preventing widowed or orphaned lines of text from a paragraph.

CHAPTER 11

Keeps, Breaks, and Columns

There seems to be an optimum amount of text that we like to find on a line. Long lines feel like a trip across the Great Plains in a covered wagon. Short ones feel like a fast trip down a ski slope covered with moguls. Many types of publications, such as newspapers, magazines, journals, and brochures, divide the page into multiple vertical columns of text. The columns divide a page into multiple virtual pages of narrower width. You will typically use columns to contain volumes of small type on large pages. The columns keep the length of the lines short enough to read easily.

The keep properties keep content together within a line, column, or page that might otherwise be separated by the end of the line, column, or page. Breaks force separation of content to a new column or page.

A Sample Input Document

The material for the examples in this chapter is excerpted from the Advisory Circular (AC) number 61-65C of the Federal Aviation Administration (FAA). ACs interpret and explain regulatory, procedural, and safety issues relevant to aviation in the United States.

The structure of the input document is as follows:

```
<?xml version="1.0"?>
<advisory-circular>
  <subject>Certification: Pilots and Flight Instructors</subject>
  <date month="2" day="11" year="1991"/>
  <number>61-65C</number>
  <section title="Purpose">
    <!— section text —>
  </section>
  <!— more section elements —>
  <section title="Pilot training and testing">
    <!— section text —>
    <paragraph>
      <e>For example, an applicant for a private pilot certificate</e>
      <!— paragraph text —>
    </paragraph>
  <!— more paragraph elements —>
  </section>
</advisory-circular>
```

The root element is `<advisory-circular>`. It contains identification elements `subject`, `date`, and `number` followed by a series of `section` elements. The `section` elements have `title` attributes that provide a kind of header for the section. They may contain `paragraph` elements following some introductory text. The `paragraph` elements use an `<e>` element to emphasize the phrase that introduces the subject of the paragraph.

The references in the text to other ACs, FAA forms, and regulatory paragraphs normally contain pointers to those documents for a number of purposes. The pointers enable style sheets to insert links to the referenced material. They also enable processing software to locate affected documents when changes occur. This example omits that level of detail.

Columns

Columns are simple to arrange in XSL. You tell the formatter how many columns you want and how much space you would like between them. The formatter takes care of the rest.

It may be easy to get them, but there are a few limitations to the use of columns. One limitation is that XSL will give you columns only in the body region of the page. There is no way to switch within the body region from the full width of the page to columns. Another limitation is that there is no way to specify columns of unequal widths. These limitations are real, but they don't prevent XSL from satisfying most practical applications of column-formatted material.

To begin, Listing 11.1 provides the root rule for a style sheet that typesets an AC. It contains the layout declarations for the document, which demonstrate a number of features discussed in the following paragraphs:

Listing 11.1 *circular-root.xsl: Layout Declaration for the AC Style Sheet*

```
<?xml version='1.0'?>
<xsl:stylesheet version="1.0"
 xmlns:xsl="http://www.w3.org/1999/XSL/Transform"
 xmlns:fo="http://www.w3.org/1999/XSL/Format">

<?xml version='1.0'?>
<xsl:stylesheet version="1.0"
 xmlns:xsl="http://www.w3.org/1999/XSL/Transform"
 xmlns:fo="http://www.w3.org/1999/XSL/Format">

  <xsl:template match="/">
    <fo:root>
      <fo:layout-master-set>
        <fo:simple-page-master master-name="title-page"
         xsl:use-attribute-sets="page-size page-geometry">
          <fo:region-body region-name="body"
           margin-top="2.5in" margin-bottom="0.5in"
           column-count="2" column-gap="3pc"/>
          <fo:region-before region-name="title"
           extent="3in"/>
        </fo:simple-page-master>
        <fo:simple-page-master master-name="body-page"
         xsl:use-attribute-sets="page-size page-geometry">
          <fo:region-body region-name="body"
           margin-top="0.5in" margin-bottom="0.5in" j
           column-count="2" column-gap="3pc"/>
          <fo:region-before region-name="header"
           extent="0.5in"/>
          <fo:region-after region-name="footer"
           extent="0.5in"/>
        </fo:simple-page-master>
        <fo:page-sequence-master master-name="circular">
          <fo:single-page-master-reference
           master-reference="title-page"/>
          <fo:repeatable-page-master-reference
           master-reference="body-page"/>
        </fo:page-sequence-master>
```

Listing 11.1 *(continued)*

```
      </fo:layout-master-set>
      <xsl:apply-templates/>
    </fo:root>
  </xsl:template>

</xsl:stylesheet>
```

The `layout-master-set` for the circular contains two page masters and a `page-sequence-master`. The page masters define a title page and a page layout for the remainder of the AC. The layout master for a document like this might normally include odd and even page layouts. Chapter 9, "Tables and Alignments," contains an example of odd and even alternating layouts.

The page size and page geometry come from the style file, `circular-xsl`, shown later in Listing 11.3. More importantly for the present, look at the `region-body` declarations in the two page masters of Listing 11.1. There is where you'll find the column settings. The `column-count` property sets the number of columns for the region. The default value is 1. This definition uses the value 2.

The `column-gap` property gives the amount of space between the columns. The value of 3 picas is ample. Some layouts use less, but these pages have a nice, open look with space between paragraphs and a wide column gap. That openness makes it easier to scan the content for needed information.

Listing 11.2 shows the template that starts composition with the `page-sequence`, `static-content`, and `flow` definitions. There are three definitions for `static-content`—one for the title and one each for the headers and footers on subsequent pages:

Listing 11.2 *circular-page.xsl:* static-content *and* flow *Definitions*

```
<?xml version='1.0'?>
<xsl:stylesheet version="1.0"
 xmlns:xsl="http://www.w3.org/1999/XSL/Transform"
 xmlns:fo="http://www.w3.org/1999/XSL/Format">

  <xsl:template match="advisory-circular">
    <fo:page-sequence master-reference="circular">
      <fo:static-content flow-name="title">
        <xsl:call-template name="format-title"/>
      </fo:static-content>
      <fo:static-content flow-name="header">
        <fo:block text-align-last="justify" font-weight="bold">
          <xsl:call-template name="format-date"/>
```

Listing 11.2 *(continued)*

```
          <fo:leader/>
          <xsl:text>AC </xsl:text>
          <xsl:value-of select="number"/>
        </fo:block>
        <fo:block>
          <fo:leader leader-length="100%" leader-pattern="rule"/>
        </fo:block>
      </fo:static-content>
      <fo:static-content flow-name="footer">
        <fo:block>
          <fo:leader leader-length="100%" leader-pattern="rule"/>
        </fo:block>
        <fo:block text-align="end" font-weight="bold">
          <fo:page-number/>
        </fo:block>
      </fo:static-content>
      <fo:flow flow-name="body">
        <xsl:apply-templates select="section"/>
      </fo:flow>
    </fo:page-sequence>
  </xsl:template>

</xsl:stylesheet>
```

The use of the `region-before` on the title page to format the full-page width title information overcomes the limitation of XSL with regard to changing from full width to column layouts on the same page. The `region-before` acts as a masthead for the document, much like the masthead on newspaper.

The first block within the `static-content` definition that selects the header contains the AC date and number separated by a `leader` FO. The default `leader-pattern` is space, so the leader serves to fill space between the start of the line and the end of the line. The next block contains a leader as well. That leader has the full width of the page and uses the `rule` pattern. It draws a horizontal rule at the bottom of the header to separate the header from the two-column content below.

The footer likewise begins with a horizontal rule. It uses end alignment to place the page number at the end edge of the page.

Listing 11.3 shows the attribute-set definitions for this style sheet. The first two attribute sets define the page size and page geometry. This is an 8.5 by 11-inch page with half-inch margins. The left margin has an extra quarter-inch space to leave room for binding:

Listing 11.3 *circular-style.xsl: Attribute Set Definitions*

```
<?xml version='1.0'?>
<xsl:stylesheet version="1.0"
 xmlns:xsl="http://www.w3.org/1999/XSL/Transform">

  <xsl:attribute-set name="page-size">
    <xsl:attribute name="page-width">8.5in</xsl:attribute>
    <xsl:attribute name="page-height">11in</xsl:attribute>
  </xsl:attribute-set>

  <xsl:attribute-set name="page-geometry">
    <xsl:attribute name="margin-top">0.5in</xsl:attribute>
    <xsl:attribute name="margin-bottom">0.5in</xsl:attribute>
    <xsl:attribute name="margin-left">0.75in</xsl:attribute>
    <xsl:attribute name="margin-right">0.5in</xsl:attribute>
  </xsl:attribute-set>

  <xsl:attribute-set name="title">
    <xsl:attribute name="font-variant">small-caps</xsl:attribute>
    <xsl:attribute name="font-weight">bold</xsl:attribute>
  </xsl:attribute-set>

  <xsl:attribute-set name="body-block">
    <xsl:attribute name="space-before">1pc</xsl:attribute>
    <xsl:attribute name="text-align">justify</xsl:attribute>
  </xsl:attribute-set>

  <xsl:attribute-set name="par-leader">
    <xsl:attribute name="font-weight">bold</xsl:attribute>
    <xsl:attribute name="font-style">italic</xsl:attribute>
  </xsl:attribute-set>

</xsl:stylesheet>
```

The remainder of the style sheet shown in Listing 11.4 contains the template used to format the title information of the AC in the `region-before` of the title page. It also contains the remaining templates that format `section` and `paragraph` elements of the document. This is the main file for the style sheet, the one you give to the formatter, because it includes the other files already shown. The other files must be present in the same directory:

Listing 11.4 *circular.xsl: The Main Style Sheet for the AC*

```
<?xml version='1.0'?>
<xsl:stylesheet version="1.0"
 xmlns:xsl="http://www.w3.org/1999/XSL/Transform"
 xmlns:fo="http://www.w3.org/1999/XSL/Format">

  <xsl:strip-space elements="*"/>
  <xsl:include href="circular-style.xsl"/>
  <xsl:include href="circular-root.xsl"/>
  <xsl:include href="circular-page.xsl"/>

  <xsl:template name="format-title">
    <fo:block>
      U.S. Department of Transportation
    </fo:block>
    <fo:block font-weight="bold">
      Federal Aviation Administration
    </fo:block>
    <fo:block font-size="3pc" font-weight="bold"
     space-after="1pc">
     Advisory Circular
    </fo:block>
    <fo:block space-before="1pc" space-after="1pc">
      <fo:leader leader-length="100%" leader-pattern="rule"
       rule-thickness="6pt"/>
    </fo:block>
    <fo:block>
      <xsl:text>Subject: </xsl:text>
      <fo:wrapper xsl:use-attribute-sets="title">
        <xsl:value-of select="subject"/>
      </fo:wrapper>
    </fo:block>
    <fo:block>
      <xsl:text>Date: </xsl:text>
      <fo:wrapper xsl:use-attribute-sets="title">
        <xsl:call-template name="format-date"/>
      </fo:wrapper>
      <fo:leader/>
      <xsl:text>AC No: </xsl:text>
      <fo:wrapper xsl:use-attribute-sets="title">
        <xsl:value-of select="number"/>
      </fo:wrapper>
    </fo:block>
```

Listing 11.4 *(continued)*

```
  </xsl:template>

  <xsl:template name="format-date">
    <xsl:value-of select="date/@month"/>
    <xsl:text>/</xsl:text>
    <xsl:value-of select="date/@day"/>
    <xsl:text>/</xsl:text>
    <xsl:value-of select="date/@year"/>
  </xsl:template>

  <xsl:template match="section" >
    <fo:block xsl:use-attribute-sets="body-block">
      <fo:inline xsl:use-attribute-sets="title">
        <xsl:number format="1. "/>
        <xsl:value-of select="@title"/>
        <xsl:text>.</xsl:text>
      </fo:inline>
      <xsl:apply-templates/>
    </fo:block>
  </xsl:template>

  <xsl:template match="paragraph">
    <fo:block xsl:use-attribute-sets="body-block">
      <fo:inline xsl:use-attribute-sets="par-leader">
        <xsl:number format="a. "/>
      </fo:inline>
      <xsl:apply-templates/>
    </fo:block>
  </xsl:template>

  <xsl:template match="e">
    <fo:inline xsl:use-attribute-sets="par-leader">
      <xsl:apply-templates/>
    </fo:inline>
  </xsl:template>

</xsl:stylesheet>
```

Not a great deal is new in the formatting of the title. It uses the `rule-thickness` attribute to get a very bold horizontal rule. To open it up and set it apart, it uses `space-before` and `space-after` for the block containing the rule. The last block in the title uses a `leader` FO to put just a little space, the 12 pt. default, between the date and the AC number.

The templates that match the `section` and `paragraph` elements both format a number for use in referencing parts of the circular. The `body-block` attribute set puts a pica of space before each section and paragraph to give the open appearance discussed earlier. Figure 11.1 shows the first page of output:

U.S. Department of Transportation
Federal Aviation Administration

Advisory Circular

Subject: **CERTIFICATION: PILOTS AND FLIGHT INSTRUCTORS**
Date: **2/11/1991** AC No: **61-65C**

1. PURPOSE. This advisory circular (AC) provides guidance for pilots and flight instructors on the certification standards, written test procedures, and other requirements contained in Federal Aviation Regulations (FAR) Part 61.

2. CANCELLATION. AC 61-65B, Certification: Pilots and Flight Instructors, dated August 6, 1984, is cancelled.

3. RELATED READING MATERIAL. AC 61-98A, Currency and Additional Qualification Requirements for Certificated Pilots; AC 61-107, Operation of Aircraft at Altitudes Above 25,000 Feet MSL and/or Mach Numbers (Mmo) Greater Than .75; and AC 61-101, Presolo Written Test

4. PILOT TRAINING AND TESTING. FAR Part 61 contains pilot training and testing procedures, flight instructor responsibilities, and requirements, priveleges, and limitatiions for each grade of certificate. Under the total operational concept of FAR Part 61, the pilot operations specified for each grade of certificate by FAR Part 61 encompass the areas of operation and tasks contained in the practical test standards (PTS). Instructors are responsible for training students to the level of competence prescribed by the PTS for each pilot operation required by FAR Part 61. The test for a pilot certificate will consist of an evaluation of the applicant's ability to demonstrate the knowledge required by the tasks in the appropriate PTS and to safely and skillfully complete each of the required tasks.

a. For example, an applicant for a private pilot certificate must have logged the flight time required by FAR Part 61 and have had his/her logbook endorsed by the certificated flight instructor (CFI) who found the pilot competent to perform each of the pilot operations listed in FAR 61.107(a)(1) through (10).

b. The flight maneuvers associated with each of the pilot operations listed in FAR 61.107 are found under similar titles in FAA-S-8081-1A, Private Pilot Practical Test Standards. The standards for successful completion of each maneuver and procedure are noted in the objective for each task in the PTS. Each of the maneuvers and procedures listed in Section 1 (Airplane) of FAA-S-8081-1A is discussed and explained in AC 61-21A, Flight Training Handbook.

5. WRITTEN TESTS. The written tests for the pilot and flight instructor certificates and ratings cover the subject areas in which aeronautical knowledge and ground instruction or home study are required by FAR Part 61.

a. Written tests are administered only to applicants who show evidence of satisfactory completion of the ground instruction or home study required by FAR Part 61 for the certificate or rating sought.

b. Applicants for ATP written tests must present an FAA Form 8060-7 Airman's Authorization for Written Test. The form can be obtained by presenting a current first-class medical and pilot logbooks or other acceptable records which document the aeronautical experience required by FAR 61.155 or 61.161, as appropriate, to a Federal Aviation Administration (FAA) inspector.

6. PRACTICAL TESTS. A practical test consisting of both oral and flight testing is conducted to evaluate the applicant's skill and knowledge. During a practial test the examiner will quiz the applicant orally on knowledge elements and ask the applicant to perform the skill elements of the test; however, oral testing may be used at any time during the test. The examiner is responsible for determining that the applicant meets the standards outlined in the objectives of each required task in the appropriate PTS.

Figure 11.1

The first page of the Advisory Circular shows two columns.

Retrieving the Marker

You can try a couple of other innovations with the AC style sheet before moving on to keeps and breaks. The first is an addition to the footer that illustrates the XSL `marker` and `retrieve-marker` FOs.

Suppose you showed the output to the administrator and she suggested that the footer contain the numbers of the sections that start and end each page. This is similar to what is done in dictionaries, which print in the header the first and last words defined on each page.

Like Scotty on *Star Trek* you say, "Well, I don't know—that might take some innovative work; I'll see what I can do." Fortunately, XSL makes it easy to deliver.

Begin by modifying the template that outputs a section (see Listing 11.4). The modified template looks like this:

```
<xsl:template match="section" >
  <fo:block xsl:use-attribute-sets="body-block">
    <fo:inline xsl:use-attribute-sets="title">
      <fo:marker marker-class-name="par">
        <xsl:number format="1"/>
      </fo:marker>
      <xsl:number format="1. "/>
      <xsl:value-of select="@title"/>
      <xsl:text>.</xsl:text>
    </fo:inline>
    <xsl:apply-templates/>
  </fo:block>
</xsl:template>
```

This new version adds a `marker` FO containing the section number. The `marker-class-name` property on the marker is the identifier, or name, for the marker. It is not unique, but it is shared by every marker that contains a section number.

The `retrieve-marker` FO references the marker class name to copy the content of the marker. The marker itself does not produce any output until it is retrieved; therefore, you have to repeat the number to get it into the body of the document. That is not a problem, because the number format differs in the body and in the footer.

Modify the `static-content` output by the style sheet for the footer as follows. This replaces code in the file circular-page.xsl, shown earlier as Listing 11.2:

```
<fo:static-content flow-name="footer">
  <fo:block>
    <fo:leader leader-length="100%" leader-pattern="rule"/>
  </fo:block>
```

```
    <fo:block text-align-last="justify" font-weight="bold">
      <xsl:text>Par </xsl:text>
      <fo:retrieve-marker retrieve-class-name="par"
       retrieve-position="first-including-carryover"/>
      <xsl:text> - </xsl:text>
      <fo:retrieve-marker  retrieve-class-name="par"
       retrieve-position="last-starting-within-page"/>
      <fo:leader/>
      <fo:page-number/>
    </fo:block>
  </fo:static-content>
```

This new version of the footer justifies the line and adds a leader to separate the paragraph numbers from the page number. Most remarkably, it uses the `retrieve-marker` FO to copy paragraph numbers from the page into the footer. The `retrieve-class-name` property on the `retrieve-marker` FO matches the `marker-class-name` on the marker. The `retrieve-position` property determines which marker to copy.

The position of the copied marker may be any one of four values. The value `first-including-carryover` copies the last marker that occurred before the beginning of the current page. The `last-starting-within-page` copies the last marker on the page. The value `first-starting-within-page` copies the first marker on the page. There may be some carried-over content before it. The value `last-ending-within-page` copies the last marker that comes before content that did not carry over onto a subsequent page.

One other property for the `retrieve-marker` FO is not used in this example. The `retrieve-boundary` property limits the search for markers to the current page, page sequence, or entire document. The default is to look for the marker only within the page sequence. You will seldom want to change the default.

Flex Space

When there are two columns on a page, an issue arises about balance. Balanced columns have their before and after edges aligned to give an even, visual line across the page. The formatter will have an easier time balancing columns and give a better looking result if you give it some flexibility. The best place for this flexibility is in the space between paragraphs. The following modification to the `body-block` attribute set in circular-style.xsl (shown as Listing 11.3) allows for as much as two picas of space between paragraphs:

```
<xsl:attribute-set name="body-block">
  <xsl:attribute name="space-before.optimum">1pc</xsl:attribute>
  <xsl:attribute name="space-before.maximum">2pc</xsl:attribute>
  <xsl:attribute name="text-align">justify</xsl:attribute>
</xsl:attribute-set>
```

It's now time to look at a subsequent page after the title page. Note the retrieved markers in the footer and the nicely balanced columns. Figure 11.2 shows page two of the output. You can also run it through a formatter yourself to try it. This output was produced by the Antenna House formatter:

2/11/1991 **AC 61-65C**

7. PREREQUISITES FOR PRACTICAL TESTS. Except for foriegn pilots; applicants for a type rating only, or a class rating with an associated type rating; or ATP applicants, each applicant must present a written statement from an appropriately certificated flight instructor certifying that the applicant has been given flight instruction in preparation for the practical test within 60 days preceding the date of application and found competent to pass the test. The written statement must also state that the applicant has satisfactory knowledge of the subject areas in which he/she was known to be deficient by the FAA airman written test report. Following the first failure of a practical test, an applicant who wishes to apply for retesting before 30 days have expired must present a written statement from an appropriately certificated and rated FAA flight instructor stating that the applicant has been given additional instruction and is competent to pass the practical test.

a. A flight instructor who completes a written statement attesting to the reqired flight instruction for a test applicant may also indicate on that statement that a review of the areas of deficientcy indicated on the written test report has been satisfactorily completed.

8. STUDENT PILOT CERTIFICATION. Specific knowledge, flight proficiency, flight experience, and endorsement requirements for the student pilot certificate are located in part 61, subpart C. See Appendix 1, endorsements 1 through 10. A student pilot certificate can be issued by a designated aviation medical examiner as part of a medical certificate. However, an aviation safety inspector (ASI) and designated pilot examiner (DPE) can also issue student pilot certificates. Whenever a student pilot certificate is issued by an ASI or DPE, the applicant must hold a current medical certificate for performing solo privileges in an airplane, rotorcraft, powered-lift, or airship. Glider pilots and balloon pilots are not required to hold a medical certificate. Additional information on the eligibility requirements for student pilots can be found in FAR ß 61.83 and the general limitations for student pilots can be found in FAR ß 61.89.

9. PRESOLO REQUIREMENTS. NOTE: Several questions have been asked about FAR ß 61.87(l)(1) to clarify that the solo endorsement on the student pilot certificate is a one-time endorsement. However, the 90-day solo endorsement that goes in the student pilot's logbook is required every 90 days for the student to be afforded continuing solo privileges [per FAR ß 61.87(l)(2)]. NOTE: Several questions have been asked for clarification on the status of solo endorsements when a person's student pilot certificate has expired. Although FAR ß 61.19(b) establishes, in pertinent part, that a student pilot certificate expires 24 calendar months from the month it was issued, the endorsements on that student pilot certificate are a matter of record forever. Granted these endorsements are required to be updated from time-to-time in the student pilot's logbook to retain solo privileges, but the endorsements on the student pilot certificate are a matter of record indefinitely. The following presolo requirements must be met:

a. Before being authorized to conduct a solo flight, a student pilot must have received and logged the flight training required by FAR ß 61.87(c) and (d) through (k), as appropriate. Satisfactory aeronautical knowledge and an acceptable performance level must have been demonstrated to an authorized instructor [per FAR ß 61.87(b)]. Advisory Circular 61-101 provides information on the required content of the presolo aeronautical knowledge test. See Appendix 1, endorsement 1.

b. Prior to solo flight, a student pilot is required to have his/her student pilot certificate and logbook endorsed for the specific make and model aircraft to be flown. Thereafter, the student pilot's logbook must be endorsed every 90 days to retain solo flight privileges. These endorsements must be given by an authorized flight instructor who has flown with the student [per FAR ß 61.87(l)]. See Appendix 1, endorsements 2 and 4.

10. ADDITIONAL SOLO PRIVILEGES. NOTE: For the purpose of ensuring clarification, it has been noted that the student pilot certificate only provides for listing the aircraft's category for the solo cross-country privileges endorsement. Per FAR ß 61.93(c)(1), the solo cross-country endorsement on the student pilot certificate must be . . . for the specific category of aircraft to be flown. However, per ß 61.93(c)(2)(i), the solo cross-country endorsement in the student pilot's logbook must be . . . for the specific make and model of aircraft to be flown. The following additional student solo privileges may be authorized:

a. A student pilot may operate an aircraft in solo flight at night provided that student has received the required flight training at night and the appropriate endorsements as required by FAR ß 61.87(m). See Appendix 1, endorsement 3.

Par 7 - 10 **2**

Figure 11.2

The second page of the AC.

When you run this yourself through a formatter, the pagination may differ slightly. The change in pagination may occur because of different default font selections in your formatter. The style settings of circular-style.xsl (shown in Listing 11.2) did not make any explicit font settings.

The disclaimer regarding the output is that it is not an official nor necessarily accurate reproduction. In addition, AC 61-65C is now obsolete, replaced by AC 61-65D. The official document is available from the Federal Aviation Administration: `http://www.faa.gov/RegulatoryAdvisory/ac_index.htm`.

Play for Keeps or Break It Up

Suppose that the title portions of the AC sections were typeset as separate blocks rather than in line with the content of the section. It would look very strange if one of these titles ended up at the bottom of a column, with the text that follows at the top of the next column. The trouble is that sooner or later that would happen. The keep properties are designed to prevent it.

There are three types of keeps. Each type constrains the action of the formatter in a specific way. The `keep-together` encourages all the content within the element on which it appears to remain within the same line, column, or page. The `keep-with-next` encourages the formatter to keep at least some of the content generated by an FO together with the content that follows. The `keep-with-previous` encourages the formatter to avoid starting a line, column, or page with the content where it appears.

Usually the formatter is able to satisfy the constraints imposed by keeps. If it cannot, it will break the constraint and format your content as well as it can. That is not a common occurrence, but it can happen. Following is an example of a keep constraint from the AC style sheet. It replaces the template that matches sections found in circular.xsl, Listing 11.4:

```
<xsl:template match="section">
  <fo:block xsl:use-attribute-sets="body-block">
    <fo:block xsl:use-attribute-sets="title"
     keep-with-next.within-column="always">
      <fo:marker marker-class-name="par">
        <xsl:number format="1. "/>
      </fo:marker>
      <xsl:value-of select="@title"/>
      <xsl:text>.</xsl:text>
    </fo:block>
    <fo:block>
      <xsl:apply-templates/>
    </fo:block>
  </fo:block>
</xsl:template>
```

This new template uses a block for the header in place of an inline and imposes a keep constraint on the block. The bolded line shows the keep constraint. Figure 11.3 shows the first page of the resulting output. Note that no title block ends up separated from its text:

U.S. Department of Transportation
Federal Aviation Administration

Advisory Circular

Subject: **Certification: Pilots and Flight Instructors**
Date: **2/11/1991** AC No: **61-65C**

1. Purpose.
This advisory circular (AC) provides guidance for pilots and flight instructors on the certification standards, written test procedures, and other requirements contained in Federal Aviation Regulations (FAR) Part 61.

2. Cancellation.
AC 61-65B, Certification: Pilots and Flight Instructors, dated August 6, 1984, is cancelled.

3. Related reading material.
AC 61-98A, Currency and Additional Qualification Requirements for Certificated Pilots; AC 61-107, Operation of Aircraft at Altitudes Above 25,000 Feet MSL and/or Mach Numbers (Mmo) Greater Than .75; and AC 61-101, Presolo Written Test

4. Pilot training and testing.
FAR Part 61 contains pilot training and testing procedures, flight instructor responsibilities, and requirements, priveleges, and limitatiions for each grade of certificate. Under the total operational concept of FAR Part 61, the pilot operations specified for each grade of certificate by FAR Part 61 encompass the areas of operation and tasks contained in the practical test standards (PTS). Instructors are responsible for training students to the level of competence prescribed by the PTS for each pilot operation required by FAR Part 61. The test for a pilot certificate will consist of an evaluation of the applicant's ability to demonstrate the knowledge required by the tasks in the appropriate PTS and to safely and skillfully complete each of the required tasks.

a. For example, an applicant for a private pilot certificate must have logged the flight time required by FAR Part 61 and have had his/her logbook endorsed by the certificated flight instructor (CFI) who found the pilot competent to perform each of the pilot operations listed in FAR 61.107(a)(1) through (10).

b. The flight maneuvers associated with each of the pilot operations listed in FAR 61.107 are found under similar titles in FAA-S-8081-1A, Private Pilot Practical Test Standards. The standards for successful completion of each maneuver and procedure are noted in the objective for each task in the PTS. Each of the maneuvers and procedures listed in Section 1 (Airplane) of FAA-S-8081-1A is discussed and explained in AC 61-21A, Flight Training Handbook.

5. Written tests.
The written tests for the pilot and flight instructor certificates and ratings cover the subject areas in which aeronautical knowledge and ground instruction or home study are required by FAR Part 61.

a. Written tests are administered only to applicants who show evidence of satisfactory completion of the ground instruction or home study required by FAR Part 61 for the certificate or rating sought.

b. Applicants for ATP written tests must present an FAA Form 8060-7 Airman's Authorization for Written Test. The form can be obtained by presenting a current first-class medical and pilot logbooks or other acceptable records which document the aeronautical experience required by FAR 61.155 or 61.161, as appropriate, to a Federal Aviation Administration (FAA) inspector.

6. Practical Tests.
A practical test consisting of both oral and flight testing is conducted to evaluate the applicant's skill and knowledge. During a practial test the examiner will quiz the applicant orally on knowledge elements and ask the applicant to perform the skill elements of the test; however, oral testing may be used at any time during the test. The examiner is responsible for determining that the applicant meets the standards outlined in the objectives of each required task in the appropriate PTS.

Figure 11.3

Section titles that keep together with their section text.

Breakin' Up Ain't Hard to Do

Neil Sedaka and Howard Greenfield wrote that breaking up is hard to do. With FO that just isn't true. There are times when you definitely want content to start or end a column or page. Those are the times to use a break. XSL makes it easy to break up content. It doesn't give you 50 ways, like Paul Simon does, but it gives you 2. That is all you need.

The `break-before` constraint encourages the formatter to start a new column or page with the content on which it appears. The `break-after` constraint encourages the formatter to end a column or page after the content on which it appears. This is simple, but just as in life, care should be taken with breaks. Things can get ugly.

A `break-before` for the page may cause the formatter to leave a small amount of content on the page before the break. That leaves a page with just a few lines of text. This may be acceptable—it sometimes happens at the end of book chapters, but it may not always be what you want. Use breaks sparingly; keeps are far more useful.

For illustration, the following creates a column break before every fourth section. This is the template that formats the sections again. If you're typing along with the chapter, you've already modified it twice, so this reproduces only the initial lines that have the added break constraint. Find this template in circular.xsl, Listing 11.4:

```
<xsl:template match="section">
  <fo:block xsl:use-attribute-sets="body-block">
    <xsl:if test="position() mod 4=0">
      <xsl:attribute name="break-before">column</xsl:attribute>
    </xsl:if>
    <fo:block xsl:use-attribute-sets="title"
     keep-with-next.within-column="always">
    <!— etc. —>
</xsl:template>
```

The `break-after` and `break-before` properties can take a value of `odd-page` or `even-page`. The setting `break-before="even-page"` causes the formatter to start the content on an even-numbered page. If the content would already appear somewhere within an even page, but not at the start, the formatter must generate a blank odd-numbered page and then start the content on the fresh, even-numbered page.

Summary

This chapter provided a style sheet for formatting a document that uses columns, keep conditions, and finally, breaks. The two-column layout is easier to scan than a layout in which the text goes all the way across the page.

Remember that keeps are much more useful than breaks. Keeps help by marrying a block that contains a section title, for example, with the first paragraph of the section text. They prevent the formatter from separating content that logically belongs together. Breaks may force the formatter to produce a page or column that contains very little content. They're most useful to ensure that a new major division, such as the chapter of a book, starts on a new page.

The next chapter will help you spiff up your documents with some graphics. Keep up the good work.

CHAPTER 12

Embedding Diagrams and Images

A picture is worth a thousand words. Charts, graphs, or a photo of Aunt Sally all belong in your documents at one time or another. FO provides two elements for getting your diagrams and images into print. Both are inline elements. They are `external-graphic` and `instream-foreign-object`.

FO also provides a property for block and inline elements that places an image in the background, behind any text, rules, and other content of the element. That image may be tiled in the background for wallpaper effects. This chapter will explore those background effects as well.

Embedding an External Resource

The `external-graphic` FO is an inline FO that must have no content. It is always empty. Use the `src` property to name the graphic. The value of the `src` property is a URI specification. It may refer to a file in the local file system or to a resource on the network. Here is a URI specification that refers to a resource on the network `url(http://www.w3.org/Icons/w3c_home)`. You can point your browser there and it will display a W3C logo.

The full syntax of URI specifications is quite involved. It is the subject of a 40-page document published by the Internet

Engineering Task Force as *RFC 2396. Uniform Resource Identifiers (URI): Generic Syntax*. The URI for that document is `http://www.ietf.org/rfc/rfc2396.txt`. A URI for a resource on the Web has form, `http://<server>/<path and file name>`. In the examples here, the `<server>` portions are `www.w3.org` and `www.ietf.org`. The `<path and file name>` portions are `Icons/w3c_home` and `rfc/rfc2396.txt`.

Just as often, you will want to specify a local file system URI as the source of your graphic. The format for a file on the local file system is `file:///`*`<path and file name>`*. One example is `file:///c:/xslTypesetting/chapter12/SkyTrailDawn.jpg`. A file may be in the same directory, or in a directory relative to the location of the XML source document. In that case, a relative URI is appropriate. An example of a relative file URI is `file://SkyTrailDawn.jpg`.

The XSL recommendation is quiet about what graphical formats are valid as the source of an `external-graphic`. It's safe to expect that many implementers will support JPEG. Some may support GIF. FOP will read an SVG (Scalable Vector Graphics) document. Other formats, such as TIFF or BMP, might be more rarely supported.

Here is a source XML example calling for an image:

```
<?xml version="1.0"?>
<test>
  <p>Image
  <img href="SkyTrailDawn.jpg"/>
  made by the author at Pt. Reyes National Seashore on August 2, 1998.</p>
</test>
```

Listing 12.1 reproduces a style sheet to display the source. The listing includes `rootrule.xsl`, developed in Chapter 4, "Hello XSL World." It also requires a style file named `docstyle.xsl`. Begin with empty attribute sets in that file as follows:

```
<?xml version='1.0'?>
<xsl:stylesheet version="1.0"
 xmlns:xsl="http://www.w3.org/1999/XSL/Transform"
 xmlns:fo="http://www.w3.org/1999/XSL/Format">

<xsl:attribute-set name="body"/>
<xsl:attribute-set name="graphic"/>
<xsl:attribute-set name="box"/>

</xsl:stylesheet>
```

Listing 12.1 *Style Sheet Displays an Image*

```
<?xml version='1.0'?>
<xsl:stylesheet version="1.0"
 xmlns:xsl="http://www.w3.org/1999/XSL/Transform"
 xmlns:fo="http://www.w3.org/1999/XSL/Format">

  <xsl:include href="rootrule.xsl"/>
  <xsl:include href="docstyle.xsl"/>

  <xsl:template match="p">
    <fo:block xsl:use-attribute-sets="body">
      <xsl:apply-templates/>
    </fo:block>
  </xsl:template>

  <xsl:template match="img">
    <fo:external-graphic xsl:use-attribute-sets="graphic">
      <xsl:attribute name="src">
        <xsl:text>url("</xsl:text>
        <xsl:value-of select="@href"/>
        <xsl:text>")</xsl:text>
      </xsl:attribute>
    </fo:external-graphic>
  </xsl:template>

</xsl:stylesheet>
```

The typeset result appears as Figure 12.1. Note that the image appears in line with the text. The `external-graphic` FO is an inline-level FO. Unless you place it within a block, it will flow in the inline progression direction with other inline content, such as text. Note also that the baseline of the image aligns with the baseline of the text. You'll learn how to change the alignment in the "Placement and Alignment" section. For now, enjoy the result.

Image  made by the author at Pt. Reyes National Seashore on August 2, 1998.

Figure 12.1

Typeset result shows the image in line with the text.

Embedding a Diagram

Some document producers may want to include graphical content in line within the source content, rather than as a separate resource. You may want to place some SVG markup in the document. You might also produce a technical document with mathematics, and include mathematical formulas in the markup.

Listing 12.2 contains sample source markup that includes markup in Mathematical Markup Language (MathML). That someone would like to produce mathematics material for online publication as well as publication in a textbook is not at all far-fetched. The example pretends to introduce a section about famous functions—and we don't mean the Academy Awards!

Listing 12.2 *Mixed markup document that uses MathML*

```
<?xml version="1.0"?>
<!DOCTYPE text [
 <!ENTITY hbar '&#x210F;'>
 <!ENTITY it '&#x2062;'>
 <!ENTITY part '&#x2202;'>
 <!ENTITY Psi '&#x03A8;'>
]>
<text>
  <p>Everyone's heard about Einstein's equation
  relating mass, energy, and the speed of light,
  <math xmlns="http://www.w3.org/1998/Math/MathML">
    <mi>E</mi>
```

Listing 12.2 *(continued)*

```
    <mo>=</mo>
    <mi>m</mi>
    <msup>
      <mi>c</mi>
      <mn>2</mn>
    </msup>
  </math>, but
  how many of us have heard of Shr&#xF6;dinger's equation,
  <math xmlns="http://www.w3.org/1998/Math/MathML">
    <mrow>
      <mo>-</mo>
      <mfrac>
        <msup> <mi>h</mi> <mn>2</mn> </msup>
        <mrow> <mn>2</mn> <mo>&it;</mo> <mi>m</mi> </mrow>
      </mfrac>
      <mfenced>
        <mrow>
          <mfrac>
            <mrow>
              <msup> <mi> &part; </mi> <mn> 2 </mn> </msup>
              <mi> &Psi; </mi>
            </mrow>
            <mrow>
              <mi> &part; </mi>
              <msup> <mi> x </mi> <mn> 2 </mn> </msup>
            </mrow>
          </mfrac>
          <mo>+</mo>
          <mfrac>
            <mrow>
              <msup> <mi> &part; </mi> <mn> 2 </mn> </msup>
              <mi> &Psi; </mi>
            </mrow>
            <mrow>
              <mi> &part; </mi>
              <msup> <mi> y </mi> <mn> 2 </mn> </msup>
            </mrow>
          </mfrac>
          <mo>+</mo>
          <mfrac>
            <mrow>
              <msup> <mi> &part; </mi> <mn> 2 </mn> </msup>
```

Listing 12.2 *(continued)*

```
            <mi> &Psi; </mi>
          </mrow>
          <mrow>
            <mi> &part; </mi>
            <msup> <mi> z </mi> <mn> 2 </mn> </msup>
          </mrow>
        </mfrac>
      </mrow>
    </mfenced>
    <mo>=</mo>
    <mrow>
      <mi>i</mi>
      <mi>&hbar;</mi>
      <mfrac>
        <mrow> <mi> &part; </mi> <mi> &Psi; </mi> </mrow>
        <mrow> <mi> &part; </mi> <mi> t </mi> </mrow>
      </mfrac>
    </mrow>
  </mrow>
</math>?
It's more likely we've heard of Shr&#xF6;dinger's cat.
</p>
</text>
```

Mathematics Typesetting with MathML

The Mathematical Markup Language (MathML) is a W3C recommendation for recording mathematical content and presentation. Use it to code math formulas in XML.

This recommendation, available at http://www.w3.org/TR/MathML2/ was first released in April 1998. It is one of the first W3C applications of XML, which became a recommendation in February of the same year.

The example for the instream-foreign-object in this chapter presents MathML markup as an example of how mathematical equations might be embedded within a document typeset with FO. There are no FO implementations that support this at time of writing. Some FO implementations support Scalable Vector Graphics (SVG). One vendor, SchemaSoft, produces a MathML to SVG converter. See http://www.schemasoft.com/MathML/.

MathML is supported in HTML browsers by a number of plug-ins available for free download or for purchase. Technical authors and publishers may find it useful if some FO implementations someday support MathML as well. See http://www.w3.org/Math for further information about MathML and implementations. A zip file containing a DTD and entity declaration files for MathML is available from http://www.w3.org/TR/REC-MathML/mmlents.zip.

The markup in Listing 12.2 contains no URI to which the `src` attribute of an `external-graphic` FO might refer. It embeds markup directly in the document. The appropriate FO with which to handle embedded markup is the `instream-foreign-object`. Use the `instream-foreign-object` FO to enclose any markup that the formatter may interpret, but that is not part of XSL. MathML is one example.

Following is a style sheet that embeds the math contained in Listing 12.2 inside of an `instream-foreign-object`. Note that the markup embedded in an `instream-foreign-object` may be any markup, not only MathML. It could be HTML. It could be SVG. It could be binary data encoded as Unicode. Any format that the formatter supports is valid within an `instream-foreign-object`.

```
<?xml version='1.0'?>
<xsl:stylesheet version="1.0"
 xmlns:xsl="http://www.w3.org/1999/XSL/Transform"
 xmlns:fo="http://www.w3.org/1999/XSL/Format"
 xmlns:mml="http://www.w3.org/1998/Math/MathML">

  <xsl:include href="rootrule.xsl"/>
  <xsl:include href="docstyle.xsl"/>

  <xsl:template match="p">
    <fo:block xsl:use-attribute-sets="body">
      <xsl:apply-templates/>
    </fo:block>
  </xsl:template>

  <xsl:template match="mml:math">
    <fo:instream-foreign-object xsl:use-attribute-sets="graphic">
      <xsl:copy-of select="."/>
    </fo:instream-foreign-object>
  </xsl:template>

</xsl:stylesheet>
```

The style sheet declares the MathML namespace on the fifth line, as `xmlns:mml="http://www.w3.org/1998/Math/MathML"`. It uses that namespace in the second template to match the MathML `math` element in the source document, `<xsl:template match="mml:math">`. The body of the template creates an `instream-foreign-object` formatting object. It copies the `math` element and all of its content into the `instream-foreign-object`.

XSL formatters don't render MathML, yet. When they do it will look something like the rendering reproduced in Figure 12.2. The rendering was produced from mixed HTML and MathML source by the W3C Amaya Web browser.

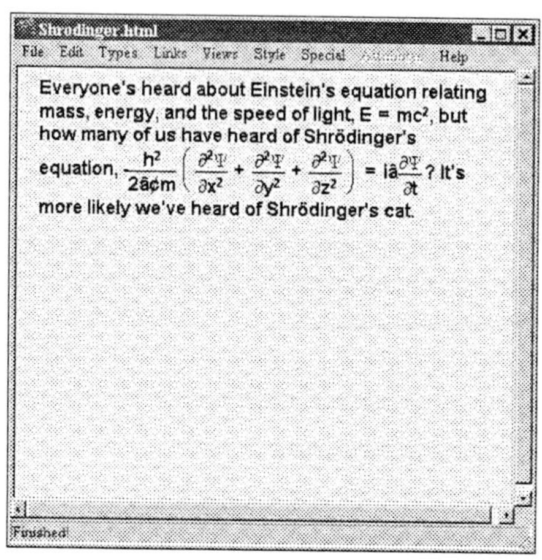

Figure 12.2
MathML rendered by the W3C Amaya Web browser.

As of this writing, the FOP formatter supports SVG markup as content of an `instream-foreign-object`.

Placement and Alignment

This discussion of embedding graphics has so far deferred discussion of placement and alignment of the embedded graphic within the surrounding text. The reason is that properties controlling these apply equally to the `external-graphic` and `instream-foreign-object` FOs. The discussion that follows demonstrates placement and alignment using the `external-graphic`, because that's the best supported FO. Everything in the discussion applies to `instream-foreign-object` as well. The first section demonstrates properties that control the size of the graphic. Later sections cover properties that control alignment with surrounding elements.

Size of the Graphic

Six properties specify size—three properties on each axis, horizontal and vertical. This is too many. You might wonder how the formatter can decide how large to make things if there are three different means to specify the size. Let's look at each, one at a time. When you get to the bottom it should be clear how to use each of them.

The `inline-progression-dimension` and `block-progression-dimension` properties specify the size of the rectangle that contains the graphical content. If you do not specify them, they are as large as is needed to fit the content, whatever the size of the content. When you do set them, set them using a length value, such as `3in` or `300px`. The length may have minimum, maximum, and optimum components. These are relative properties. The axis to which they refer changes based on the writing mode.

The `height` and `width` properties are absolute properties corresponding to the `block-progression-dimension` and `inline-progression-dimension` properties. The absolute properties override any setting of the relative ones. Which relative property they override depends on the writing-mode setting. Chapter 6, "Block and Inline," contains a detailed discussion of corresponding properties and writing mode. The safe policy is to use `height` and `width` or `block` and `inline-progression-dimension`, but not both.

The `content-height` and `content-width` properties specify the size to which the formatter will scale the graphic. If you do not specify `content-height` or `content-width`, the formatter will leave the graphic at its natural size. The natural size depends on the graphics format. Some formats include size information. A JPEG or GIF image has a size in pixels.

Content Width and Height

The `content-height` and `content-width` dimensions apply to the graphic. They do not apply to the amount of real estate reserved for it by the `height`, `width`, `block-progression-dimension`, or `inline-progression-dimension` properties. The graphic may be smaller or larger than the space reserved for it.

That opens the question of what the formatter does with a graphic that is larger or smaller than the area allocated for it; but let's not go there, yet. The usual behavior is to display the entire graphic in an area that is exactly the size required to fit. One way to do that is to leave the graphic at its natural size and specify none of the size properties. The other way is to specify the `content-width` or `content-height` property only. The result reproduced in Figure 12.1 set the `content-width` property to 3 inches, as follows:

```
<xsl:attribute-set name="graphic">
  <xsl:attribute name="content-width">3in</xsl:attribute>
</xsl:attribute-set>
```

In this case, the `inline` and `block-progression-dimension` properties default to the value `auto`. The formatter computes them to be equal to the size of the content. The formatter scales the graphic equally in width and height so that the width equals the 3 inches specified while the graphical proportions remain constant. It's just that simple.

Scaling

The `scaling` property may alter this behavior. The `scaling` property determines whether the formatter scales width and height equally. Its default value, `uniform`, requires equal scaling. The value, `non-uniform` allows the formatter to scale the unspecified dimension any way it wants. If your style sheet specifies both `content-width` and `content-height`, the value for scaling has no effect. The formatter will scale to both the height and width specified.

Figure 12.3 demonstrates the effect of specifying both the `content-width` and `content-height`. To do this, you modify the graphic attribute set in `docstyle.xsl` as follows:

```
<xsl:attribute-set name="graphic">
  <xsl:attribute name="content-width">3in</xsl:attribute>
  <xsl:attribute name="content-height">1in</xsl:attribute>
</xsl:attribute-set>
```

Sky Trail, Pt. Reyes. Sunlight behind trees. Mist captures its pattern of light and shadow.

Without a thought we know this is dawn. Why?

Figure 12.3
Non-uniform scaling of a graphic.

Overflow

The next possible case is that the graphic is larger than the area made available to display it. The natural size of SkyTrailDawn.jpg is larger than 3 inches, so let's try setting the `inline-progression-dimension` to 3 inches instead, like this:

```
<xsl:attribute-set name="graphic">
  <xsl:attribute name="inline-progression-dimension">3in</xsl:attribute>
</xsl:attribute-set>
```

What happens now depends on the value of the overflow property. Be default, the auto settings will have the formatter clip the image to the size of the box and provide a scrollbar to scroll the clipped portions into view. If the output is to a device that is not interactive, the implementation can do what it wants. It would probably be better if it clipped.

A setting of scroll should force the formatter to present scrollbars whether the image is too large for the box. A setting of hidden should cause the formatter to always clip and never show scrollbars. A setting of visible should cause the formatter to print the entire image, overprinting nearby areas.

The final case is that the graphic is too small for the area made available to display it. The formatter will position the graphic such that all of it is visible. How it aligns with the edges of the box depends on the alignment properties.

Alignment

The display-alignment property determines the alignment edge for the graphic in the block-progression dimension. If the value is before, the top of the graphic aligns with the before edge of the available box. If the value is center, the formatter places equal space before and after the graphic. If the value is after, the bottom edge of the image aligns with the after edge of the display area. The default value is before.

The text-align property determines the alignment of the graphic in the inline-progression dimension. The text-align property has behavior as with text, which is covered in Chapter 6. The justify value is equivalent to the value start because the formatter cannot split the graphic to align both sides.

Use the alignment-baseline property to change the alignment of the containing box relative to the text around it. The default value aligns the bottom of the graphic with the baseline of the surrounding text. That is the so-called alphabetic baseline. A value of central centers the graphic at the center of the text. The second equation in Figure 12.2 has a central alignment-baseline.

Block Placement

So far, we have allowed the graphic placement to be in line with other inline elements. At times, you might like the graphic to appear by itself with other content before and after it. In that case, all you have to do is enclose the external-graphic or instream-object-object within a block, like this:

```
<xsl:template match="img">
  <fo:block xsl:use-attribute-sets="box">
    <fo:external-graphic xsl:use-attribute-sets="graphic">
      <xsl:attribute name="src">
```

```
          <xsl:text>url("</xsl:text>
          <xsl:value-of select="@href"/>
          <xsl:text>")</xsl:text>
        </xsl:attribute>
      </fo:external-graphic>
    </fo:block>
  </xsl:template>
```

Figure 12.4 demonstrates the result.

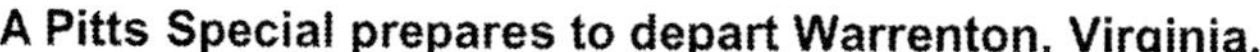

A Pitts Special prepares to depart Warrenton, Virginia.

Another contest weekend comes to an end.

Figure 12.4
A graphic enclosed within a block gets its own line.

Character

Now here's an FO with character. The `character` FO typesets a single character identified by the `character` property. The source fragment, `<fo:character character="a"/>`, will typeset a lowercase a.

All the font properties apply. All the border, padding, and background properties apply as well. You might use it to typeset an elaborate capital at the beginning of the first word of a chapter. You might use it to typeset symbols from a symbol font. Use it to typeset a bullet of a list.

You've seen it used as a bullet in Chapter 10, when we talked about lists and leaders. It's mentioned here because it's a great way to put symbols into your document. Suppose that you have all the Aresti aerobatic symbols in a font. A font is scalable. It's based on splines. We can now print the Aresti symbols at any size and not worry too much about rough problems with scaling. This is much more flexible than a collection of images in some directory. Images don't scale as well, especially if you're going larger.

To demonstrate, the following is a fragment of source XML that contains an Aresti diagram:

```
<?xml version="1.0"?>
<!DOCTYPE test [
 <!ENTITY a6.1.1 'q'>
]>
<test>
  <p>Every figure has a level of difficulty known as
  its <quote>K-factor.</quote> The tail slide,
  catalog 6.1.1 <aresti cat="&a6.1.1;"/>
  has a K factor of 15.  Optional rolls on the
  up and down lines may increase the difficulty.</p>
</test>
```

The document type defines the entity "a6.1.1" as the character in the Aresti font that displays the given figure. In this case, a lowercase q in the Aresti font will diagram a tail slide. The style sheet matches the Aresti element and outputs a character FO as follows:

```
<xsl:template match="aresti">
  <fo:character
   font-family="aresti, sans-serif">
    <xsl:attribute name="character">
      <xsl:value-of select="@cat"/>
    </xsl:attribute>
  </fo:character>
</xsl:template>
```

Without a font full of Aresti symbols, the example will simply print a lowercase q using the sans-serif font. Supposing that you did have an Aresti font, the output might look like that in Figure 12.5, which is simulated in HTML with an image file:

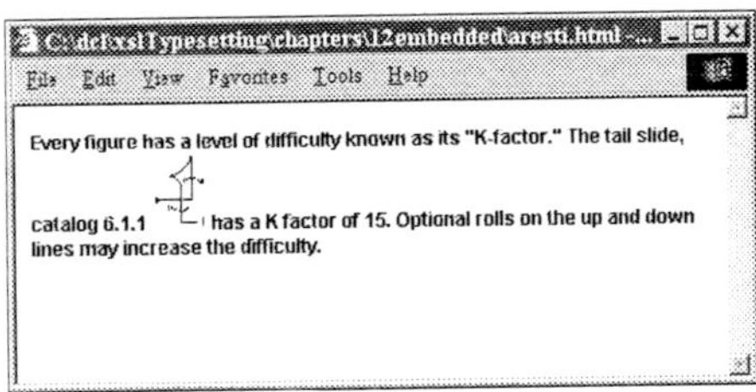

Figure 12.5
An Aresti symbol in line with text.

The same scenario may be handled just as well using a collection of SVG files called for by an external graphic that contains a reference to the file. Perhaps giving the character example is a stretch, but not too much of one. Many times, a font may be preferable to a directory full of SVG files. In any case, following is the style sheet fragment for typesetting the same example using SVG:

```
<xsl:template match="aresti">
  <fo:external-graphic content-height="0.75in">
    <xsl:attribute name="src">
      <xsl:text>url(aresti/</xsl:text>
      <xsl:value-of select="@cat"/>
      <xsl:text>.svg)</xsl:text>
    </xsl:attribute>
  </fo:external-graphic>
</xsl:template>
```

This example refers to a graphic in an Aresti subdirectory. If the graphic is not there, the formatter will either print nothing or print a placeholder for the missing graphic.

Background Effects

As in HTML, it's possible in XSL to tile images in the background. Any FO that supports borders will also support background images and background color. This includes most of the block and inline level FOs. The background properties are available wherever you would want to use them.

Use the `background-image` property to specify an image for the background. Its value is a URI specification, just as with the `external-graphic` FO discussed earlier in this chapter. When you specify a background image, that image will repeat or tile by default across the entire background of the FO on which you specify it. The background extends from border to border. That means the image will paint in the padding rectangle.

Figure 12.6 shows an example in which the `background-image` property is specified along with 24-point padding all around. The inner rectangle has 12-point padding all around, but no specified background. Note that the image shows through the padding of the overlying block. This illustrates that the default background is transparent.

Figure 12.6
Background image.

Here are the style settings for `docstyle.xsl` that produced the example:

```
<xsl:attribute-set name="body">
  <xsl:attribute name="text-align">center</xsl:attribute>
  <xsl:attribute name="background-image">plane32.bmp</xsl:attribute>
  <xsl:attribute name="border-before-style">solid</xsl:attribute>
  <xsl:attribute name="border-after-style">solid</xsl:attribute>
  <xsl:attribute name="border-start-style">solid</xsl:attribute>
  <xsl:attribute name="border-end-style">solid</xsl:attribute>
  <xsl:attribute name="padding-before">24pt</xsl:attribute>
  <xsl:attribute name="padding-after">24pt</xsl:attribute>
  <xsl:attribute name="padding-start">24pt</xsl:attribute>
  <xsl:attribute name="padding-end">24pt</xsl:attribute>
</xsl:attribute-set>

<xsl:attribute-set name="graphic">
  <xsl:attribute name="border-before-style">solid</xsl:attribute>
  <xsl:attribute name="border-after-style">solid</xsl:attribute>
  <xsl:attribute name="border-start-style">solid</xsl:attribute>
  <xsl:attribute name="border-end-style">solid</xsl:attribute>
  <xsl:attribute name="padding-before">12pt</xsl:attribute>
  <xsl:attribute name="padding-after">12pt</xsl:attribute>
  <xsl:attribute name="padding-start">12pt</xsl:attribute>
  <xsl:attribute name="padding-end">12pt</xsl:attribute>
</xsl:attribute-set>
```

Background Color and Background Image Position

If you add one line to the graphic attribute set, `<xsl:attribute name="background-color">gray</xsl:attribute>`, the padding between the image and the inner border will hide the background image of the outer box. Let's save showing that to investigate the background-position properties.

The `background-position-horizontal` property will shift the background image to the right by a specified amount. It will also justify the image to the `left`, `center`, or `right` of the padding rectangle. The default justifies the image to the left, as you've seen. You can specify any length value, but use the keyword value, `center` for this example.

The `background-position-vertical` property is analogous to the `background-position-horizontal` property in the vertical dimension. A positive length provides an offset from the top of the padding rectangle. The keyword values are `top`, `center`, and `bottom`. Negative lengths for these properties move the image up or to the left.

Here are the elaborated property settings, including the background color for the image rectangle. Figure 12.7 demonstrates the rendered result:

```
<xsl:attribute-set name="body">
  <xsl:attribute name="text-align">center</xsl:attribute>
  <xsl:attribute name="background-image">plane32.bmp</xsl:attribute>
  <xsl:attribute name="background-position-horizontal">center</xsl:attribute>
  <xsl:attribute name="background-position-vertical">center</xsl:attribute>
  <xsl:attribute name="border-before-style">solid</xsl:attribute>
  <xsl:attribute name="border-after-style">solid</xsl:attribute>
  <xsl:attribute name="border-start-style">solid</xsl:attribute>
  <xsl:attribute name="border-end-style">solid</xsl:attribute>
  <xsl:attribute name="padding-before">24pt</xsl:attribute>
  <xsl:attribute name="padding-after">24pt</xsl:attribute>
  <xsl:attribute name="padding-start">24pt</xsl:attribute>
  <xsl:attribute name="padding-end">24pt</xsl:attribute>
</xsl:attribute-set>

<xsl:attribute-set name="graphic">
  <xsl:attribute name="background-color">gray</xsl:attribute>
  <xsl:attribute name="border-before-style">solid</xsl:attribute>
  <xsl:attribute name="border-after-style">solid</xsl:attribute>
  <xsl:attribute name="border-start-style">solid</xsl:attribute>
  <xsl:attribute name="border-end-style">solid</xsl:attribute>
  <xsl:attribute name="padding-before">12pt</xsl:attribute>
  <xsl:attribute name="padding-after">12pt</xsl:attribute>
```

```
  <xsl:attribute name="padding-start">12pt</xsl:attribute>
  <xsl:attribute name="padding-end">12pt</xsl:attribute>
</xsl:attribute-set>
```

Figure 12.7
Centered background image and opaque border.

Background Repeat

If you don't want the image to tile, you'll need one more property—`background-repeat`. Override the default value of the `background-repeat` property with one of the keywords: `repeat-x`, `repeat-y`, or `no-repeat`. The value `repeat-x` causes the formatter to repeat the image in one line across the box. The value `repeat-y` causes the formatter to repeat the image in one line down the box. The value `no-repeat` causes the formatter to place the image only once.

The values of the `background-position-horizontal` and `background-position-vertical` properties still apply. If you use the settings as follows:

```
<xsl:attribute name="background-position-horizontal">center</xsl:attribute>
<xsl:attribute name="background-position-vertical">center</xsl:attribute>
<xsl:attribute name="background-repeat">repeat-y</xsl:attribute>
```

You will see one line of little airplanes dividing the box from top to bottom. One of the little airplanes will be centered in the box behind the image.

Summary

Now you can insert images and diagrams with confidence anywhere in your documents. You can embed foreign markup such as MathML or SVG. You can control the transparency of the background to put together very nice framing effects.

This chapter discussed the `external-graphic` and `instream-object-object` FOs as well as the `background-image`, `background-color`, `background-position-horizontal`, `background-position-vertical`, and `background-repeat` properties. You have now worked with a substantial number of properties that control the appearance of content on the page.

Something new is afoot, and you won't have to be Sherlock Holmes to get to the bottom of it. It's footnotes and floats. When you need content to float to the top or the bottom of the page rather than stay where it's put, read on to Chapter 13, "Footnotes and Floats."

CHAPTER 13

Footnotes and Floats

Footnotes and floats, floats and footnotes. It is not only because they make a nice alliteration that they appear together in this chapter. The two are conceptually related. Both have a kind of phantom behavior. You code them at one place in the style sheet, but the formatter typesets them separately somewhere else. The XSL recommendation refers to these as "out of line" FOs. The formatter removes them from their place in line with other FOs and places them apart.

An Epistle with Footnotes and Floats

> According to the *Dictionary of Unitarian and Universalist Biography*, Robert Burns founded in 1780 a debating society among his friends which they named the Tarbolton Bachelor's Club. They used the club to discuss among themselves many questions that young men may companionably discuss concerning the pursuit of a happy life. The biography quotes Burns as writing in the club charter, "Every man proper for a member of this society must have a frank, honest, open heart; above any thing dirty or mean; and must be a professed lover of one or more of the female sex."
>
> —*The Tarbolton Bachelor's Club*

"Green grow the rashes," Burns wrote. "The finest hours that e'er I spent, I spent among the lasses, O." Burns also wrote a poem he titled "Epistle to a Young Friend," an excerpt of which serves as the example for this chapter. Listing 13.1 demonstrates the, markup, with most of the text elided for brevity:

Listing 13.1 *Markup for Demonstration of Footnotes and Floats*

```
<collection>
  <author>
    <name>Robert Burns</name>
    <bio>
      Robert Burns was born on January 25, 1759
      <!— more bio —>
      <q>Lord, grant that we may lead a gude life</q>
    </bio>
  </author>
  <poem>
    <title>Epistle to a Young Friend</title>
    <note>
      Burns wrote this poem to Andrew Hunter Aitken,
    </note>
    <stanza>
      <line>I lang hae thought, my youthfu friend, </line>
      <line>A something to have sent you,</line>
      <line>Tho it should serve nae ither end</line>
      <line>Than just a kind memento:</line>
      <line>But how the subject-theme may <d>gang</d>,</line>
      <!— more lines —>
    </stanza><stanza>
      <line>I'll no say, men are villains a':</line>
      <!— more lines —>
    </stanza>
    <!— mare stanzas —>
  </poem>
  <definitions>
    <def>
      <phrase>gang</phrase>
      <translation>go</translation>
    </def>
    <!— more definitions —>
  </definitions>
</collection>
```

The collection contains author elements followed by poem and definition elements. It relies on document order to associate authors with poems.

The poem elements contain a title and stanzas much like the example concerning white space used in Chapter 7, "White Space and Line Handling." Unlike the example in that chapter, these stanzas contain line elements to demarcate each line of the poem.

A note element may appear within a poem. This serves as an example for side floats later in the chapter. The `<d>` elements enclose terms defined in the definitions. The `<def>` elements have the defined phrase followed by a translation. These will serve as footnote examples. The `<bio>` element within the `<author>` element will serve as an example for top floats.

Footnotes

Footnotes are brief, items of information not directly relevant to the purpose of the paragraph or sentence where they are noted. An inconspicuous mark in the body text indicates the presence of a footnote. Call that mark the footnote reference. The note itself appears at the bottom of the page. Call the note itself the footnote body.

XSL provides two FOs for inserting footnotes into a document. They are the `footnote` and `footnote-body`. The `footnote` FO introduces the footnote. It contains a single `inline` FO that acts as the footnote reference. The `footnote-body` FO must appear after the `inline` within the `footnote`. The `footnote-body` contains one or more blocks. The basic form is this:

```
<fo:footnote>
  <fo:inline>
    <!— footnote reference —>
  </fo:inline>
  <fo:footnote-body>
    <fo:block>
      <!— footnote body —>
    </fo:block>
  </fo:footnote-body>
</fo:footnote>
```

Look for the pattern in Listing 13.2. It appears within the template that matches the `<d>` element. Recall that the input source uses the `<d>` element around one occurrence of a word or phrase in the poem that has a definition. The full listing for the file poemstyle.xsl appears later, in Listing 13.3. Focus on the footnote for now:

Listing 13.2 *Style Sheet Formats a Collection of Poems*

```
<?xml version='1.0'?>
<xsl:stylesheet version="1.0"
 xmlns:xsl="http://www.w3.org/1999/XSL/Transform"
 xmlns:fo="http://www.w3.org/1999/XSL/Format">

  <xsl:include href="rootrule.xsl"/>
  <xsl:include href="poemstyle.xsl"/>

  <xsl:template match="collection">
    <xsl:apply-templates select="poem"/>
  </xsl:template>

  <xsl:template match="title">
    <fo:block xsl:use-attribute-sets="title">
      <xsl:apply-templates/>
    </fo:block>
  </xsl:template>

  <xsl:template match="stanza">
    <fo:block xsl:use-attribute-sets="stanza">
      <xsl:apply-templates/>
    </fo:block>
  </xsl:template>

  <xsl:template match="line">
    <fo:block>
      <xsl:apply-templates/>
    </fo:block>
  </xsl:template>

  <xsl:template match="note">
  </xsl:template>

  <xsl:template match="d">
    <xsl:variable name="term">
      <xsl:value-of select="text()"/>
    </xsl:variable>
    <fo:footnote>
      <fo:inline>
        <xsl:value-of select="text()"/>
        <fo:character baseline-shift="super"
```

Listing 13.2 *(continued)*

```
          font-size="60%" font-weight="light"
          character="&#x2020;"/>
      </fo:inline>
      <fo:footnote-body>
        <xsl:apply-templates
         select="/collection/definitions/def
                 [contains(phrase/text(),$term)]"/>
      </fo:footnote-body>
    </fo:footnote>
  </xsl:template>

  <xsl:template match="def">
    <fo:block font-size="80%">
      <xsl:value-of select="phrase"/>
      <xsl:text>: </xsl:text>
      <xsl:value-of select="translation"/>
    </fo:block>
  </xsl:template>

</xsl:stylesheet>
```

The XSL that formats the body of the footnote is very likely the cleverest bit of XSL wizardry so far. It may not top the recursive numbering scheme developed for outline numbering in Chapter 10, "Lists and Leaders," but perhaps it comes close. You'll find the clever bit in the select clause for the `apply-templates` element of the `footnote-body` FO:

```
<fo:footnote-body>
  <xsl:apply-templates
   select="/collection/definitions/def
           [contains(phrase/text(),$term)]"/>
</fo:footnote-body>
```

The select clause contains an XPath expression that works as follows. It finds the root of the input using the leading slash. It then selects all the `def` elements by navigating their ancestry from the top down, `/collection/definitions/def`. The part in square brackets is called a predicate. It selects only the `def` elements that have a `phrase` child and which phrase contains text matching the term found in the text `[contains(phrase/text(),$term)]`.

The `$term` expression is a variable reference. The XSL `variable` declaration at the beginning of the template associated the text content of the `<d>` element with the variable named `term`:

```
<xsl:variable name="term">
  <xsl:value-of select="text()"/>
</xsl:variable>
```

If this doesn't convince you that XSL is a powerful tool for restructuring and formatting XML content, perhaps nothing will. Enough self-congratulation. Figure 13.1 shows the result. Try reading it out loud. The sound of the words helps reveal the meaning of the oddly spelled words:

Epistle to a Young Friend

I lang hae thought, my youthfu friend,
A something to have sent you,
Tho it should serve nae ither end
Than just a kind memento:
But how the subject-theme may gang † ,
Let time and chance determine:
Perhaps it may turn out a sang:
Perhaps, turn out a sermon.

Ye'll try the world soon, my lad:
And, Andrew dear, believe me,
Ye'll find mankind an unco squad,
And muckle they may grieve ye:
For care and trouble set your thought,
Ev'n when your end's attained:
And a' your views may come to nought,
Where ev'ry nerve is strained.

I'll no say, men are villains a':
The real, harden'd wicked,
Wha hae nae check but human law,
Are to a few restricked:
But, och! mankind are unco † weak,
An little to be trusted:
If self the wavering balance shake,
It's rarely right adjusted!

Adieu, dear, amiable youth!
Your heart can ne'er be wanting!
May prudence, fortitude, and truth,
Erect your brow undaunting!
In ploughman phrase, 'God send you speed,'
Still daily to grow wiser:
And may ye better reck the rede † ,
Than ever did th' adviser!

gang: go
unco: extremely, mightily
reck the rede: play the tune

Figure 13.1

A fragment of Burns's "Epistle to a Young Friend" with footnotes.

Be sure to note the footnotes at the bottom of the page. Looking back at Listing 13.2, you may see that the term came from the content of the <d> element in the stanzas. The definition came from the `def/translation` element in the definitions. The footnote references in the body are superscript small daggers.

Many times you may want to use numbered footnotes. Chapter 10, which discussed lists, contained detailed examples for numbering list items. You may apply the same techniques for numbering footnotes.

Separating Footnotes from the Body

The footnotes might look, better if they were set off from the body of the page in some way. The offset should appear only when there is a footnote; otherwise, it will be extraneous. It should give a clean separation from the body text and the list of footnotes.

XSL reserves the special flow name `xsl-footnote-separator` for content that will separate footnotes from the body. Define the content for the separator with a `static-content` element in the `page-sequence`. The formatter will place that content above the group of footnotes on any page that contains them.

The page sequence comes from the root template in `rootrule.xsl`, unfortunately. Returning to Listing 13.2, delete the include of `rootrule.xsl`, paste the content of the rule into the style sheet, and modify it as follows:

```
<xsl:template match="/">
  <fo:root>
    <fo:layout-master-set>
      <fo:simple-page-master
       master-name="page"
       page-with="8.5"
       page-height="11">
        <fo:region-body
         region-name="body"
         margin-top="0.5in"
         margin-bottom="0.5in"
         margin-left="1.0in"
         margin-right="0.5in"/>
      </fo:simple-page-master>
    </fo:layout-master-set>
    <fo:page-sequence master-reference="page">
      <fo:static-content flow-name="xsl-footnote-separator">
        <fo:block start-indent="4pc" end-indent="4pc"
         space-after="8pt" text-align-last="justify">
          <fo:leader leader-pattern="rule"/>
```

```
            <fo:leader leader-length="1pc"/>
            <fo:character character="."/>
            <fo:leader leader-length="1pc"/>
            <fo:leader leader-pattern="rule"/>
          </fo:block>
        </fo:static-content>
        <fo:flow flow-name="body">
          <xsl:apply-templates/>
        </fo:flow>
      </fo:page-sequence>
    </fo:root>
  </xsl:template>
```

The changes include adding a page size to the `simple-page-master` and adjusting the margins on the `region-body`. The most important change is the addition of a `static-content` section within the `page-sequence`. The `static-content` has the XSL reserved `flow-name` value of `xsl-footnote-separator` to indicate that this is content to appear between the body and the footnotes. It contains a single block that formats a fancy broken rule.

Peek ahead to Figure 13.2 to see the formatted result. For now, before going on to floats, you may want to look at Listing 13.3. It contains the source for the attribute sets included by `poemstyle.xsl`:

Listing 13.3 *poemstyle.xsl—Attribute Sets for the Style Sheet*

```
<?xml version='1.0'?>
<xsl:stylesheet version="1.0"
 xmlns:xsl="http://www.w3.org/1999/XSL/Transform"
 xmlns:fo="http://www.w3.org/1999/XSL/Format">

  <xsl:attribute-set name="title">
    <xsl:attribute name="space-before">1pc</xsl:attribute>
    <xsl:attribute name="font-size">14pt</xsl:attribute>
    <xsl:attribute name="font-family">Georgia, serif</xsl:attribute>
    <xsl:attribute name="font-weight">bold</xsl:attribute>
  </xsl:attribute-set>

  <xsl:attribute-set name="bio">
    <xsl:attribute name="font-size">12pt</xsl:attribute>
    <xsl:attribute name="space-after">6pt</xsl:attribute>
    <xsl:attribute name="border-before-style">ridge</xsl:attribute>
```

Listing 13.3 *(continued)*

```
    <xsl:attribute name="border-after-style">ridge</xsl:attribute>
    <xsl:attribute name="border-start-style">ridge</xsl:attribute>
    <xsl:attribute name="border-end-style">ridge</xsl:attribute>
    <xsl:attribute name="border-before-width">6pt</xsl:attribute>
    <xsl:attribute name="border-after-width">6pt</xsl:attribute>
    <xsl:attribute name="border-start-width">6pt</xsl:attribute>
    <xsl:attribute name="border-end-width">6pt</xsl:attribute>
    <xsl:attribute name="padding-before">8pt</xsl:attribute>
    <xsl:attribute name="padding-after">8pt</xsl:attribute>
    <xsl:attribute name="padding-start">8pt</xsl:attribute>
    <xsl:attribute name="padding-end">8pt</xsl:attribute>
  </xsl:attribute-set>

  <xsl:attribute-set name="note">
    <xsl:attribute name="inline-progression-dimension">1.5in</xsl:attribute>
    <xsl:attribute name="font-size">8pt</xsl:attribute>
    <xsl:attribute name="space-after">6pt</xsl:attribute>
    <xsl:attribute name="border-before-style">solid</xsl:attribute>
    <xsl:attribute name="border-after-style">solid</xsl:attribute>
    <xsl:attribute name="border-start-style">solid</xsl:attribute>
    <xsl:attribute name="border-end-style">solid</xsl:attribute>
    <xsl:attribute name="border-before-width">3pt</xsl:attribute>
    <xsl:attribute name="border-after-width">3pt</xsl:attribute>
    <xsl:attribute name="border-start-width">3pt</xsl:attribute>
    <xsl:attribute name="border-end-width">3pt</xsl:attribute>
    <xsl:attribute name="padding-before">4pt</xsl:attribute>
    <xsl:attribute name="padding-after">4pt</xsl:attribute>
    <xsl:attribute name="padding-start">4pt</xsl:attribute>
    <xsl:attribute name="padding-end">4pt</xsl:attribute>
  </xsl:attribute-set>

  <xsl:attribute-set name="author">
    <xsl:attribute name="font-size">18pt</xsl:attribute>
    <xsl:attribute name="font-style">italic</xsl:attribute>
    <xsl:attribute name="space-after">3pt</xsl:attribute>
  </xsl:attribute-set>

  <xsl:attribute-set name="stanza">
    <xsl:attribute name="font-size">14pt</xsl:attribute>
    <xsl:attribute name="font-family">Book Antiqua, sans-serif</xsl:attribute>
    <xsl:attribute name="space-before">6pt</xsl:attribute>
```

Listing 13.3 *(continued)*

```
    <xsl:attribute name="keep-together.within-page">always</xsl:attribute>
  </xsl:attribute-set>

</xsl:stylesheet>
```

Before Floats

The elements known as "before floats" are out-of-line elements that move to the top of the page. The formatter places them at the top of the page on which they occur, except in extreme cases of real-estate shortage. When it runs low on space, the formatter may move a float to the top of a subsequent page.

Use the `float` FO with a `float` property setting of `before` to generate a before float. The content of the float is one or more blocks. As an example, the following template will match the `bio` element in the example source to output a before float:

```
<xsl:template match="bio">
  <fo:float float="before">
    <fo:block xsl:use-attribute-sets="bio">
      <xsl:apply-templates/>
    </fo:block>
  </fo:float>
</xsl:template>
```

That is all there is to making the float. The content of the biography should float to the top of the page. To make it work in the style sheet, you will need to modify the template that matches the `collection` element to have it process the `author` section from the input. You will also need to add templates to match the `<q>` element and the `name` element, as follows:

```
<xsl:template match="collection">
  <xsl:apply-templates select="author"/>
  <xsl:apply-templates select="poem"/>
</xsl:template>

<xsl:template match="q">
  <fo:character character="&quot;"/>
  <xsl:apply-templates/>
  <fo:character character="&quot;"/>
</xsl:template>
```

```
<xsl:template match="author/name">
  <fo:block xsl:use-attribute-sets="author">
    <xsl:apply-templates/>
  </fo:block>
</xsl:template>
```

Separating Before Floats from the Body

As with the footnotes, XSL provides a means to add a separator between any before float and the body of the page. The reserved flow name for this purpose is `xsl-before-float-separator`. The following `static-content` element added to the `page-sequence` will create a 4 pt. rule between the before float and the body:

```
<fo:static-content flow-name="xsl-before-float-separator">
  <fo:block space-after="8pt">
    <fo:leader leader-pattern="rule"
     leader-pattern-width="4pt"
     leader-length="100%"/>
  </fo:block>
</fo:static-content>
```

In this case, the before float separator is overkill because the float itself has a border around it. The output shown in Figure 13.2 omits it.

Side Floats

Side floats move to the start or end edge of the page or reference area in which they occur. Use the `float` FO with a `float` property setting of `start` or `end` to generate a side float. The formatter will place the float at the start edge or the end edge as indicated. The content of the float, as with before floats, is one or more blocks. To see an example, replace the template in Listing 13.2 that matches the `note` element with the following:

```
<xsl:template match="note">
  <fo:float float="after">
    <fo:block xsl:use-attribute-sets="note">
      <xsl:apply-templates/>
    </fo:block>
  </fo:float>
</xsl:template>
```

Figure 13.2 shows the result output. This output is not 100% in agreement with the expected output. The floating elements do not move out of line as they should. The formatter places the floats in progression with the rest of the blocks. Your mileage may improve by the time you read this.

Note the differences between Figure 13.1 and Figure 13.2. The before float and author name took space formerly used to typeset the fourth stanza. That stanza and the footnotes associated with it moved to the next page. Remember to notice the footnote separator as well.

Robert Burns

Robert Burns was born on January 25, 1759 in Alloway, Ayrshire, Scotland. He is the national poet of Scotland, revered for his rakish spirit and for his preservation of Scots language and song. Burns published his first volume of poems in 1786. A year later he began a project to collect and write songs of Scotland. The most famous of these songs is Auld Lang Syne, a perennial on New Year's Eve. Burns died in 1796, only 37 years old. He wrote, "Lord, grant that we may lead a gude life; for a gude life makes a gude end; at least it helps weel!"

Epistle to a Young Friend

Burns wrote this poem to Andrew Hunter Aitken, who became a merchant in Liverpool and then a British consul in Riga. Aitken died in 1831.

I lang hae thought, my youthfu friend,
A something to have sent you,
Tho it should serve nae ither end
Than just a kind memento:
But how the subject-theme may gang † ,
Let time and chance determine:
Perhaps it may turn out a sang;
Perhaps, turn out a sermon.

Ye'll try the world soon, my lad;
And, Andrew dear, believe me,
Ye'll find mankind an unco squad,
And muckle they may grieve ye:
For care and trouble set your thought,
Ev'n when your end's attained;
And a' your views may come to nought,
Where ev'ry nerve is strained.

I'll no say, men are villains a':
The real, harden'd wicked,
Wha hae nae check but human law,
Are to a few restricked;
But, och! mankind are unco † weak,
An little to be trusted;
If self the wavering balance shake,
It's rarely right adjusted!

---

gang: go
unco: extremely, mightily

Adieu, dear, amiable youth!
Your heart can ne'er be wanting!
May prudence, fortitude, and truth,
Erect your brow undaunting!
In ploughman phrase, 'God send you speed,'
Still daily to grow wiser;
And may ye better reck the rede † ,
Than ever did th' adviser!

reck the rede: play the tune

Figure 13.2
A fragment of Burns's "Epistle to a Young Friend" with floats.

Summary

Floats are useful for setting apart long portions of content that are outside of the primary thrust or purpose of the text in the body. They are sometimes called sidebars. Callouts in magazines are also floating elements. These take a pithy quote from the text to draw interest and visually break up the page.

You may also use floats to set apart tables or figures if they need not appear exactly in progression with the text. Footnotes have a purpose similar to floats, except they generally contain short references or annotations. Unlike floats, they contain a direct reference at some specific place in the body text.

The next chapter describes scrolling and other dynamic behaviors available when your FO document appears on an interactive device such as a notebook computer. It describes how to specify hyperlinks with FO and a few other, extraordinary effects that you may not have expected from a formatter.

CHAPTER 14

Dynamic Effects

The XSL working group did not limit itself to producing paper documents, not by any means. The Adobe company has strong participation in the working group. Adobe's Portable Document Format (PDF) is a powerful format for print and for browsing. You may be aware that PDF has a number of interactive features, and so does FO.

FOs can produce a styled document for an interactive device. FOs have been used to simulate displays of an HTML browser and a WML (Wireless Markup Language) device. XSL combines transformations with strong typesetting semantics to reproduce the presentation of a data result or document with true fidelity on every client.

Scrolling

One of the common behaviors of an interactive document display is scrolling. Scrolling is so common that Microsoft marketed a mouse with a scroll wheel between its buttons. Every user of the Web is familiar with the browser's vertical scrollbar. We reach for it as often or more frequently than the Back button.

Content rendered with FOs can scroll vertically or horizontally on a display device such as your computer screen much the same way as HTML content does within a Web browser. Several properties influence this behavior. They are the `clip`, `media-usage`, `page-height`, `page-width`, and `overflow` properties.

The media-usage Property

The `media-usage` property provides the first clue to the formatter about whether to paginate or scroll content. If it paginates, it might treat one screenful as a page. If it scrolls, there will be no page breaks and a scrollbar will be present, much the same as with an HTML browser.

The default value for `media-usage` is `auto`, which causes most formatters to paginate content. Settings on the `page-width` or `page-height` properties may affect this decision by the formatter. In particular, if the style sheet specifies one or the other of `page-width` or `page-height` and the display device is an interactive one, the formatter may choose to bind the size of the page in the specified dimension and treat the other dimension as indefinite. It will then scroll in the direction that extends indefinitely.

An indefinite `page-height` or `page-width` may mean that the formatter does no pagination of the document. If the `block-progression-dimension` for the document is top to bottom and the `page-height` is indefinite, the formatter will render in very much the same way that a browser renders. It will typeset the content onto an infinite scroll.

With `media-usage` set to paginate, the formatter will break pages at the dimensions set by the `page-height` and `page-width`. If either the `page-height` or `page-width` is not specified, the formatter will use defaults for the given device. With `media-usage` set to `bounded-in-one-dimension` the formatter will always scroll.

Overflow and Clipping

Sometimes content will be too large to fit in the area allocated by the formatter. It is hard to overflow an area with wrapped text, but overflow may occur with an `external-graphic` or on a long line with the `wrap-option` property set to `no-wrap`.

In this case the formatter may do one of several things, all under your control. If the `overflow` property has the value `hidden`, it will clip the content at the edge of the area. The overflowed content will disappear.

If the `overflow` property has the value `scroll`, the formatter presents scrollbars so that you can scroll the overflowed content into view. If the media does not support interactive viewing, it clips the content.

If the `overflow` property has the value `visible`, the overflowed content will overwrite the padding, border, and margin of the area containing it and any areas around it all the way to the edge of the media.

Clipping occurs at the edges of the content rectangle, within the border and padding. Use the `clip` property to specify clipping offsets from the top, right, bottom, and left edges of the content rectangle. The setting, `clip="rect(6pt, 4pt, -6pt, -4pt)"` will offset the clipping rectangle six points down and four points left of the content rectangle. The `rect(<top>, <right>, <bottom>, <left>)` syntax is the only syntax valid for the `clip` property, except for the keywords `auto` and `inherit`.

Hyperlink

The `basic-link` FO acts as the source of traversal to some target. The target may be another place within the document, or another document. The `basic-link` is roughly equivalent to the anchor tag `<a>` in HTML. Clicking the content of a `basic-link` FO may cause the formatter to display a different part of the document, or a different document, or launch another viewer to display some other type of document.

Write a `basic-link` around any content to make that content active for traversal to the target. The `basic-link` is an inline-level element that renders in the same way as the inline FO. It may have borders and padding, background images or color, and all the other properties associated with inline.

Additional properties on the `basic-link` FO define the target of the link. Specify the `internal-destination` property to link to content elsewhere in the same FO result document. Specify the `external-destination` property to link to content in a separate document.

Internal Links

The `internal-destination` property references the value of the `id` property from some other FO. The `id` property must be unique for all FOs in the document; therefore, the id reference uniquely determines another location in the document. As an example, consider the HTML or PDF output for the XSL FO recommendation. The sections that describe an FO contain links to sections that describe the valid properties for the FO.

The style rule that outputs the property description must output an `id` attribute on the section header. It might do something like the following:

```
<xsl:template match="property-description">
 <fo:block xsl:use-attribute-sets="heading">
  <xsl:attribute name="id">
   <xsl:value-of select="property-name/>
   <xsl:text>.property-description</xsl:text>
  </xsl:attribute>
```

```
   <!— some statements to produce the section number —>
   <xsl:value-of select="property-name"/>
  </fo:block>
  <xsl:apply-templates/>
</xsl:template>
```

That template uses the property name prefixed to an arbitrary string to establish a unique id for the block that contains the heading. The template that produces the link within a FO description might then look something like this:

```
<xsl:template match="property">
 <fo:block xsl:use-attribute-sets="property-item">
  <fo:basic-link>
   <xsl:attribute name="internal-destination">
    <xsl:value-of select="property-name/>
    <xsl:text>.property-description</xsl:text>
   </xsl:attribute>
   <xsl:value-of select="property-name"/>
  </fo:basic-link>
 </fo:block>
</xsl:template>
```

Note that the statements to generate the value of the `internal-destination` property in the `basic-link` match the statements to generate the `id` property in the target. That ensures that the reference will match the target. Activation of the link in the FO description will cause the renderer to display the property description.

External Links

The `external-destination` property defines a link to an external source. Its value must be a Universal Resource Identifier (URI). This is the same type of identifier used to designate an external graphic or background image. The action of the formatter is implementation dependent. Some implementations may be able to access the system and find an application that will display the externally linked content based on the URI or the MIME type. MIME is an Internet standard for identifying content types.

The target document given by an `external-destination` may contain XML markup. It may be SVG, MathML, or some other nondocument markup such as a data source. FO supplies a number of properties to help the formatter interpret the external target and format a presentation for it.

The `target-processing-context` specifies a location within the target document where display processing should begin. This accepts a URI with a target expression to an element within the document, typically an XPointer.

The target-stylesheet property contains a URI that locates a style sheet. The formatter uses the target style sheet to begin a transform of the external-destination at the target-processing-context. First, it locates the style sheet and target document. Second, it locates the processing context within the target document. Third, it executes the transform. Finally, it displays the result.

The target-presentation-context is a fourth property for externally linked content. It determines the point within the processed result at which the formatter should actually begin presentation. Consider an entirely fantastic example:

```
<fo:basic-link
 external-destination="http://dcl/collections/mathEquations.xml"
 target-processing-context="//equation[@name='schrodinger']"
 target-stylesheet="http://dcl/magic/eq2math.xsl"
 target-presentation-context="//math">
 Here be Shrodinger's equation
</fo:basic-link>
```

This locates a collection of equations at the imaginary location, dcl/collections/. It finds the equation element within that target document with a name attribute equal to "shrodinger." It uses the style sheet eq2math.xsl to transform the target beginning at the Shrodinger equation entry. The result contains some descriptive text followed by the equation. The target-presentation-context selects only the equation for display.

Other Link Properties

You may have had the experience of clicking a link in a browser, perhaps a link in a table of contents to a section of the document. For some inexplicable reason, the browser displays the header of the section at the bottom of the page, forcing you to scroll down to see the text to which you intended to navigate by clicking the link. Call it "click then scroll."

The destination-placement-offset property determines the location on the page where the formatter should display the target content. It gives a distance from the top of the page for presentation of the target. It accepts a length, such as 1in.

The show-destination property allows you to open a new presentation window for display of the linked content. Set it to the value new to open a new presentation. The default value, replace, causes the document containing the link to be replaced by the target document, either by scrolling, if the target is merely out of view, or by reformatting, if the target is a separate document.

Set the indicate-destination property with the value true to cause the formatter to highlight the content of the link in some way. It may underline it, change its color, reverse the background and foreground colors, or place a marquis of chaser lights around it. The method is open to the implementation. By default, the `indicate-destination` property is `false`, meaning that the formatter makes no special presentation of the link. You may change formatting attributes yourself to indicate the link.

This link will have no special formatting at all:

```
<fo:basic-link
 internal-destination="wizard">
  <xsl:apply-templates/>
</fo:basic-link>
```

This link relies on the formatter to show its presence:

```
<fo:basic-link
 internal-destination="wizard"
 indicate-destination="true">
  <xsl:apply-templates/>
</fo:basic-link>
```

This one uses a bold font to show the link:

```
<fo:basic-link
 internal-destination="wizard">
  <fo:wrapper font-style="bold">
    <xsl:apply-templates/>
  </fo:wrapper>
</fo:basic-link>
```

The example that begins the next section shows how to format a link with different properties, depending on whether that link has been visited.

Altered States

The `multi-properties` and `multi-property-set` FOs allow you to define alternative presentations of some content based on the state of a link or the state of a pointer. The FO allows you to change only the properties, not the structure or content of the content rendered within. You can use `multi-properties` to alter border width, background color, or font weight, for example.

You can use the `multi-properties` FO to change presentations dynamically when certain events occur. In the example that follows, you will define several alternative presentations for a basic-link FO. The formatter will initially render the link with blue text. When you move a pointer over it, the formatter will add a green border. When you click down with the pointer, the border will change to red. After visiting the target of the link, the formatter will render it with fuchsia text.

Structure the `multi-properties` FO as follows. Begin with one or more `multi-property-set` FOs. Define an `active-state` property with a different value on each `multi-property-set`. The possible values for the `active-state` property are `link`, `visited`, `hover`, `active`, and `focus`. Define any other properties on the `multi-property-set` that you would like the formatter to alter for the active state. In the example that follows, a link has blue text and a visited link has fuchsia text. The explanation following the example will make clear the meaning of the values for the `active-state` property.

Finish the content of the `multi-properties` with a single wrapper FO. Place within the `wrapper` all the content affected by the alternative property sets. Listing 14.1 contains an example:

Listing 14.1 *Sample Application of* multi-properties

```
<fo:multi-properties>
 <fo:multi-property-set
  active-state="link"
  color="blue">
 <fo:multi-property-set
  active-state="visited"
  color="fuchsia"/>
 <fo:multi-property-set
  active-state="hover"
  xsl:use-attribute-sets="green-border"/>
 <fo:multi-property-set
  active-state="active"
  xsl:use-attribute-sets="red-border"/>
 <fo:multi-property-set
  active-state="focus"
  border-start-style="solid"
  border-start-width="4pt"
  border-end-style="solid"
  border-end-width="4pt"/>
 <fo:wrapper
  border-start-style="merge-property-values()"
  border-end-style="merge-property-values()"
  border-before-style="merge-property-values()"
  border-after-style="merge-property-values()"
  border-start-width="merge-property-values()"
  border-end-width="merge-property-values()"
```

Listing 14.1 *(continued)*

```
    border-before-width="merge-property-values()"
    border-after-width="merge-property-values()"
    border-start-color="merge-property-values()"
    border-end-color="merge-property-values()"
    border-before-color="merge-property-values()"
    border-after-color="merge-property-values()"
    color="merge-property-values()">
    <fo:inline>
     This is the content of the multi-properties with a
     <fo:basic-link
      internal-destination="link-ref"
      show-destination="new">
      link
     </fo:basic-link>
     to a target internal to this document.
    </fo:inline>
  </fo:wrapper>
</fo:multi-properties>
```

Each `multi-property-set` defines an active state for which it is valid together with properties that the formatter should use to format within that state. The `wrapper` contains the content affected by the altered properties. It must specify which properties may be altered by setting those property values with the `merge-property-values()` function.

Here's what will happen in an interactive formatter that implements `multi-property-set`:

The content of the inline will initially appear with blue text because it contains a link. You have not yet visited the link; therefore, the formatter merges properties from the `multi-property-set` with `active-state` set to the value `link`.

When you track the mouse over the content of the inline, the formatter will merge all the properties of the `green-border` attribute set into the `wrapper` and display the inline with a green border. The merge selects the `multi-property-set` with `active-state` equal to `hover`. The blue color will revert to the text color inherited by the `multi-properties` FO.

When you click down the content of the inline, the formatter merges all the properties of the `red-border` attribute set into the `wrapper`. The color of the border around the inline will change from green to red. The `active-state` has the value `active`.

When you release the mouse, the inline will have focus. The formatter will merge the start and end border properties defined on the `multi-property-set` with `active-state` set to the value `focus`.

When you click the word "link," the formatter executes the `basic-link` FO. It displays the portion of the document referenced by the `internal-destination` in a new window. The color of the text in the inline will change to fuchsia. The inline no longer has focus, and the link contained within the `wrapper` has been activated. The formatter merges values from the `multi-property-set` with `active-state` set to the value `visited`.

The FOs described in this chapter belong to the group called Dynamic Effects for good reason. The `multi-properties` example demonstrates that you can use them to get a lot of activity on the screen in response to pointer movements, clicks, and link activations. The next section demonstrates dynamic effects FOs for showing and hiding content in response to mouse clicks.

Toggle Switch

The `multi-switch`, `multi-case`, and `multi-toggle` FOs provide the means to display alternative presentations based on the setting of a switch. This section uses them to make an expanding and collapsing list. This presents one record of eleven. It contains data about an Apollo flight taken from Andrew Chaikin's history, *A Man on the Moon.* Begin with some content such as the following:

```
<?xml version="1.0"?>
<apollo>
 <mission number="12">
  <dates>November 14-24, 1969</dates>
  <crew>
   <commander>
    <surname>Conrad</surname>
    <given>Charles</given>
    <suffix>Jr.</suffix>
   </commander>
   <CM name="Yankee Clipper">
    <surname>Gordon</surname>
    <given>Richard</given>
    <middle>F</middle>
    <suffix>Jr.</suffix>
   </CM>
   <LM name="Intrepid">
    <surname>Bean</surname>
    <given>Alan</given>
```

```
    <middle>L</middle>
   </LM>
  </crew>
  <purpose>Pinpoint Lunar landing; Ocean of Storms</purpose>
 </mission>
</apollo>
```

The XML data source contains one record for each Apollo mission. The `number` attribute on the `mission` element gives the mission number. The `dates` element contains the dates of the flight from start to finish. The crew includes a Commander, Command Module pilot, and Lunar Module pilot. The `name` attributes on the `CM` and `LM` elements give the names of the two space vehicles launched by the Apollo rocket for each mission.

One way to start with a `multi-switch` is to test separately all the alternative renderings. That done, it is a small matter to add the `multi-case` and `multi-toggle` entries. Here is a style sheet that does most of the rendering. The style sheet in Listing 14.2 uses very little that was not already presented in earlier chapters:

Listing 14.2 *Style Sheet Forms a Basis for the* multi-switch

```
<?xml version='1.0'?>
<xsl:stylesheet version="1.0"
 xmlns:xsl="http://www.w3.org/1999/XSL/Transform"
 xmlns:fo="http://www.w3.org/1999/XSL/Format">

 <xsl:strip-space elements="*"/>
 <xsl:include href="rootrule.xsl"/>

 <xsl:attribute-set name="list-geometry">
  <xsl:attribute name="provisional-distance-between-starts">
   5pc
  </xsl:attribute>
  <xsl:attribute name="provisional-label-separation">
   4pt
  </xsl:attribute>
 </xsl:attribute-set>

 <xsl:template match="middle">
  <xsl:value-of select="text()"/>
  <xsl:text> </xsl:text>
 </xsl:template>

 <xsl:template match="suffix">
```

Listing 14.2 *(continued)*

```
 <xsl:text>, </xsl:text>
 <xsl:value-of select="text()"/>
</xsl:template>

<xsl:template match="@name">
 <xsl:value-of select="."/>
 <xsl:text>, </xsl:text>
</xsl:template>

<xsl:template match="commander|CM|LM">
 <xsl:value-of select="given"/>
 <xsl:text> </xsl:text>
 <xsl:apply-templates select="middle"/>
 <xsl:value-of select="surname"/>
 <xsl:apply-templates select="suffix"/>
</xsl:template>

<xsl:template name="list-item-label">
 <fo:list-item-label end-indent="label-end()">
  <fo:block
   text-align="start"
   font-weight="bold">
   <xsl:text>Apollo </xsl:text>
   <xsl:value-of select="@number"/>
  </fo:block>
 </fo:list-item-label>
</xsl:template>

<xsl:template name="case-expanded">
 <xsl:call-template name="list-item-label"/>
 <fo:list-item-body start-indent="body-start()">
  <fo:block>
   <xsl:value-of select="dates"/>
  </fo:block>
  <fo:block>
   <xsl:text>Commander </xsl:text>
   <xsl:apply-templates select="crew/commander"/>
  </fo:block>
  <fo:block>
   <xsl:text>Command Module </xsl:text>
   <xsl:apply-templates select="crew/CM/@name"/>
```

Listing 14.2 *(continued)*

```
    <xsl:text> pilot </xsl:text>
    <xsl:apply-templates select="crew/CM"/>
   </fo:block>
   <fo:block>
    <xsl:text>Lunar Module </xsl:text>
    <xsl:apply-templates select="crew/LM/@name"/>
    <xsl:text> pilot </xsl:text>
    <xsl:apply-templates select="crew/LM"/>
   </fo:block>
   <fo:block>
    <xsl:apply-templates select="purpose"/>
   </fo:block>
  </fo:list-item-body>
 </xsl:template>

 <xsl:template name="case-collapsed">
  <xsl:call-template name="list-item-label"/>
  <fo:list-item-body start-indent="body-start()">
   <fo:block>
    <xsl:value-of select="dates"/>
   </fo:block>
  </fo:list-item-body>
 </xsl:template>

 <xsl:template match="mission">
  <fo:list-item>
   <xsl:call-template name="case-expanded"/>
  </fo:list-item>
 </xsl:template>

 <xsl:template match="apollo">
  <fo:list-block xsl:use-attribute-sets="list-geometry">
   <xsl:apply-templates/>
  </fo:list-block>
 </xsl:template>

</xsl:stylesheet>
```

One or two new tricks exist here. The following two lines appear separately in the template named `case-expanded`. They process the `name` attribute of the `CM` and `LM` elements if that attribute is present:

```
<xsl:apply-templates select="crew/CM/@name"/>
<xsl:apply-templates select="crew/LM/@name"/>
```

If the `name` attribute is not present, nothing will happen. No output will occur. When a `name` attribute is present, the following template matches it:

```
<xsl:template match="@name">
 <xsl:value-of select="."/>
 <xsl:text>, </xsl:text>
</xsl:template>
```

This template outputs the name, followed by a comma and a space. The benefit of this strategy over a `value-of` construct like `<xsl:value-of select="crew/CM/@name"/>` followed by the `<xsl:text>` is that the comma and the space will not appear when the `CM` does not have a name. The style sheet uses the same strategy for the `middle` and `suffix` elements of crew member names.

The template that matches the `mission` element occurs near the bottom of the listing. Change the third line of that template to test the two cases. The line

```
<xsl:call-template name="case-expanded"/>
```

tests the case when the data item for every Apollo flight is expanded. Figure 14.1 shows the typeset result. Change the value of the `name` property to `case-collapsed`. The style sheet now renders the collapsed view shown in Figure 14.2.

The "J" missions had expanded capacity for lunar exploration, including a greater supply of air and water to enable three moon walks of seven-plus hours. They also included an electric, four-wheeled vehicle to take the astronauts far afield of the landing site. Astronauts Schmitt and Cernan drove about five miles away from the lander on the second walk of the final mission, Apollo 17. The two studied the geology of the moon for three full days.

After you have tested the alternative presentations, you can modify the style sheet to get the toggle behavior. There are two cases for the toggle—expanded and collapsed. Represent this by writing a `multi-switch` FO with two `multi-case` FOs within. A `multi-switch` may have only `multi-case` children. No other FO will do.

Each `multi-case` FO has a `name` property naming the state at which the formatter should select it from among the other cases in the `multi-switch`. The formatter initially displays the first case with the `starting-state` property set to `show`. In fact, the value `show` is the default. If you want the formatter to initially display a `multi-case` other than the first, all cases preceding the desired case must have `starting-state="hide"`.

Apollo 7	October 11-22, 1968 Commander Walter M Schirra Command Module pilot Donn F Eisele Lunar Module pilot R Walter Cunningham First Earth orbital test
Apollo 8	December 21-27, 1968 Commander Frank Borman Command Module pilot James A Lovell, Jr. Lunar Module pilot William A Anders First Lunar orbital test
Apollo 9	March 3-13, 1969 Commander James A McDivitt Command Module Gumdrop, pilot David R Scott Lunar Module Spider, pilot Russell L Schweickart Earth orbital test with space rendevous maneuvers
Apollo 10	May 18-26, 1969 Commander Thomas P Stafford Command Module Charlie Brown, pilot John W Young Lunar Module Snoopy, pilot Eugene A Cernan Lunar orbital test with Lunar Module
Apollo 11	July 16-24, 1969 Commander Neil A Armstrong Command Module Columbia, pilot Michael Collins Lunar Module Eagle, pilot Edwin E Aldrin, Jr. First Moon landing, July 20, 1969; Sea of Tranquility
Apollo 12	November 14-24, 1969 Commander Charles Conrad, Jr. Command Module Yankee Clipper, pilot Richard F Gordon, Jr. Lunar Module Intrepid, pilot Alan L Bean Pinpoint Lunar landing; Ocean of Storms
Apollo 13	April 11-17, 1970 Commander James A Lovell, Jr. Command Module Odyssey, pilot John L Swigert, Jr. Lunar Module Aquarius, pilot Fred W Haise, Jr. Third Lunar landing attempt aborted due to service module explosion.
Apollo 14	January 31-February 9, 1971 Commander Alan B Shepard, Jr. Command Module Kitty Hawk, pilot Stuart A Roosa Lunar Module Anteres, pilot Edgar D Mitchell Third Lunar landing; Fra Mauro, Sea of Rains
Apollo 15	July 26-August 7, 1971 Commander David R Scott Command Module Endeavor, pilot Alfred M Worden Lunar Module Falcon, pilot James B Irwin First extended scientific J-mission; Hadley-Apennine, Sea of Rains
Apollo 16	April 16-27, 1972 Commander John W Young Command Module Casper, pilot Kenneth Mattingly, III Lunar Module Orion, pilot Charles M Duke Second J-mission explored the Decartes highlands
Apollo 17	December 7-19, 1972 Commander Eugene A Cernan Command Module America, pilot Ronald E Evans Lunar Module Challenger, pilot Harrison H Schmitt Last Lunar mission explored Taurus-Littrow near the Sea of Serenity

Figure 14.1

Expanded view of the Apollo mission data.

Apollo 7	October 11-22, 1968
Apollo 8	December 21-27, 1968
Apollo 9	March 3-13, 1969
Apollo 10	May 18-26, 1969
Apollo 11	July 16-24, 1969
Apollo 12	November 14-24, 1969
Apollo 13	April 11-17, 1970
Apollo 14	January 31-February 9, 1971
Apollo 15	July 26-August 7, 1971
Apollo 16	April 16-27, 1972
Apollo 17	December 7-19, 1972

Figure 14.2
Collapsed view of the Apollo mission data.

The content of the `multi-case` is the content typeset for that case. That content may be any content valid in the context where the `multi-switch` appears. If the `multi-switch` appears where only inline content is valid, the content of the `multi-case` must be inline. In this case, the `multi-switch` appears as the first child of a `list-item`. That means that the content of the `multi-case` must consist of a `list-item-label` and `list-item-body`. Listing 14.3 shows the completed template matching each mission. Substitute this for the mission template in Listing 14.2 if you're following along:

Listing 14.3 *Mission Template Implements the* multi-switch

```
<xsl:template match="mission">
 <fo:list-item>
  <fo:multi-switch>
   <fo:multi-case name="collapsed" starting-state="show">
    <fo:multi-toggle switch-to="expanded">
     <xsl:call-template name="case-collapsed"/>
    </fo:multi-toggle>
   </fo:multi-case>
   <fo:multi-case name="expanded">
    <fo:multi-toggle switch-to="collapsed">
     <xsl:call-template name="case-expanded"/>
    </fo:multi-toggle>
   </fo:multi-case>
  </fo:multi-switch>
 </fo:list-item>
</xsl:template>
```

This is the only template that need be changed to effect the toggle behavior. The only part of this not yet explained is the `multi-toggle`. The `multi-toggle` contains content that is active. That is the content that may be clicked. When it is clicked, the formatter changes the current case to the case named by the `switch-to` property of the `multi-toggle`. It then reformats the `multi-switch`, selecting the new case.

A click on the expanded display selects the case with the name `case-collapsed`. A click on the collapsed display selects the case with the name `case-expanded`. The toggle does not expand or collapse every entry. The change occurs entirely within the `multi-switch` ancestor of the `multi-toggle`. It toggles one entry only. Figure 14.3 shows the appearance of the result with one element expanded:

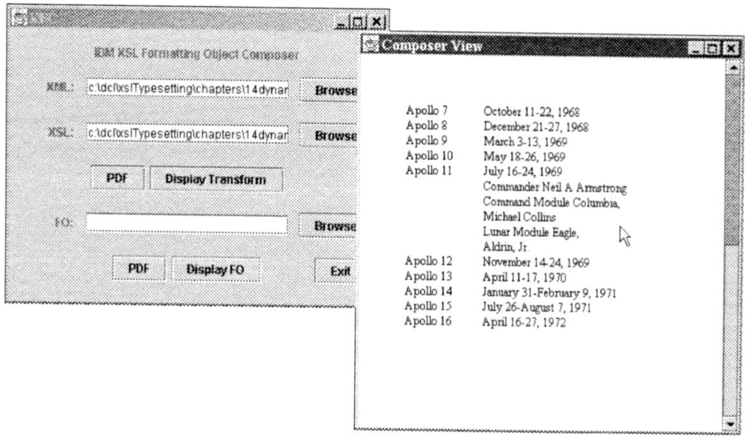

Figure 14.3

An expanding and collapsing list with one item expanded.

An early version of the IBM XFC program from alphaworks (see Chapter 3, "Tools and Implementations") had some support for `multi-switch`. At some point it may have complete support. If you want to experiment with `multi-switch`, that is one place to check for an implementation that supports it.

Nothing prevents you from embedding a `multi-switch` within a `multi-case` to achieve multiple levels of expansion. In this case, the style sheet will look like a combination of the one just demonstrated and the one shown in the Enumerated List example of Chapter 11, "Keeps, Breaks, and Columns." Try modifying that style sheet to add `multi-switch` behavior. If you make that challenge, you're getting to be expert.

Summary

An interactive formatter can potentially provide many dynamic behaviors from link activation to alternating link colors to alterative presentations. You can specify all this in FO without resorting to proprietary extensions, programming, or scripting languages. An interactive formatter may scroll content much the same as a hypertext browser does, and it may introduce scrollbars within areas of the page that overflow their available space.

We've covered just about everything there is to see in XSL FOs. Take it for a flight around the world in the next chapter, "Going Global." After that, you're on your own. Stop at your home port or any port of call to set up shop writing XSL style sheets.

CHAPTER 15

Going Global

One of the great features of XSL FO is that it was designed to typeset any of the world's written languages supported by the Unicode character standard. It can handle Russian and Chinese. It can handle Telagu (an Indic script) and Arabic. Some of these languages are written in different directions. Traditional Chinese is written from the top of the page to the bottom, with the first line beginning on the right side. Today, it is often written left to right. FO can handle it all.

Writing Direction

The distinction between traditional and simplified Chinese arises because more and more publishers and writers of Chinese are changing from writing vertically to writing from left to right and top to bottom, just like English. To understand what that is like for a reader accustomed to traditional Chinese

imagine
we
were
writing
this
text
from
top
to
bottom
and
right
to
left
like
this.

Many American Chinese miss the top-down, left-right traditional Chinese writing. FOs may be a little late to alter the trend. Mao Tse Tung started the trend with the Communist revolution in 1949. Some Chinese think of the left-to-right, top-to-bottom writing direction as Communist. HTML does not support top-to-bottom, right-to-left display, so Web sites have been perpetuating the trend for several years.

FOs provide the `writing-mode` property to control the direction of writing. You may set a value for the `writing-mode` property on the `simple-page-master`, `block-container`, `inline-container`, `table`, or any of the region FOs. Specify the value `lr-tb` to get Latin-style lines reading from left to right and from top to bottom. Specify the value `rl-tb` to get Arabic- or Hebrew-style lines reading from right to left and from top to bottom.

The first letter pair in the value for the `writing-mode` property is the pair before the hyphen. That pair determines the inline-progression direction, or `ipd`. The `ipd` may be any of `lr`, `rl`, `tb`, or `bt`. Those four values correspond to left-to-right, right-to-left, top-to-bottom, and bottom-to-top directions of writing for the lines.

The letter pair after the hyphen determines the block-progression direction, or `bpd`. The `bpd` may be one of the directions at right angles to the `ipd`. If the `ipd` is `lr` or `rl`, the `bpd` may be `tb` or `bt`. If the `ipd` is `tb` or `bt`, the `bpd` may be `lr` or `rl`.

These combinations lead to eight possible values for the writing mode. They are `lr-tb`, `lr-bt`, `rl-tb`, `rl-bt`, `tb-rl`, `tb-lr`, `bt-rl`, `bt-lr`. The three required for the most widely recognized printed languages are `lr-tb` for Latin, `rl-tb` for Arabic and Hebrew, and `tb-rl` for Chinese, Korean, and Japanese. Writers may abbreviate those three to only the first two letters, but there's really no reason to do so. Use the full designations and practice the mantra— inhale, ipd; exhale, bpd. Follow the eyes. The direction they move to read lines of words is first. The direction they move to read from one line to the next is second.

Why not reproduce an example of traditional Chinese? The *Tao Te Ching* is a philosophical work written in the sixth century B.C. by the sagacious archivist, Lao Tsu. Following are the first few lines of the Tao in an XML source:

```
<?xml version="1.0" encoding="UTF-8"?>
<tao>
  <chapter number="1">
&#x9053;&#x53ef;&#x9053;&#x975e;&#x5e38;
&#x9053;&#x540d;&#x53ef;&#x540d;&#x975e;
&#x5e38;&#x540d;&#x65e0;&#x540d;&#x5929;
&#x5730;&#x4e4b;&#x59cb;&#x6709;&#x540d;
&#x4e07;&#x7269;&#x4e4b;&#x6bcd;
  </chapter>
</tao>
```

All the Unicode Chinese characters here are shown as character entities because they would otherwise typeset as gibberish. This will also help you easily reproduce the input. The lines include breaks to keep them within the page width limit. The file would more commonly contain UTF-8 encoded Unicode characters without line breaks. The file used to produce the output shown in Figure 15.1 had no line breaks between the begin and end tags of the chapter element.

Listing 15.1 contains a simple style sheet to typeset the source. Rather than import `rootrule.xsl`, as many of the other style sheets in the book have, this style sheet produces the full layout declaration. This layout declaration defines a page size and a writing mode in the `simple-page-master`:

Listing 15.1 *Stylesheet to Typeset Some Traditional Chinese*

```
<?xml version="1.0"?>
<xsl:stylesheet version="1.0"
 xmlns:xsl="http://www.w3.org/1999/XSL/Transform"
 xmlns:fo="http://www.w3.org/1999/XSL/Format">

  <xsl:strip-space elements="*"/>
  <xsl:include href="tao-style.xsl"/>

  <xsl:template match="/">
    <fo:root>
      <fo:layout-master-set>
        <fo:simple-page-master master-name="page"
```

Listing 15.1 *(continued)*

```
         page-width="4in" page-height="5in"
         writing-mode="tb-rl">
          <fo:region-body region-name="body"
           xsl:use-attribute-sets="body-margin"/>
        </fo:simple-page-master>
      </fo:layout-master-set>
      <fo:page-sequence master-reference="page">
        <fo:flow flow-name="body">
          <xsl:apply-templates/>
        </fo:flow>
      </fo:page-sequence>
    </fo:root>
  </xsl:template>

  <xsl:template match="chapter">
    <fo:block
     xsl:use-attribute-sets="blue-border"
     font-weight="bold"
     font-size="24pt">
      <xsl:apply-templates/>
    </fo:block>
  </xsl:template>

</xsl:stylesheet>
```

The style sheet does not differ much in other respects from other style sheets. The `simple-page-master` sets the `writing-mode` property to `tb-lr`; top-to-bottom, left-to-right; ipd, bpd. Remember the mantra? Have a look at Figure 15.1 to see the beautiful result:

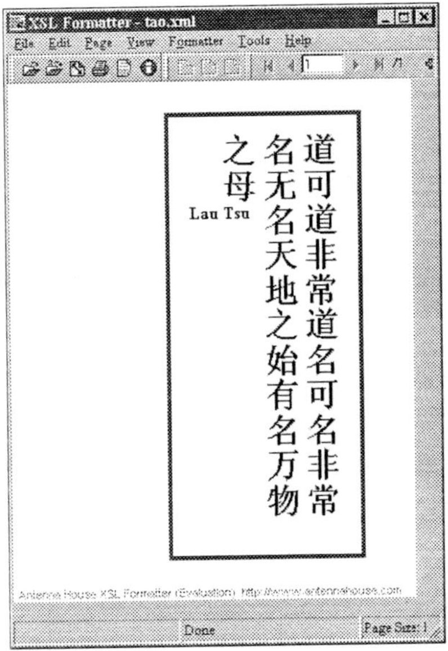

Figure 15.1
The beginning of the Tao Te Ching *in traditional Chinese.*

For completeness, Listing 15.2 contains the attribute sets read by the previous listing to style the output. By now you would have no trouble coming up with this on your own:

Listing 15.2 *The Style File* tao-style.xsl *Included in Listing 15.1.*

```
<?xml version="1.0"?>
<xsl:stylesheet version="1.0"
 xmlns:xsl="http://www.w3.org/1999/XSL/Transform">

  <xsl:attribute-set name="body-margin">
    <xsl:attribute name="margin-top">0.5in</xsl:attribute>
    <xsl:attribute name="margin-bottom">0.6in</xsl:attribute>
    <xsl:attribute name="margin-left">0.5in</xsl:attribute>
    <xsl:attribute name="margin-right">0.5in</xsl:attribute>
  </xsl:attribute-set>
```

Listing 15.2 *(continued)*

```
  <xsl:attribute-set name="blue-border">
    <xsl:attribute name="padding-start">1pc</xsl:attribute>
    <xsl:attribute name="padding-end">1pc</xsl:attribute>
    <xsl:attribute name="padding-before">1pc</xsl:attribute>
    <xsl:attribute name="padding-after">1pc</xsl:attribute>
    <xsl:attribute name="border-before-style">solid</xsl:attribute>
    <xsl:attribute name="border-before-color">blue</xsl:attribute>
    <xsl:attribute name="border-after-style">solid</xsl:attribute>
    <xsl:attribute name="border-after-color">blue</xsl:attribute>
    <xsl:attribute name="border-start-style">solid</xsl:attribute>
    <xsl:attribute name="border-start-color">blue</xsl:attribute>
    <xsl:attribute name="border-end-style">solid</xsl:attribute>
    <xsl:attribute name="border-end-color">blue</xsl:attribute>
  </xsl:attribute-set>

</xsl:stylesheet>
```

Altering the Writing Mode

You may set the writing mode on the page master or on a region. Different regions may have different writing modes. In addition, the `block-container` and `inline-container` FOs accept the `writing-mode` property. The following template alters the writing mode with an `inline-container`. Add it to the style sheet given in Listing 15.2:

```
<xsl:template match="author">
  <fo:inline-container
   inline-progression-dimension="4pc"
   alignment-baseline="text-before-edge"
   font-size="12pt"
   writing-mode="lr-tb">
   <fo:block>
    <xsl:apply-templates/>
   </fo:block>
  </fo:inline-container>
</xsl:template>
```

The template matches an `author` element that you can add to the input just before the closing tag for the `chapter` element, as follows:

```
<author>Lau Tsu</author>
```

Figure 15.2 shows the result. The setting for `alignment-baseline` keeps the `inline-container` aligned with the before edge of the line. The "Alignment of Scripts" section near the end of this chapter describes the `alignment-baseline` property more fully:

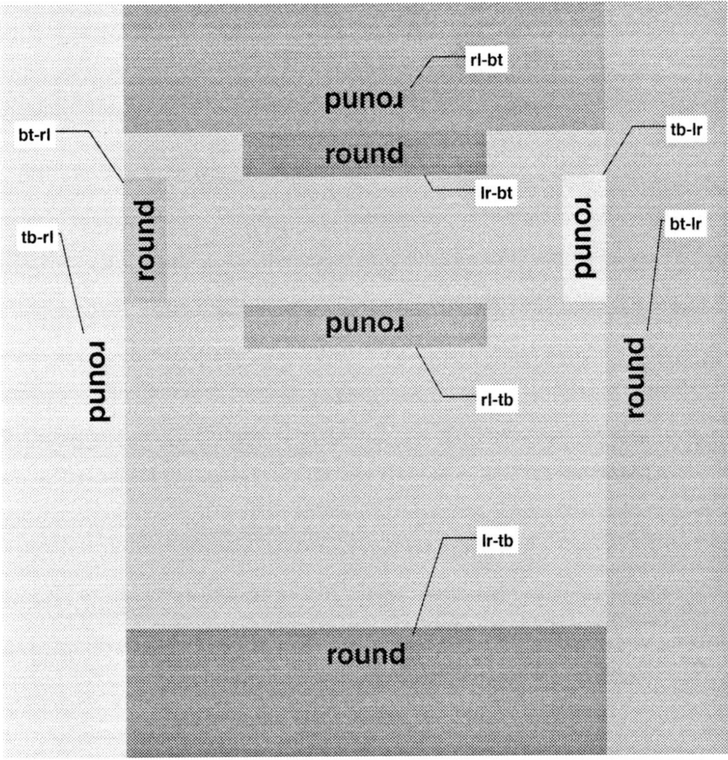

Figure 15.2
Writing mode on an inline-container.

Mixing Scripts

Some scripts write right to left (rtl), such as Arabic and Hebrew. The writing mode sets the direction of writing on a line, either left to right (ltr) or right to left. The `direction` property on an inline may override the writing direction within that inline FO.

The Unicode standard specifies an algorithm called bidi (short for bidirectional) that will reorder rtl text that occurs in a context with writing direction ltr, and vice versa. When the direction is rtl and the formatter encounters ltr text, the bidi algorithm reorders the ltr text so that it formats ltr. This works almost 100% of the time the way it is supposed to and the way you expect it to. Rarely, you may want to override the behavior of the bidi algorithm.

The `unicode-bidi` property can override the text reversal. Its default value is `normal`. That value allows the bidi algorithm to do its thing. The values `embed` and `bidi-override` will alter the behavior of the bidi algorithm.

The value `embed` sets the writing direction to the value of the `direction` property, regardless of the direction determined by the bidi algorithm. It resets the direction currently in use by the bidi algorithm, but allows the algorithm to go on reordering if it encounters some text that normally writes opposite the new direction.

The value `bidi-override` also sets the direction according to the current value of the `direction` property. Unlike `embed`, the bidi algorithm is essentially disabled and all text will appear in order for the direction given.

Alignment of Scripts

Different scripts such as Indic, Arabic, Latin, and CJK align along different baselines. Latin scripts align along an alphabetic baseline. Many Indic scripts align at the top, along a hanging baseline. The CJK scripts align on an ideographic baseline.

When scripts mix on a line, there is potential for adjustments to determine which baselines will align. This changes the vertical positioning of some of the text. The `alignment-adjust` and `alignment-baseline` properties interact to determine which of the baselines align between two elements. The `baseline-shift` property will move the alignment up or down. Use it to create superscripts and subscripts.

You can experiment if you have a result that contains mixed scripts. The example that produced Figure 15.2 uses the `alignment-baseline` property to control alignment of the author's name with the Chinese text.

Summary

This is the final chapter of this adventure with XSL FOs. I hope you have had an entertaining and informative trip. We started in Chapter 4 with a simple greeting, Hello XSL World. We end with a visit to China to experience the truly global scope of XSL FO.

I hope that you have enjoyed the journey. You have joined a noble lineage. In the fifteenth century, Johannes Gutenberg invented movable type. Before then, every book was copied by hand. Books were rare. Writing belonged to an elite group while the rest enjoyed a purely oral tradition. Gutenberg's moveable type enabled him to make dozens of copies of a printed work in the time it took a monk to transcribe two copies.

Gutenberg started a written tradition that is a cornerstone for the richly informed and knowledgeable society we enjoy today. As a person skilled with XSL, you perpetuate that tradition. Every time you typeset something, you contribute to the foundation of our successful civilization—a freely informed and knowledgeable public. Keep up the good work.

APPENDIX A
Basics of the XSL Transform

The W3C XSL working group designed XSL as a styling facility in two major parts—Transformations and FO. The FOs and their properties capture the semantics of presentation. The transformation language provides a way to convert a content form into a presentation form.

XSL Transformations (XSLT) had attracted use as a generalized XML-to-XML transformation language by the time it became a W3C recommendation in November of 1999. That recommendation states that XSLT was designed primarily with function needed for styling, however far it went as a generalized XML-to-XML transform. Nevertheless, it has been widely adopted for that purpose.

The style sheet transformation language may stand on its own; however, FOs were never intended to be written anywhere other than as result elements in a style sheet. As far as FO is concerned, there is no separation from the transform. It is almost inconceivable that someone would write an entire document, such as a chapter of this book, using FOs. Working with FO means working with all of XSL as an integrated whole. Working with FO means working with style sheets.

The Processing Model

XSLT works by matching elements in the input, outputting something, and then matching further elements in the input. It allows the input to drive the structure of the result. Here is an input example that will help illustrate this processing behavior:

```
<?xml version="1.0"?>
<house>
 <carton>
  <eggs/>
 </carton>
</house>
```

An XSL style sheet consists of templates. Each template matches some part of the input and produces some part of the output. Here is a very small style sheet with one template that matches the `<house>` element of the input sample. The body of the template creates an element named `<t1>`. That will help you identify output from the first template:

```
<?xml version='1.0'?>
<xsl:stylesheet version="1.0"
 xmlns:xsl="http://www.w3.org/1999/XSL/Transform">

  <xsl:template match="house">
    <t1>
      <xsl:text>Template matched on a</xsl:text>
    </t1>
  </xsl:template>

</xsl:stylesheet>
```

All style sheets are XML. The first line identifies this as an XML source, and the second line opens the style sheet with a style sheet element. This element contains the XSLT version for the style sheet. As of this writing there is only the one recommended version.

The third line declares a namespace prefix of `xsl` for all the XSL transform elements. This means that everything you read in the style sheet that begins with the characters `xsl:` has to do with transformation.

The five lines in the middle represent an XSL "template." The match attribute on the template represents the name of an element from the input. The template will respond to input elements with that name. In this case, the template will respond to elements from the input with name `a`.

The XSL `text` element declares verbatim text that will appear in the output. Use this element especially when you need leading or trailing white space or embedded linefeed characters in the result. XSLT otherwise ignores leading space and newlines.

The result of running an XSLT processor with the preceding two inputs is this:

```
<?xml version="1.0" encoding="UTF-8"?>
<t1>Template matched on a</t1>
```

The transform engine happily outputs an XML declaration. XSLT starts with XML and outputs XML by default. It matched the `<house>` element, output the `<t1>` element containing the text, and then terminated. When a template matches an input element and executes we will say that it "fires." The input element is the trigger. The body of the template is the response.

Suppose you add a template to the style sheet to match the `<carton>` element as follows:

```
  <xsl:template match="carton">
    <t2>
      <xsl:text>Template matched on ab</xsl:text>
    </t2>
  </xsl:template>
```

When you run the transform, you will find that the output is the same. This is odd that nothing changed. Why did this not match the `<carton>` element and output another line of text? Why did the template that matches `<carton>` not fire?

The answer is that the transform engine matched the `<house>` element, output the text content of that template, and received no further instruction to do anything else. It therefore stopped altogether and did nothing more.

Oddly, if the template matching the `<carton>` element was the only template in the style sheet, it would then fire and the output would be the following:

```
<?xml version="1.0" encoding="UTF-8"?>

 <t2>Template matched on ab</t2>
```

Try writing the template as follows and run it against the sample input. Somehow the transform engine gets past the input `<house>` element, where it has no instruction from the style sheet to do anything. It then gets to the input `<carton>` where it finds a template to match. Here is the entire style sheet, just to ensure that you're in synch:

```
<?xml version='1.0'?>
<xsl:stylesheet version="1.0"
 xmlns:xsl="http://www.w3.org/1999/XSL/Transform">
```

```
  <xsl:template match="carton">
    <t2>
      <xsl:text>Template matched on ab</xsl:text>
    </t2>
  </xsl:template>

</xsl:stylesheet>
```

Set aside why that works for a minute and add back the rule that matched <house>. Modify that rule by adding an XSL `apply-templates` command as follows:

```
  <xsl:template match="house">
    <t1>
      <xsl:text>Template matched on a</xsl:text>
      <xsl:apply-templates/>
    </t1>
  </xsl:template>
```

Run the transform, and the result output now looks like this:

```
<?xml version="1.0" encoding="UTF-8"?>
<t1>Template matched on a
 <t2>Template matched on ab</t2>
</t1>
```

Both templates matched some input and responded by producing their text content. This worked because the XSL `apply-templates` command caused the transform engine to process the child elements of <house>. That means it processed the input element <carton> and executed the template that matches <carton>.

Consider now what would happen if you changed the template that matches <carton> to a template that matches <eggs>. The element <eggs> is nested at a second level below the template that matches <house>. If you guess that it will fire, you guessed right. It fires for the same reason the template that matched <carton> fired in the absence of any other templates.

The processor has default behavior for elements not matched by any template in the style sheet. Whenever the processor has an element not matched by any template, it continues to examine children of the unmatched element.

In the example that matched <carton> only, the processor found no template to match <house>. It then went on to examine the children of <house> and found a template that matched <carton>.

In the example that matched <house> and <eggs> the processor found no template to match <carton>. It therefore processed the children of <carton> and found a template to match <eggs>.

In the example that matched <house> but not <carton> the processor found a rule to match <house>. That rule cut it short. The rule did not contain an XSLT `apply-templates` directive to continue processing of the children.

That completes a first discussion of the fundamental processing model of the XSL transform. The processor begins with the root element of the input. It finds the first template that matches the root element and fires that template.

When the processor reaches an XSL `apply-templates` directive, it processes all children of the currently matched node, finding templates that match those children. When the processor does not find a template to match an element, it processes the children of that element by default.

Reorganizing the Input

The preceding section hinted at one or two methods of reordering or reorganizing elements from the input. This section will now look explicitly at methods for ignoring elements from the input, adding levels to the output not present in the input, and for processing input elements in a different order than that in which they appear.

Skipping Elements

The XSL transform can prune whole subtrees from the input and ignore them completely. It can also ignore individual elements while processing all their children. You have already seen examples of both in the section that illustrated the processing model. This section will revisit these pruning behaviors with a new focus on the practical effects rather than on how the processing progresses.

Consider the following input. The <carton> element occurs at multiple levels. The <fridge> element contains a repetition of the first subtree of the <house> element:

```
<?xml version="1.0"?>
<house>
 <carton>
  <eggs/>
 </carton>
 <fridge>
   <carton>
```

```
      <eggs/>
    </carton>
  </fridge>
</house>
```

The repeated subtree is the one that has an <eggs> element within an <carton> element. The style sheet of Listing A.1 will eliminate the repeated subtree when it occurs beneath the <fridge> element. It does so by matching the <fridge> element and doing no processing:

Listing A.1 *A Style Sheet That Filters Input*

```
<?xml version='1.0'?>
<xsl:stylesheet version="1.0"
 xmlns:xsl="http://www.w3.org/1999/XSL/Transform">

  <xsl:output indent="yes"/>

  <xsl:template match="house">
    <have-house>
      <xsl:apply-templates/>
    </have-house>
  </xsl:template>

  <xsl:template match="carton">
    <have-carton>
      <xsl:apply-templates/>
    </have-carton>
  </xsl:template>

  <xsl:template match="eggs">
    <have-eggs>
      <xsl:apply-templates/>
    </have-eggs>
  </xsl:template>

  <xsl:template match="fridge"/>

</xsl:stylesheet>
```

The last template before the close of the style sheet does the deed. It matches the <fridge> element and then does nothing. No further processing of children occurs beneath this node. The output appears as follows:

```
<?xml version="1.0" encoding="UTF-8"?>
<have-house>
 <have-carton>
  <have-eggs/>
 </have-carton>

</have-house>
```

The output may even has a blank line in place of the missing subtree. To get only the `<fridge>` element without the subtree, adjust the last template as follows:

```
<xsl:template match="fridge">
  <have-fridge/>
</xsl:template>
```

The revised template outputs the `<have-fridge>` element, but contains no `apply-templates` to further process children of the `<fridge>` element. The result output looks like this:

```
<?xml version="1.0" encoding="UTF-8"?>
<have-house>
 <have-carton>
  <have-eggs/>
 </have-carton>
 <have-fridge/>
</have-house>
```

The third possibility is to have the `<fridge>` element output nothing but process all its children. Do this by modifying that template once again, as follows:

```
<xsl:template match="fridge">
  <xsl:apply-templates/>
</xsl:template>
```

In this case, the equivalent behavior would be achieved by deleting the template altogether. That is because the template as now written has the same behavior that results when the processor finds no match for an element. It processes all the children of that element. The result output contains the `<have-carton>` subtree repeated twice, like this:

```
<?xml version="1.0" encoding="UTF-8"?>
<have-house>
 <have-carton>
  <have-eggs/>
 </have-carton>
```

```
    <have-carton>
      <have-eggs/>
    </have-carton>

</have-house>
```

Note that this result, produced with Xalan Java 2.0.1, contains phantom space for the skipped element and extra indentation for the repeated subtree. There are two reasons for this. The first is that the processor by default treats the newlines and spaces from the input as text. The second is that the default template for matching text copies the text to the output.

The best way to eliminate the phantom space is to ask the processor to ignore it. XSL contains the special `skip-space` directive for this purpose. Use the XSL `strip-space` directive to have the processor ignore leading and trailing spaces and newlines in the input. The `strip-space` directive accepts an `elements` attribute that lists all elements within which the processor should ignore the space. Place the directive below the style sheet element, before any template elements. The following construction occurs many times in the style sheets of the book:

```
<xsl:strip-space elements="*"/>
```

That construction has the processor ignore space and newlines in all elements. Include it inside the style sheet element before the first template. Delete the `<xsl:output indent="yes"/>` directive and the output closes up, as follows:

```
<?xml version="1.0" encoding="UTF-8"?>
<have-house><have-carton><have-eggs/></have-carton><have-carton><have-eggs/>
➥</have-carton></have-house>
```

That is exactly what you want for FO. Chapter 7, "White Space and Line Handling," discusses in detail why it is usually best not to pass along white space from the input when styling.

Extracting a Subtree

Consider again the example of the preceding section. Suppose you would like to have the `<carton>` subtree within the `<fridge>` element produce content outside of that element rather than within it. Here is the input:

```
<?xml version="1.0"?>
<house>
 <carton>
  <eggs/>
```

```
 </carton>
 <fridge>
   <carton>
     <eggs/>
   </carton>
 </fridge>
</house>
```

The desired output places the <have-fridge> element before, rather than around, the <have-carton> subtree—like this:

```
<?xml version="1.0" encoding="UTF-8"?>
<have-house>
 <have-carton>
  <have-eggs/>
 </have-carton>
 <have-fridge/>
   <have-carton>
     <have-eggs/>
   </have-carton>

</have-house>
```

The method for achieving this in the XSL source is as follows. This template places the <have-fridge> element before, rather than around, the apply-templates:

```
  <xsl:template match="fridge">
    <have-fridge/>
    <xsl:apply-templates/>
  </xsl:template>
```

By now you may be catching on that the structure of the output from a style sheet directly follows the structure of the elements within the templates. The apply-templates element is a sort of include, placeholder, or opening into which further templates pour further output.

Adding Elements

An XSL template may add any number of elements it likes when matching a single element of input. It can produce any arbitrary XML. Here is a simple input sample:

```
<?xml version="1.0"?>
<house>
 <carton/>
```

```
  <toaster/>
</house>
```

That is not much, and this is an example taken in the abstract, but a style sheet can do something more with it. The style sheet shown in Listing A.2 expands the `<carton>` element into the header and the `<toaster>` element into the body of a styled document:

Listing A.2 *A Style Sheet That Expands Input*

```
<?xml version='1.0'?>
<xsl:stylesheet version="1.0"
 xmlns:xsl="http://www.w3.org/1999/XSL/Transform">

  <xsl:template match="house">
    <styled-output>
      <xsl:apply-templates/>
    </styled-output>
  </xsl:template>

  <xsl:template match="carton">
    <head-material>
      <title>Title Text</title>
      <version>1</version>
    </head-material>
  </xsl:template>

  <xsl:template match="toaster">
    <body-material>
      <heading>A heading</heading>
      <block>Some content in a block
      within the body of the styled result.
      </block>
    </body-material>
  </xsl:template>

</xsl:stylesheet>
```

The `head-material` and the `body-material` subtrees are in no way present in the input. The style sheet manufactures them completely using the input elements as triggers only. The first template, the one that matches `<house>`, places the root element that will hold all the rest of the content. The other two manufacture content when the processor encounters an `<carton>` or `<toaster>` element. The result is a perfectly plausible styled document:

```
<?xml version="1.0" encoding="UTF-8"?>
<styled-output>
 <head-material><title>Title Text</title><version>1</version></head-material>
 <body-material><heading>A heading</heading><block>Some content in a block
      within the body of the styled result.
      </block></body-material>
</styled-output>
```

Note that all the line breaks come from the input, except for line breaks from text within an element of the style sheet. This is still a bit of a mystery. The section further on, called "Processing Text," will address some of the text mysteries. First, there's one more detail to reveal about `apply-templates`.

Ordering Element Processing

The `apply-templates` operation in an XSL style sheet gathers all the children of the currently matched element of input and processes them in order, one at a time. It starts the matching process with every one of the children of the current element.

Sometimes you might want to process only some of the children of an element. Sometimes you might want to process the children of an element in an order different from the order in which they appear in the input. The `apply-templates` operation accepts an attribute named `select`. That attribute contains a formula for selecting specific children, for narrowing the selection from all the children to just some of the children of the current element.

Now consider this input. It has a root element with three children, in order `<carton>`, `<toaster>`, and `<fridge>`:

```
<?xml version="1.0"?>
<house>
 <carton/>
 <toaster/>
 <fridge/>
</house>
```

The style sheet of Listing A.3 reorders the three children of `<house>`. It does so by explicitly selecting each child in the `select` attribute of the `apply-templates` operator:

Listing A.3 *A Style Sheet Reorders Elements*

```
<?xml version='1.0'?>
<xsl:stylesheet version="1.0"
 xmlns:xsl="http://www.w3.org/1999/XSL/Transform">
```

Listing A.3 *(continued)*

```
  <xsl:template match="house">
    <have-house>
      <xsl:apply-templates select="fridge"/>
      <xsl:apply-templates select="carton"/>
      <xsl:apply-templates select="toaster"/>
    </have-house>
  </xsl:template>

  <xsl:template match="carton|toaster|fridge">
    <xsl:copy-of select="."/>
  </xsl:template>

</xsl:stylesheet>
```

The second template contains two new tricks as well. It matches any of the three elements `<carton>`, `<toaster>`, or `<fridge>` using the `or` operator, `'|'`. Its content template copies the currently selected node to the output using the XSL `copy-of` command. The result looks like this:

```
<?xml version="1.0" encoding="UTF-8"?>
<have-house><fridge/><carton/><toaster/></have-house>
```

The `<fridge>` element precedes the `<carton>` element because the template matching `<house>` selected it first for processing. The `<carton>` and `<toaster>` elements follow likewise in the order of selection.

Processing Text

The XML recommendation refers to text within an element as PCDATA or CDATA. We also sometimes call it a "text node." By any name, text has a special place in the processing of a style sheet. First, the processor has a default behavior of copying text to the output. That behavior gives expected results, rather than surprising results. You probably did not think twice in the earlier examples that the text appeared in the output.

The style sheet can match a text node from the input as easily as it matches an element. Use the `text()` function to match a text node. Here are two examples:

```
<xsl:template match="text()"/>
<xsl:template match="carton/text()"/>
```

The first example matches any text node. Its effect in a style sheet is to suppress all text. The second example matches a text node child of an <carton> element. Its effect in a style sheet is to suppress text within an <carton>. The following input will serve to demonstrate:

```
<?xml version="1.0"?>
<house>
 <carton>Text within the &lt;carton></carton>
 <toaster>Text within the &lt;toaster>
   pastry><pastry>Text within the &lt;pastry></pastry>
 </toaster>
</house>
```

The following simple style sheet places the text from the input elements within blocks. Try it "as is" first to verify that the output contains all the text, as expected:

```
<?xml version='1.0'?>
<xsl:stylesheet version="1.0"
 xmlns:xsl="http://www.w3.org/1999/XSL/Transform">

  <xsl:template match="carton|toaster|pastry">
    <block><xsl:apply-templates/></block>
  </xsl:template>

</xsl:stylesheet>
```

Now add one of the preceding templates that matched text. Start with the first, `<xsl:template match="text()"/>`. All the text from the input will disappear from the output:

```
<?xml version="1.0" encoding="UTF-8"?>
<block/><block><block/></block>
```

Now substitute the second template example for the first. Replace the template that matches `text()` with the template `<xsl:template match="carton/text()"/>`. Now only the text within the <carton> element disappears:

```
<?xml version="1.0" encoding="UTF-8"?>

 <block/>
 <block>Text within the &lt;toaster&gt;
   <block>Text within the &lt;pastry&gt;</block>
 </block>
```

The empty block in the preceding output came from the `<carton>` element. The processor copied the text nodes from the other elements into the blocks generated by them. The `apply-templates` command within the block picks up the text nodes.

Pulling Text

XSL specifies an operator that will expand to the text nodes nested within an element, which means that you can still get the text content of a node, even if you suppress copying using one of the methods just discussed. Use the XSL `value-of` operation to copy all the text node children of an element to the result.

Begin with the sample input used previously, repeated here:

```
<?xml version="1.0"?>
<house>
 <carton>Text within the &lt;carton></carton>
 <toaster>Text within the &lt;toaster>
   pastry><pastry>Text within the &lt;pastry></pastry>
 </toaster>
</house>
```

Apply the following style sheet to the sample input. It matches the `<house>` element only and uses the `value-of` command to extract the text content of the `<carton>` element. It does not do any further processing of the input after matching the `<house>` element:

```
<?xml version='1.0'?>
<xsl:stylesheet version="1.0"
 xmlns:xsl="http://www.w3.org/1999/XSL/Transform">

  <xsl:template match="house">
    <block><xsl:value-of select="carton"/></block>
  </xsl:template>

</xsl:stylesheet>
```

The result of running the sample style sheet against the sample input is one line of text within a block. The block comes from the body of the template that matched the `<house>` element. The text comes from the XSL `value-of` applied to the selected `<carton>` element:

```
<?xml version="1.0" encoding="UTF-8"?>
<block>Text within the &lt;ab&gt;</block>
```

The next result may surprise you. Modify the template matching `<house>` so that the `value-of` operator selects the `<toaster>` element instead of the `<carton>` element. The new template will look as follows. Only the value of the select attribute has changed:

```
<xsl:template match="house">
  <block><xsl:value-of select="toaster"/></block>
</xsl:template>
```

You may expect the text value of the `<toaster>` element to contain only the immediate text node children of the element. In fact, it contains the concatenation of all the text node children of the subtree rooted at the `<toaster>` element:

```
<?xml version="1.0" encoding="UTF-8"?>
<block>Text within the &lt;toaster&gt;
   Text within the &lt;pastry&gt;
 </block>
```

Use the `value-of` operator to extract text when you do not want to match templates. Use the `apply-templates` operator when you want to match templates to the children of an element.

Generating Text

Earlier examples in this appendix included text in the content of a style sheet template that likewise appeared in the result document. XSL provides the `text` command to make text output explicit. The main advantage of the `text` command is that it helps control extra newlines and white space in the result. Begin with an example as follows:

```
<?xml version="1.0"?>
<house>
 <carton>
   Text within the &lt;carton>
 </carton>
 <toaster>
   Text within the &lt;toaster>
 </toaster>
</house>
```

Listing A.4 presents a style sheet that has two templates.

Listing A.4 *A Style Sheet That Demonstrates* xsl:text

```
<?xml version='1.0'?>
<xsl:stylesheet version="1.0"
 xmlns:xsl="http://www.w3.org/1999/XSL/Transform">

  <xsl:template match="carton">
    <block>
      <xsl:apply-templates/>
      This is text from the template
      matching &lt;carton>
    </block>
  </xsl:template>

  <xsl:template match="toaster">
    <block>
      <xsl:apply-templates/>
      <xsl:text>This is text from the template
      matching &lt;toaster></xsl:text>
    </block>
  </xsl:template>
</xsl:stylesheet>
```

The result contains two blocks. The first block contains newline characters present in the text nodes of the style sheet. The second does not.

```
<?xml version="1.0" encoding="UTF-8"?>

 <block>
   Text within the &lt;carton&gt;

      This is text from the template
      matching &lt;carton&gt;
    </block>
 <block>
   Text within the &lt;toaster&gt;
 This is text from the template
      matching &lt;toaster&gt;</block>
```

The XSL processor strips away any text nodes that contain only white space before generating the output. In the first template, the text node after the `apply-templates` contains newline characters as well as non-white-space characters. The only text node in the second template that is not entirely made of white space is within the XSL `text` element. The output contains only the newline characters that occur within the XSL `text` element.

Processing Attributes

There will be times in a style sheet when you will want to test the value of an attribute or copy the value of an attribute to the output. XSL uses an "at" symbol (@) to prefix the name of an attribute and distinguish it from the name of an element.

First, have a look at a few tests. The match expression in `<xsl:template match="locale[@type]">` selects `locale` elements that have a `type` attribute. The expression in `<xsl:template match="locale[@type="int"]">` selects `locale` elements with a type attribute set to the value `int`. The bracket notation denotes a test. The test must be true for the element preceding the opening bracket ([). The template will not fire if the test is not true.

You may also use the @ notation with XSL `value-of` to output the value of an attribute. The expression `<xsl:value-of select='@type'/>` outputs the value of the type attribute on the currently selected node.

Put all this together in an example, as follows. Begin with some XML source that has an element without an attribute and two elements with the same attribute but with different values:

```
<?xml version="1.0"?>
<parent>
  <locale>
    has no attribute
  </locale>
  <locale type="int">
    has attribute value
  </locale>
  <locale type="ext">
    has attribute value
  </locale>
</parent>
```

Now write a template to match each of the three `locale` elements. If the element has a `type` attribute, output the value of that attribute. The style sheet also demonstrates the use of the XSL `priority` attribute in a template, although priority isn't used often in the examples of the book. Listing A.5 has the content of the style sheet:

Listing A.5 *A Style Sheet That Demonstrates Attribute Handling*

```
<?xml version='1.0'?>
<xsl:stylesheet version="1.0"
 xmlns:xsl="http://www.w3.org/1999/XSL/Transform">

  <xsl:output indent="yes"/>

  <xsl:template match="/">
    <root>
      <xsl:apply-templates/>
    </root>
  </xsl:template>

  <xsl:template match="locale[@type='int']" priority="2">
    <t1>
      <xsl:value-of select="."/>
      <xsl:value-of select="@type"/>
    </t1>
  </xsl:template>

  <xsl:template match="locale[@type]" priority="1">
    <t2>
      <xsl:value-of select="."/>
      <xsl:value-of select="@type"/>
    </t2>
  </xsl:template>

  <xsl:template match="locale">
    <t3>
      <xsl:value-of select="."/>
    </t3>
  </xsl:template>

</xsl:stylesheet>
```

The first template of the style sheet matches the `root` element and outputs a root element for the result. That root element serves as a container for the elements output by the other templates. Remember than an XML document must have one, and only one, element at its root.

The second template matches the `locale` element with a `type` attribute set to the value `int`. It has a priority setting greater than the default of zero because it would otherwise conflict with the next two templates. Both of those also select `locale` elements.

The third template matches a `locale` element that has a `type` attribute set to any value. It has a priority value less than the first but higher than the last.

The fourth template matches any `locale`, whether or not it has an attribute. This matches all three elements, but has a lower priority than the prior templates. Those will take precedence if they also match. The result of running the style sheet of Listing A.5 against the sample input will look something like the following:

```
<?xml version="1.0" encoding="UTF-8"?>
<root>
  <t3>
    has no attribute
  </t3>
  <t1>
    has attribute value
  int</t1>
  <t2>
    has attribute value
  ext</t2>
</root>
```

Never mind the strange indentation. That is the perennial white space and newline problem cropping up again. What is germane here is the number of the "t" element output by the transform. The `<t3>` template matched the input element with no attribute. The `<t1>` template matched the input element with a `type` attribute equal to `int`. The `<t2>` template matched the input element with `type` attribute equal to `ext`.

Summary

This appendix should have provided enough background about XSLT to help you understand the basics of an XSL transform. The examples in the book apply the transform to produce FO. Knowing the fundamentals of XSLT will help you follow the examples. However, there is more to know about the transform language than was covered in this appendix. You will pick up some of that by way of example through working with the rest of the book. The rest is the subject of numerous books and Web resources about XSLT.

The best place to get going is to try applying the style sheet language to actual styling tasks. Chapter 4, "Hello XSL World," introduces a transform that produces the first output with XSL FO. If you have not done so already, that is a great place to go from here.

APPENDIX B

A Concise Listing of Formatting Objects

This appendix provides summary information about Formatting Objects (FO) for quick reference. It contains two major sections. The first organizes the FOs into functional groups. The second provides an alphabetical listing of FOs. Each entry in the listing includes a short description followed by a list of properties that apply to the FO described.

The property lists refer to property groups when all the properties in a group apply. The applicable groups appear first, before individual properties. Appendix C, "A Concise Listing of Properties," contains descriptions of the property groups and lists the properties that belong to them.

Formatting Object Categories

Declarations and Pagination and Layout Formatting Objects

The FOs in this group form the top-level structure of the FO document, define page layout masters, and define sequences of page layout masters for the document.

`fo:color-profile, fo:conditional-page-master-reference, fo:declarations, fo:flow, fo:layout-master-set, fo:page-sequence, fo:page-sequence-master, fo:region-after, fo:region-before, fo:region-body, fo:region-end, fo:region-start, fo:repeatable-page-master-alternatives, fo:repeatable-page-master-reference, fo:root, fo:simple-page-master, fo:single-page-master-reference, fo:static-content, fo:title`

Block-Level Formatting Objects

Block-level FOs stack in the block-progression direction. Use them to format paragraphs, titles, headings, and other elements that stack from before to after (top to bottom).

`fo:block, fo:block-container`

Inline-Level Formatting Objects

Inline-level FOs pack in the inline-progression direction. Use them to decorate a portion of text or to produce rules or leaders.

`fo:bidi-override, fo:character, fo:external-graphic, fo:initial-property-set, fo:inline, fo:inline-container, fo:instream-foreign-object, fo:leader, fo:page-number, fo:page-number-citation`

Formatting Objects for Tables

All the formatting objects that structure tables.

`fo:table, fo:table-and-caption, fo:table-body, fo:table-caption, fo:table-cell, fo:table-column, fo:table-footer, fo:table-header, fo:table-row`

Formatting Objects for Lists

The four FOs that structure lists.

`fo:list-block, fo:list-item, fo:list-item-body, fo:list-item-label`

Dynamic Effects: Link and Multi Formatting Objects

FOs that work in interactive formatters to change presentation or jump to linked content within or external to the document.

`fo:basic-link, fo:multi-case, fo:multi-properties, fo:multi-property-set, fo:multi-switch, fo:multi-toggle`

Out-of-Line Formatting Objects

FOs that float content to the edges of the page, out of line from the normal flow of content.

`fo:float, fo:footnote, fo:footnote-body`

Other Formatting Objects

A catchall group for the remaining three.

`fo:marker, fo:retrieve-marker, fo:wrapper`

Formatting Objects

basic-link

Use the `basic-link` FO as the source of a link. Interactive user agents may display the internal or external destination of the link on a pointer click.

`Common Accessibility Properties; Common Aural Properties; Common Border, Padding, and Background Properties; Common Margin Properties-Inline; Common Relative Position Properties; alignment-adjust, alignment-baseline, baseline-shift, destination-placement-offset, dominant-baseline, external-destination, id, indicate-destination, internal-destination, keep-together, keep-with-next, keep-with-previous, line-height, show-destination, target-presentation-context, target-processing-context, target-stylesheet`

bidi-override

Use the `bidi-override` inline FO to override Unicode bidirectional behavior. The `direction` property determines whether text prints left to right or right to left.

`Common Aural Properties; Common Font Properties; Common Relative Position Properties; color, direction, id, letter-spacing, line-height, score-spaces, unicode-bidi, word-spacing`

block

Use the `block` FO to format paragraphs, titles, headlines, captions, table cell contents, and so forth.

`Common Accessibility Properties; Common Aural Properties; Common Border, Padding, and Background Properties; Common Font Properties; Common Hyphenation Properties; Common Margin Properties-Block;`

Common Relative Position Properties; break-after, break-before, color, hyphenation-keep, hyphenation-ladder-count, id, intrusion-displace, keep-together, keep-with-next, keep-with-previous, last-line-end-indent, linefeed-treatment, line-height, line-height-shift-adjustment, line-stacking-strategy, orphans, span, text-align, text-align-last, text-altitude, text-depth, text-indent, visibility, white-space-collapse, white-space-treatment, widows, wrap-option

block-container

Use the block-container FO to change the writing mode, reference orientation, or absolute position of a block.

Common Absolute Position Properties; Common Border, Padding, and Background Properties; Common Margin Properties-Block; block-progression-dimension, break-after, break-before, clip, display-align, height, id, inline-progression-dimension, intrusion-displace, keep-together, keep-with-next, keep-with-previous, overflow, reference-orientation, span, width, writing-mode, z-index

character

Use the character inline FO to place a decorated character in line with regular text.

Common Aural Properties; Common Border, Padding, and Background Properties; Common Font Properties; Common Hyphenation Properties; Common Margin Properties-Inline; Common Relative Position Properties; alignment-adjust, alignment-baseline, baseline-shift, character, color, dominant-baseline, glyph-orientation-horizontal, glyph-orientation-vertical, id, keep-with-next, keep-with-previous, letter-spacing, line-height, score-spaces, suppress-at-line-break, text-altitude, text-decoration, text-depth, text-shadow, text-transform, treat-as-word-space, visibility, word-spacing

color-profile

Use color-profile in the declarations portion of the style sheet to reference an ICC color profile.

color-profile-name, rendering-intent, src

conditional-page-master-reference

Use `conditional-page-master-reference` within `repeatable-page-master-alternatives` to conditionally select a `simple-page-master`.

`blank-or-not-blank, master-reference, odd-or-even, page-position`

declarations

Use `declarations` under the root element to group color profile references.

external-graphic

Use the `external-graphic` inline FO to reference a graphic, such as a JPEG or GIF format data file.

`Common Accessibility Properties; Common Aural Properties; Common Border, Padding, and Background Properties; Common Margin Properties-Inline; Common Relative Position Properties; alignment-adjust, alignment-baseline, baseline-shift, block-progression-dimension, clip, content-height, content-type, content-width, display-align, dominant-baseline, height, id, inline-progression-dimension, keep-with-next, keep-with-previous, line-height, overflow, scaling, scaling-method, src, text-align, width`

float

Use `float` to place content above or beside the normal flow of content.

`clear, float`

flow

Use `flow` within a `page-sequence` to denote content that flows from page to page.

`flow-name`

footnote

Use the `footnote` inline FO to format a footnote citation together with the content of the footnote.

`Common Accessibility Properties;`

footnote-body

Use `footnote-body` within a footnote FO to format the content of the footnote.

`Common Accessibility Properties;`

initial-property-set

Use `initial-property-set` as the immediate child of a block (following any markers) to specify properties for the first line of the block.

`Common Accessibility Properties; Common Aural Properties; Common Border, Padding, and Background Properties; Common Font Properties; Common Relative Position Properties; color, id, letter-spacing, line-height, score-spaces, text-decoration, text-shadow, text-transform, word-spacing`

inline

Use the `inline` FO to put a background or border around some text that should flow within a line of text. Use it to format a footnote reference.

`Common Accessibility Properties; Common Aural Properties; Common Border, Padding, and Background Properties; Common Font Properties; Common Margin Properties-Inline; Common Relative Position Properties; alignment-adjust, alignment-baseline, baseline-shift, block-progression-dimension, color, dominant-baseline, height, id, inline-progression-dimension, keep-together, keep-with-next, keep-with-previous, line-height, text-decoration, visibility, width, wrap-option`

inline-container

Use `inline-container` to change the writing mode or reference orientation of content that should flow within a line of text.

`Common Border, Padding, and Background Properties; Common Margin Properties-Inline; Common Relative Position Properties; alignment-adjust, alignment-baseline, baseline-shift, block-progression-dimension, clip, display-align, dominant-baseline, height, id, inline-progression-dimension, keep-together, keep-with-next, keep-with-previous, line-height, overflow, reference-orientation, width, writing-mode`

instream-foreign-object

Use the `instream-foreign-object` FO to contain XML markup that is not XSL FO. MathML and SVG are examples of foreign markup that might appear here.

`Common Accessibility Properties; Common Aural Properties; Common Border, Padding, and Background Properties; Common Margin Properties-Inline; Common Relative Position Properties; alignment-adjust, alignment-baseline, baseline-shift, block-progression-dimension, clip, content-height, content-type, content-width, display-align, dominant-baseline, height, id, inline-progression-dimension, keep-with-next, keep-with-previous, line-height, overflow, scaling, scaling-method, text-align, width`

layout-master-set

Use the `layout-master-set` within the root to enclose page masters defined for the document.

leader

Use the `leader` inline FO to generate a rule or line of repeating characters from one inline FO to another.

`Common Accessibility Properties; Common Aural Properties; Common Border, Padding, and Background Properties; Common Font Properties; Common Margin Properties-Inline; Common Relative Position Properties; alignment-adjust, alignment-baseline, baseline-shift, color, dominant-baseline, id, keep-with-next, keep-with-previous, leader-alignment, leader-length, leader-pattern, leader-pattern-width, letter-spacing, line-height, rule-style, rule-thickness, text-altitude, text-depth, text-shadow, visibility, word-spacing`

list-block

Use a `list-block` to enclose the items of a list.

`Common Accessibility Properties; Common Aural Properties; Common Border, Padding, and Background Properties; Common Margin Properties-Block; Common Relative Position Properties; break-after, break-before, id, intrusion-displace, keep-together, keep-with-next, keep-with-previous, provisional-distance-between-starts, provisional-label-separation`

list-item

Use the `list-item` FO within a `list-block` to format one item of a list.

`Common Accessibility Properties; Common Aural Properties; Common Border, Padding, and Background Properties; Common Margin Properties-Block; Common Relative Position Properties; break-after, break-before, id, intrusion-displace, keep-together, keep-with-next, keep-with-previous, relative-align`

list-item-body

Use the `list-item-body` FO to format the substantive content of a `list-item`.

`Common Accessibility Properties; id, keep-together`

list-item-label

Use the `list-item-label` to format the bullet or number that labels a `list-item`.

`Common Accessibility Properties; id, keep-together`

marker

Use `marker` to enclose content to be copied by a `retrieve-marker` element.

`marker-class-name`

multi-case

Use `multi-case` within a `multi-switch` to enclose alternative content for selection by the switch.

`Common Accessibility Properties; case-name, case-title, id, starting-state`

multi-properties

Use `multi-properties` with an interactive renderer to provide alternative appearance for some content based on the position of the mouse or state of a `basic-link`.

`Common Accessibility Properties; id`

multi-property-set

Use `multi-property-set` to specify an alternative appearance within multiproperties.

`active-state, id`

multi-switch

Use `multi-switch` with an interactive renderer to contain alternative content for selection with clicks of the mouse.

`Common Accessibility Properties; auto-restore, id`

multi-toggle

Use `multi-toggle` within a `multi-case` to switch rendering to another case when the content within the `multi-toggle` receives a mouse click.

`Common Accessibility Properties; id, switch-to`

page-number

Use the `page-number` FO to typeset the current page number.

```
Common Accessibility Properties; Common Aural Properties; Common Border,
Padding, and Background Properties; Common Font Properties;
Common Margin Properties-Inline; Common Relative Position Properties;
alignment-adjust, alignment-baseline, baseline-shift, dominant-baseline,
id, keep-with-next, keep-with-previous, letter-spacing, line-height,
score-spaces, text-altitude, text-decoration, text-depth, text-shadow,
text-transform, visibility, word-spacing, wrap-option
```

page-number-citation

Use the `page-number-citation` FO to reference the page on which some other content appears. This is the page number, for example, printed in a table of contents.

```
Common Accessibility Properties; Common Aural Properties; Common Border,
Padding, and Background Properties; Common Font Properties;
Common Margin Properties-Inline; Common Relative Position Properties;
alignment-adjust, alignment-baseline, baseline-shift, dominant-baseline,
id, keep-with-next, keep-with-previous, letter-spacing, line-height,
ref-id, score-spaces, text-altitude, text-decoration, text-depth,
text-shadow, text-transform, visibility, word-spacing, wrap-option
```

page-sequence

Use the `page-sequence` FO to contain the entire content of the document or to contain each chapter or section of a document.

```
country, force-page-count, format, grouping-separator, grouping-size,
id, initial-page-number, language, letter-value, master-reference
```

page-sequence-master

Use `page-sequence-master` within the `layout-master-set` to specify sequences of page master references.

`master-name`

region-after

Use `region-after` to describe a region on the after edge of a page.

`Common Border, Padding, and Background Properties; clip, display-align, extent, overflow, precedence, reference-orientation, region-name, writing-mode`

region-before

Use `region-before` to describe a region on the before edge of a page.

`Common Border, Padding, and Background Properties; clip, display-align, extent, overflow, precedence, reference-orientation, region-name, writing-mode`

region-body

Use `region-body` to describe a region in the center of a page.

`Common Border, Padding, and Background Properties;`
`Common Margin Properties-Block; clip, column-count, column-gap, display-align, overflow, reference-orientation, region-name, writing-mode`

region-end

Use `region-end` to describe a region on the end edge of a page.

`Common Border, Padding, and Background Properties; clip, display-align, extent, overflow, reference-orientation, region-name, writing-mode`

region-start

Use `region-start` to describe a region on the start edge of a page.

`Common Border, Padding, and Background Properties; clip, display-align, extent, overflow, reference-orientation, region-name, writing-mode`

repeatable-page-master-alternatives

Use `repeatable-page-master-alternatives` to define alternative page layouts selected repeatedly for some number of pages or for the entire content of the flow. One common use is to code separate layouts for even and odd pages.

`maximum-repeats`

repeatable-page-master-reference

Use `repeatable-page-master-reference` to repeat a single page master for some number of pages or for the entire content of the flow.

`master-reference, maximum-repeats`

retrieve-marker

Use `retrieve-marker` in static content to copy the first or last occurrence of marked content from the page.

`retrieve-boundary, retrieve-class-name, retrieve-position`

root

For good or evil, this is the root of it all.

`media-usage`

simple-page-master

Use the `simple-page-master` to define a single page layout.

`Common Margin Properties-Block; master-name, page-height, page-width, reference-orientation, writing-mode`

single-page-master-reference

The `single-page-master-reference` contains a name that matches the name of a `simple-page-master`.

`master-reference`

static-content

Use the `static-content` FO for repeating or running headers and footers or any other content to be repeated on every page that contains a region named by the `flow-name` attribute.

`flow-name`

table

The `table` FO is the root of a table. Use it to define inherited properties common to most of the content of the table.

`Common Accessibility Properties; Common Aural Properties; Common Border, Padding, and Background Properties; Common Margin Properties-Block; Common Relative Position Properties; block-progression-dimension, border-after-precedence, border-before-precedence, border-collapse, border-end-precedence, border-separation, border-start-precedence, break-after, break-before, height, id, inline-progression-dimension, intrusion-displace, keep-together, keep-with-next, keep-with-previous, table-layout, table-omit-footer-at-break, table-omit-header-at-break, width, writing-mode`

table-and-caption

Use the `table-and-caption` FO to place a caption together with a table.

`Common Accessibility Properties; Common Aural Properties; Common Border, Padding, and Background Properties; Common Margin Properties-Block; Common Relative Position Properties; break-after, break-before, caption-side, id, intrusion-displace, keep-together, keep-with-next, keep-with-previous, text-align`

table-body

Enclose the data rows of a table within the `table-body` FO.

`Common Accessibility Properties; Common Aural Properties; Common Border, Padding, and Background Properties; Common Relative Position Properties; border-after-precedence, border-before-precedence, border-end-precedence, border-start-precedence, id, visibility`

table-caption

Use the `table-caption` FO within `table-and-caption` to define the caption associated with the table.

`Common Accessibility Properties; Common Aural Properties; Common Border, Padding, and Background Properties; Common Relative Position Properties; block-progression-dimension, height, id, inline-progression-dimension, intrusion-displace, keep-together, width`

table-cell

Group content of one table cell with a `table-cell` FO.

`Common Accessibility Properties; Common Aural Properties; Common Border, Padding, and Background Properties; Common Relative Position Properties; block-progression-dimension, border-after-precedence, border-before-precedence, border-end-precedence, border-start-precedence, column-number, display-align, empty-cells, ends-row, height, id, inline-progression-dimension, number-columns-spanned, number-rows-spanned, relative-align, starts-row, width`

table-column

Define properties for all cells within one column with `table-column`.

`Common Border, Padding, and Background Properties; border-after-precedence, border-before-precedence, border-end-precedence, border-start-precedence, column-number, column-width, number-columns-repeated, number-columns-spanned, visibility`

table-footer

Use the `table-footer` FO for rows repeated at the end of a table and at the bottom of every page break in the table body.

`Common Accessibility Properties; Common Aural Properties; Common Border, Padding, and Background Properties; Common Relative Position Properties; border-after-precedence, border-before-precedence, border-end-precedence, border-start-precedence, id, visibility`

table-header

Use the `table-header` FO for rows repeated at the start of a table and at the top of every page start in the table body.

`Common Accessibility Properties; Common Aural Properties; Common Border, Padding, and Background Properties; Common Relative Position Properties; border-after-precedence, border-before-precedence, border-end-precedence, border-start-precedence, id, visibility`

table-row

Use the `table-row` FO to group instances of table-cell into rows.

`Common Accessibility Properties; Common Aural Properties; Common Border, Padding, and Background Properties; Common Relative Position Properties; block-progression-dimension, border-after-precedence, border-before-precedence, border-end-precedence, border-start-precedence, break-after, break-before, height, id, keep-together, keep-with-next, keep-with-previous, visibility`

title

An interactive formatter may display the text of the title in the title bar of its window.

`Common Accessibility Properties; Common Aural Properties; Common Border, Padding, and Background Properties; Common Font Properties; Common Margin Properties-Inline; color, line-height, visibility`

wrapper

Use the `wrapper` FO to change properties without introducing structural change in the document. Use it to make text bold, italic, or underlined without introducing an inline, for example. Use it to enclose content affected by a `multi-property-set`.

`Id`

APPENDIX C

A Concise Listing of Properties

This appendix provides summary information about formatting object (FO) properties. It contains three major sections. The first organizes properties into functional groups. The second describes property value types. These short sections provide background for the big kahuna—an alphabetical listing of all 248 properties.

Each entry in the properties listing includes a short description followed by the groups that contain the property, the FOs that recognize it, the allowed values, and the default or initial value.

The properties in the group below titled Shorthand Properties provide means to specify several of the other, non-shorthand properties at once. The best example is `border`, which allows specification of border color, width, and style for all four sides of the border. Shorthand properties do not have default values. The properties they stand for in shorthand notation provide the defaults.

Shorthand properties may not be supported in all implementations. The recommendation classifies them as optional for all but a complete implementation. Even implementations that implement extended features need not support them. Shorthand properties were included for CSS compatibility. The XSL `attribute-set` and recursive application of templates eliminate repetitive typing of property names when using style sheets. You should avoid them.

Property Categories

Area Alignment Properties

Properties to align inline areas vertically given differing baselines of mixed scripts. The `display-align` and `relative-align` properties specify the horizontal alignment of blocks.

`alignment-adjust, alignment-baseline, baseline-shift, display-align, dominant-baseline, relative-align`

Area Dimension Properties

Properties control the dimensions of block and inline areas.

`block-progression-dimension, content-height, content-width, height, inline-progression-dimension, max-height, max-width, min-height, min-width, scaling, scaling-method, width`

Block and Line-Related Properties

Properties to control white space, line breaking, and the alignment of text within blocks.

`hyphenation-keep, hyphenation-ladder-count, last-line-end-indent, linefeed-treatment, line-height, line-height-shift-adjustment, line-stacking-strategy, text-align, text-align-last, text-indent, white-space-collapse, white-space-treatment, wrap-option`

Character Properties

Properties control the presentation of text.

`character, letter-spacing, suppress-at-line-break, text-decoration, text-shadow, text-transform, treat-as-word-space, word-spacing`

Color-Related Properties

Properties specify colors.

`color, color-profile-name, rendering-intent`

Common Absolute-Position Properties

Properties specify absolutely the position and size of formatted areas. The properties `top`, `bottom`, `left`, and `right` are members of the Relative Position Properties group as well.

`absolute-position, bottom, left, right, top`

Common Accessibility Properties

Properties aid in nonvisual rendering of the document.

`role, source-document`

Common Aural Properties

Properties control the aural rendition of the document with a text-to-speech engine.

`azimuth, cue-after, cue-before, elevation, pause-after, pause-before, pitch, pitch-range, play-during, richness, speak, speak-header, speak-numeral, speak-punctuation, speech-rate, stress, voice-family, volume`

Common Border, Padding, and Background Properties

Properties specify backgrounds and borders on block and inline areas. Properties with top, bottom, left, or right correspond to properties with before, after, start, or end, according to the value of the `writing-mode` property.

`background-attachment, background-color, background-image, background-position-horizontal, background-position-vertical, background-repeat, border-after-color, border-after-style, border-after-width, border-before-color, border-before-style, border-before-width, border-bottom-color, border-bottom-style, border-bottom-width, border-end-color, border-end-style, border-end-width, border-left-color, border-left-style, border-left-width, border-right-color, border-right-style, border-right-width, border-start-color, border-start-style, border-start-width, border-top-color, border-top-style, border-top-width, padding-after, padding-before, padding-bottom, padding-end, padding-left, padding-right, padding-start, padding-top`

Common Font Properties

Properties select the font for text in the document.

`font-family, font-model, font-selection-strategy, font-size, font-size-adjust, font-stretch, font-style, font-variant, font-weight`

Common Hyphenation Properties

Properties control hyphenation and line breaking.

`country, hyphenate, hyphenation-character, hyphenation-push-character-count, hyphenation-remain-character-count, language, script`

Common Margin Properties—Block

Properties set the space around block FOs.

`end-indent, margin-bottom, margin-left, margin-right, margin-top, space-after, space-before, start-indent`

Common Margin Properties—Inline

Properties set the space around inline FOs.

`margin-bottom, margin-left, margin-right, margin-top, space-end, space-start`

Common Relative Position Properties

Properties specify the relative position of formatted areas. The properties `top`, `bottom`, `left`, and `right` are members of the Absolute Position Properties group as well.

`bottom, left, relative-position, right, top`

Float-Related Properties

Properties specify the page edge for placement of floating elements.

`clear, float, intrusion-displace`

Keeps and Breaks Properties

Properties manage the location of breaks in lines, columns, or pages.

`break-after, break-before, keep-together, keep-with-next, keep-with-previous, orphans, widows`

Layout-Related Properties

Some miscellaneous layout properties control the top of the page, clipping, overflow, and column spanning.

`clip, overflow, reference-orientation, span`

Leader and Rule Properties

Properties affect leaders and horizontal rules.

`leader-alignment, leader-length, leader-pattern, leader-pattern-width, rule-style, rule-thickness`

Miscellaneous Properties

Assorted properties not otherwise categorized.

`content-type, id, provisional-distance-between-starts, provisional-label-separation, ref-id, score-spaces, src, visibility, z-index`

Pagination and Layout Properties

Properties that define page masters and control their selection.

`blank-or-not-blank, column-count, column-gap, extent, flow-name, force-page-count, initial-page-number, master-name, master-reference, maximum-repeats, media-usage, odd-or-even, page-height, page-position, page-width, precedence, region-name`

Properties for Dynamic Effects

Properties define the actions of the `basic-link` and `multi- formatting` objects in interactive renderers.

`active-state, auto-restore, case-name, case-title, destination-placement-offset, external-destination, indicate-destination, internal-destination, show-destination, starting-state, switch-to, target-presentation-context, target-processing-context, target-stylesheet`

Properties for Markers

Properties for the `marker` and `retrieve-marker` FOs.

`marker-class-name, retrieve-boundary, retrieve-class-name, retrieve-position`

Properties for Number-to-String Conversions

Properties of page numbers.

`format, grouping-separator, grouping-size, letter-value`

Shorthand Properties

Shorthand properties expand to some number of individual properties. Only complete implementations must support them.

`background, background-position, border, border-bottom, border-color, border-left, border-right, border-spacing, border-style,` border-top, border-width, cue, font, margin, padding, page-break-after, page-break-before, page-break-inside, pause, position, size, vertical-align, white-space, xml:lang

Table Properties

Properties of table column definitions, table rows, and table cells.

border-after-precedence, border-before-precedence, border-collapse, border-end-precedence, border-separation, border-start-precedence, caption-side, column-number, column-width, empty-cells, ends-row, number-columns-repeated, number-columns-spanned, number-rows-spanned, starts-row, table-layout, table-omit-footer-at-break, table-omit-header-at-break

Writing-Mode Related Properties

Properties that control the direction of flow for inline, text, and block elements.

direction, glyph-orientation-horizontal, glyph-orientation-vertical, text-altitude, text-depth, unicode-bidi, writing-mode

Property Types

Values that appear in angle brackets, such as <percentage>, refer to types. Types are names for a set, a numeric range, or a compound form that may appear as a value for a given property.

Compound properties have components. Specify a component of a property with the property name, a period (.), and the name of the component. Refer to the component within-page of the keep property as keep.within-page.

The following types apply to more than a few of the properties. The properties section describes rare types when they occur.

<border-style>: A place holder for the constants none, hidden, dotted, dashed, solid, double, groove, ridge, inset, and outset.

<border-width>: May have the values thin, medium, thick, or <length>.

<color>: A CSS2 color specification familiar to HTML writers. Valid color notations are #rgb, #rrggbb, rgb(255, 255, 255), rgb(100%, 100%, 100%), and the following HTML4 color names (not case sensitive): black, silver, gray, white, maroon, red,

purple, fuchsia, green, lime, olive, yellow, navy, blue, teal, and aqua. Have fun with fuchsia.

<id>: A name that begins with a letter or underscore (_) followed by any number of letters, digits, combining characters, extenders, period (.) or underscore(_). A single colon may appear as a "namespace" separator within the name. The letters, digits, combining characters, and extenders are Unicode standard character classifications. An id is always unique within the document.

<idref>: Has the same value specification as id. An idref always has a value shared by some id in the document.

<integer>: An optional plus (+) or minus (–) followed by some number of digits.

<keep>: A compound type with three components: within-page, within-column, and within-line. Each may have the value, auto, always, or <integer>.

<length>: A <number> followed by length units. Length units are pt, pc, in, cm, mm, px, em (points, picas, inches, centimeters, millimeters, pixels, and em-box size). Here are a few sample lengths: 1cm, +0.5in, 2pt, 1.25em, -12mm.

<length-conditional>: A compound type with length and conditionality components. The length component has a <length> value. The values for conditionality are discard and retain.

<length-range>: A compound type with minimum, optimum, and maximum components. All three components have <length> values. Formatters constrain the values such that minimum <= optimum <= maximum.

<margin-width>: May be auto, a <length>, or a <percentage>.

<name>: Has the same value specification as id. A name may occur more than once in the document. The value may match the value of some other property.

<number>: An optional plus (+) or minus (–) followed by some number of digits, followed by an optional decimal point (.), and some number of digits.

<percentage>: A number followed by a percent sign (%). The descriptions indicate the measure to which the percentage applies for each property that may have a percentage value.

<space>: A compound type with components— minimum, optimum, maximum, conditionality, and precedence. The first are the same as for <length-conditional>. The precedence component may be an <integer> or the value force.

<string>: A sequence of characters enclosed in single or double quotation marks.

`<uri-specification>`: The character sequence URL (followed by an optional space and single or double quote, a URI, a quote to match any which appeared before the URI, and a close parenthesis (")"). The URI specification is described in IETF RFC 2396. It is essentially the string you would type into a browser to view a resource on the Internet. The string `http://www.w3.org/1999/XSL/Transform` is a URI. The string `file://C|/Program Files/Adobe/Acrobat 4.0/Help/accessPDF.htm` is a URI.

Properties

absolute-position

Use this property to fix the position of `block-container`.

Common Absolute Position Properties

Applies to:	block-container
Values:	auto | absolute | fixed | inherit
Default:	auto

active-state

The state for which a `multi-property-set` applies.

Group(s):	Properties for Dynamic Effects Formatting Objects
Applies to:	multi-property-set
Values:	link | visited | active | hover | focus
Default:	None. Supply a value.

alignment-adjust

Identifies the baseline alignment point of the element, especially `external-graphic` and `instream-foreign-object` elements.

Group(s):	Area Alignment Properties
Applies to:	all inline-level FOs
Values:	auto | baseline | before-edge | text-before-edge | middle | central | after-edge | text-after-edge | ideographic | alphabetic | hanging | mathematical | <percentage> | <length> | inherit

Percent: external-graphic and instream-foreign-object: refers to the computed "height"; character: refers to the font-size; otherwise refers to the line-height

Default: auto

alignment-baseline

Identifies the baseline of the containing line area to which this element will align.

Group(s): Area Alignment Properties

Applies to: all inline-level FOs

Values: auto | baseline | before-edge | text-before-edge | middle | central | after-edge | text-after-edge | ideographic | alphabetic | hanging | mathematical | inherit

Default: auto

auto-restore

Whether to reset the initial case of an embedded multi-switch when it becomes hidden by an outer multi-switch.

Group(s): Properties for Dynamic Effects Formatting Objects

Applies to: multi-switch

Values: true | false

Default: inherits from the parent

Initial: false

azimuth

The horizontal direction from which the listener should perceive the reader's voice. <angle> is a number in the range –360 to 360 followed by the letters deg. The value 0deg is directly in front.

Group(s): Common Aural Properties

Applies to: all elements

Values: <angle> | [[left-side | far-left | left | center-left | center | center-right | right | far-right | right-side] || behind] | leftwards | rightwards | inherit

Default: inherits from the parent

Initial: center

background

Shorthand for `background-color`, `background-image`, `background-repeat`, `background-attachment`, `background-position-horizontal`, and `background-position-vertical`.

Group(s):	Shorthand Properties
Applies to:	all elements
Values:	[<background-color> || <background-image> || <background-repeat> || <background-attachment> || <background-position>]] | inherit
Default:	see individual properties

background-attachment

Whether any background image moves with scrolling or remains fixed in the frame.

Group(s):	Common Border, Padding, and Background Properties
Applies to:	all elements
Values:	scroll | fixed | inherit
Default:	scroll

background-color

A solid color for the background.

Group(s):	Common Border, Padding, and Background Properties
Applies to:	all elements
Values:	<color> | transparent | inherit
Default:	transparent

background-image

An image for the background.

Group(s):	Common Border, Padding, and Background Properties
Applies to:	all elements
Values:	<uri-specification> | none | inherit
Default:	none

background-position

Shorthand for `background-position-horizontal` and `background-position-vertical`.

Group(s):	Shorthand Properties
Applies to:	block-level and replaced elements
Values:	[[<percentage> | <length>]{1,2} | [[top | center | bottom] || [left | center | right]]] | inherit
Percent:	refers to the size of the box itself
Default:	see individual properties

background-position-horizontal

The offset from the left edge of the padding rectangle for the left edge of any background image.

Group(s):	Common Border, Padding, and Background Properties
Applies to:	all elements
Values:	<percentage> | <length> | left | center | right | inherit
Percent:	refers to the size of the padding-rectangle
Default:	0%

background-position-vertical

The offset from the top edge of the padding rectangle for the top edge of any background image.

Group(s):	Common Border, Padding, and Background Properties
Applies to:	all elements
Values:	<percentage> | <length> | top | center | bottom | inherit
Percent:	refers to the size of the padding-rectangle
Default:	0%

background-repeat

Whether and in which directions any background image should repeat.

Group(s):	Common Border, Padding, and Background Properties
Applies to:	all elements
Values:	repeat | repeat-x | repeat-y | no-repeat | inherit
Default:	repeat

baseline-shift

An offset for the baseline relative to where it would normally align with the baseline of the line area.

Group(s):	Area Alignment Properties
Applies to:	all inline-level FOs
Values:	baseline | sub | super | <percentage> | <length> | inherit
Percent:	refers to the "line-height" of the parent area
Default:	Baseline

blank-or-not-blank

Whether the master may be used for a blank page, a nonblank page, or either.

Group(s):	Pagination and Layout Properties
Applies to:	conditional-page-master-reference
Values:	blank | not-blank | any | inherit
Default:	any

block-progression-dimension

The size of the content rectangle in the `block-progression dimension`.

Group(s):	Area Dimension Properties
Applies to:	elements that produce areas
Values:	auto | <length> | <percentage> | <length-range> | inherit
Percent:	refers to the block-progression-dimension of the closest ancestor block if specified; otherwise treated as auto
Default:	auto

border

Shorthand for border-X-color, border-X-style, and border-X-width in which X is top, bottom, left, or right.

Group(s):	Shorthand Properties
Applies to:	all elements
Values:	[<border-width> || <border-style> || <color>] | inherit
Default:	see individual properties

border-after-color

The color of the border on the after edge.

Group(s):	Common Border, Padding, and Background Properties
Applies to:	block and inline elements
Values:	<color> | inherit
Default:	the value of the color property

border-after-precedence

Precedence of the border after. Higher precedence wins over lower precedence.

Group(s):	Table Properties
Applies to:	table, table-body, table-header, table-footer, table-column, table-row, table-cell
Values:	force | <integer> | inherit
Default:	table: 6, table-cell: 5, table-column: 4, table-row: 3, table-body: 2, table-header: 1, table-footer: 0

border-after-style

The style of the border on the after edge.

Group(s):	Common Border, Padding, and Background Properties
Applies to:	block and inline elements
Values:	<border-style> | inherit
Default:	none

border-after-width

The width of the border on the after edge.

Group(s):	Common Border, Padding, and Background Properties
Applies to:	block and inline elements
Values:	<border-width> | <length-conditional> | inherit
Default:	medium

border-before-color

The color of the border on the before edge.

Group(s):	Common Border, Padding, and Background Properties
Applies to:	block and inline elements
Values:	<color> | inherit
Default:	the value of the color property

border-before-precedence

Precedence of the border before. Higher precedence wins over lower precedence.

Group(s):	Table Properties
Applies to:	table, table-body, table-header, table-footer, table-column, table-row, table-cell
Values:	force | <integer> | inherit
Default:	table: 6, table-cell: 5, table-column: 4, table-row: 3, table-body: 2, table-header: 1, table-footer: 0

border-before-style

The style of the border on the before edge.

Group(s):	Common Border, Padding, and Background Properties
Applies to:	block and inline elements
Values:	<border-style> | inherit
Default:	none

border-before-width

The width of the border on the before edge.

Group(s): Common Border, Padding, and Background Properties
Applies to: block and inline elements
Values: <border-width> | <length-conditional> | inherit
Default: medium

border-bottom

Shorthand for `border-bottom-color`, `border-bottom-style`, and `border-bottom-width`.

Group(s): Shorthand Properties
Applies to: all elements
Values: [<border-width> || <border-style> || <color>] | inherit
Default: see individual properties

border-bottom-color

The color of the border on the bottom edge.

Group(s): Common Border, Padding, and Background Properties
Applies to: all elements
Values: <color> | inherit
Default: the value of the color property

border-bottom-style

The style of the border on the bottom edge.

Group(s): Common Border, Padding, and Background Properties
Applies to: all elements
Values: <border-style> | inherit
Default: none

border-bottom-width

The width of the border on the bottom edge.

Group(s):	Common Border, Padding, and Background Properties
Applies to:	all elements
Values:	<border-width> | inherit
Default:	medium

border-collapse

Whether borders in the table are separated, collapsed together, or collapsed with conflict resolution based on the border precedence values.

Group(s):	Table Properties
Applies to:	table
Values:	collapse | collapse-with-precedence | separate | inherit
Default:	inherits from the parent
Initial:	collapse

border-color

Shorthand for `border-X-color` in which X is top, bottom, left, or right.

Group(s):	Shorthand Properties
Applies to:	all elements
Values:	[<color> | transparent]{1,4} | inherit
Default:	see individual properties

border-end-color

The color of the border on the end edge.

Group(s):	Common Border, Padding, and Background Properties
Applies to:	block and inline elements
Values:	<color> | inherit
Default:	the value of the color property

border-end-precedence

Precedence of the border end. Higher precedence wins over lower precedence.

Group(s): Table Properties

Applies to: table, table-body, table-header, table-footer, table-column, table-row, table-cell

Values: force | <integer> | inherit

Default: table: 6, table-cell: 5, table-column: 4, table-row: 3, table-body: 2, table-header: 1, table-footer: 0

border-end-style

The style of the border on the end edge.

Group(s): Common Border, Padding, and Background Properties

Applies to: block and inline elements

Values: <border-style> | inherit

Default: none

border-end-width

The width of the border on the end edge.

Group(s): Common Border, Padding, and Background Properties

Applies to: block and inline elements

Values: <border-width> | <length-conditional> | inherit

Default: medium

border-left

Shorthand for `border-left-color`, `border-left-style`, and `border-left-width`.

Group(s): Shorthand Properties

Applies to: all elements

Values: [<border-width> || <border-style> || <color>] | inherit

Default: see individual properties

border-left-color

The color of the border on the left edge.

Group(s): Common Border, Padding, and Background Properties
Applies to: all elements
Values: <color> | inherit
Default: the value of the color property

border-left-style

The style of the border on the left edge.

Group(s): Common Border, Padding, and Background Properties
Applies to: all elements
Values: <border-style> | inherit
Default: none

border-left-width

The width of the border on the left edge.

Group(s): Common Border, Padding, and Background Properties
Applies to: all elements
Values: <border-width> | inherit
Default: medium

border-right

Shorthand for `border-right-color`, `border-right-style`, and `border-right-width`.

Group(s): Shorthand Properties
Applies to: all elements
Values: [<border-width> || <border-style> || <color>] | inherit
Default: see individual properties
Group(s): Shorthand Properties
Applies to: all elements
Values: [<border-width> || <border-style> || <color>] | inherit
Default: see individual properties

border-right-color

The color of the border on the right edge.

Group(s): Common Border, Padding, and Background Properties
Applies to: all elements
Values: <color> | inherit
Default: the value of the color property

border-right-style

The style of the border on the right edge.

Group(s): Common Border, Padding, and Background Properties
Applies to: all elements
Values: <border-style> | inherit
Default: none

border-right-width

The width of the border on the right edge.

Group(s): Common Border, Padding, and Background Properties
Applies to: all elements
Values: <border-width> | inherit
Default: medium

border-separation

Distance separating cell borders when border-collapsed has the value separated. The type `<length-bp-ip-direction>` is a compound type with two components—`block-progression-direction` and `inline-progression-direction`. Each component has a value of type `<length>`.

Group(s): Table Properties
Applies to: table
Values: <length-bp-ip-direction> | inherit
Default: inherits from the parent
Initial: .block-progression-direction="0pt" .inline-progression-direction="0pt"

border-spacing

Shorthand for `border-separation`.

Group(s):	Shorthand Properties
Applies to:	table
Values:	<length> <length>? | inherit
Default:	inherits from the parent
Initial:	0pt

border-start-color

The color of the border on the start edge.

Group(s):	Common Border, Padding, and Background Properties
Applies to:	block and inline elements
Values:	<color> | inherit
Default:	the value of the color property

border-start-precedence

Precedence of the border start. Higher precedence wins over lower precedence.

Group(s):	Table Properties
Applies to:	table, table-body, table-header, table-footer, table-column, table-row, table-cell
Values:	force | <integer> | inherit
Default:	table: 6, table-cell: 5, table-column: 4, table-row: 3, table-body: 2, table-header: 1, table-footer: 0

border-start-style

The style of the border on the start edge.

Group(s):	Common Border, Padding, and Background Properties
Applies to:	block and inline elements
Values:	<border-style> | inherit
Default:	none

border-start-width

The width of the border on the start edge.

Group(s): Common Border, Padding, and Background Properties
Applies to: block and inline elements
Values: <border-width> | <length-conditional> | inherit
Default: medium

border-style

Shorthand for border-X-style in which X is top, bottom, left, or right.

Group(s): Shorthand Properties
Applies to: all elements
Values: <border-style>{1,4} | inherit
Default: see individual properties

border-top

Shorthand for `border-top-color`, `border-top-style`, and `border-top-width`.

Group(s): Shorthand Properties
Applies to: all elements
Values: [<border-width> || <border-style> || <color>] | inherit
Default: see individual properties

border-top-color

The color of the border on the top edge.

Group(s): Common Border, Padding, and Background Properties
Applies to: all elements
Values: <color> | inherit
Default: the value of the color property

border-top-style

The style of the border on the top edge.

Group(s): Common Border, Padding, and Background Properties
Applies to: all elements
Values: <border-style> | inherit
Default: none

border-top-width

The width of the border on the top edge.

Group(s): Common Border, Padding, and Background Properties
Applies to: all elements
Values: <border-width> | inherit
Default: medium

border-width

Shorthand for `border-X-color`, `border-X-style`, and `border-X-width` in which X is top, bottom, left, or right.

Group(s): Shorthand Properties
Applies to: all elements
Values: <border-width>{1,4} | inherit
Default: see individual properties

bottom

Specifies the offset of a block's bottom edge above the bottom edge of the referenced element.

Group(s): Common Absolute Position Properties and Common Relative Position Properties
Applies to: absolute or relative positioned elements
Values: <length> | <percentage> | auto | inherit
Percent: refers to the height of the containing block
Default: auto

break-after

Whether to place a column or page break after this element.

Group(s):	Keeps and Breaks Properties
Applies to:	block-level FOs, list-item, and table-row.
Values:	auto | column | page | even-page | odd-page | inherit
Default:	auto

break-before

Whether to place a column or page break before this element.

Group(s):	Keeps and Breaks Properties
Applies to:	block-level FOs, list-item, and table-row.
Values:	auto | column | page | even-page | odd-page | inherit
Default:	auto

caption-side

The edge of the table for the table caption.

Group(s):	Table Properties
Applies to:	table-and-caption
Values:	before | after | start | end | top | bottom | left | right | inherit
Default:	inherits from the parent
Initial:	before

case-name

The name of a `multi-case`.

Group(s):	Properties for Dynamic Effects Formatting Objects
Applies to:	multi-case
Values:	<name>
Default:	None. Supply a value.

case-title

Descriptor for a `multi-case`.

Group(s): Properties for Dynamic Effects Formatting Objects
Applies to: multi-case
Values: <string>
Default: None. Supply a value.

character

The character to display; `<character>` is a Unicode character.

Group(s): Character Properties
Applies to: character
Values: <character>
Default: None. Supply a value.

clear

Whether to position a block so that it does not overlap floating elements generated by prior blocks.

Group(s): Float-Related Properties
Applies to: block-level elements
Values: start | end | left | right | both | none | inherit
Default: none

clip

The rectangle within which the overflow property applies. The value for `<shape>` uses functional notation as follows: `rect (<top>, <left>, <bottom>, <right>)`. The parameters, `<top>`, `<left>`, `<bottom>`, and `<right>` are offsets from the sides of the enclosing box. The offsets are `<length>` valued or may be the keyword `auto`. Formatters treat the value, `auto` the same as zero.

Group(s): Layout-Related Properties
Applies to: block-level and replaced elements
Values: <shape> | auto | inherit
Default: auto

color

The color of text.

Group(s):	Color-Related Properties
Applies to:	all elements
Values:	<color> | inherit
Default:	inherits from the parent
Initial:	The implementation determines the initial color, usually black.

color-profile-name

The name of an ICC color profile.

Group(s):	Color-Related Properties
Applies to:	color-profile
Values:	<name> | inherit
Default:	None. Supply a value.

column-count

The number of columns in the body of the page.

Group(s):	Pagination and Layout Properties
Applies to:	region-body
Values:	<number> | inherit
Default:	1

column-gap

The space between columns.

Group(s):	Pagination and Layout Properties
Applies to:	region-body
Values:	<length> | <percentage> | inherit
Percent:	refers to the width of the region being divided into columns
Default:	12.0pt

column-number

Refers to a column for formatting or for cell placement.

Group(s):	Table Properties
Applies to:	table-column, table-cell
Values:	<number>
Default:	The current column number

column-width

The width of the column referred to by `column-number`.

Group(s):	Table Properties
Applies to:	table-column
Values:	<length> | <percentage>
Percent:	refers to the width of table
Default:	None. Supply a value.

content-height

The height of imported graphic elements.

Group(s):	Area Dimension Properties
Applies to:	external-graphic, instream-foreign-object
Values:	auto | scale-to-fit | <length> | <percentage> | inherit
Percent:	refers to the intrinsic height
Default:	auto

content-type

A mime type or namespace URI to provide a clue for rendering non-FO content.

Group(s):	Miscellaneous Properties
Applies to:	external-graphic, instream-foreign-object
Values:	<string> | auto
Default:	auto

content-width

The width of imported graphic elements.

Group(s): Area Dimension Properties

Applies to: external-graphic, instream-foreign-object

Values: auto | scale-to-fit | <length> | <percentage> | inherit

Percent: refers to the intrinsic width

Default: auto

country

The country code for the intended reader; `<country>` is a country code defined in IETF. RFC 3066, "Tags for the Identification of Languages." Available at `http://www.ietf.org/rfc/rfc3066.txt`.

Group(s): Common Hyphenation Properties

Applies to: block, character, page-sequence

Values: none | <country> | inherit

Default: inherits from the parent

Initial: none

cue

Shorthand for `cue-before` and `cue-after`.

Group(s): Shorthand Properties

Applies to: all elements

Values: <cue-before> || <cue-after> | inherit

Default: see individual properties

cue-after

A sound the reader must produce after reading the content.

Group(s): Common Aural Properties

Applies to: all elements

Values: <uri-specification> | none | inherit

Default: none

cue-before

A sound the reader must produce before reading the content.

Group(s): Common Aural Properties
Applies to: all elements
Values: <uri-specification> | none | inherit
Default: none

destination-placement-offset

The distance from the top at which to display the destination when a user activates the link.

Group(s): Properties for Dynamic Effects Formatting Objects
Applies to: basic-link
Values: <length>
Default: 0pt

direction

Whether the inline progression direction is left to right or right to left.

Group(s): Writing-Mode-Related Properties
Applies to: all elements
Values: ltr | rtl | inherit
Default: Inherits from the parent
Initial: ltr

display-align

Group(s): Area Alignment Properties
Applies to: table-cell, region-body, region-before, region-after, region-start, region-end, block-container, inline-container, external-graphic, instream-foreign-object
Values: auto | before | center | after | inherit
Default: inherits from the parent
Initial: auto

dominant-baseline

Group(s): Area Alignment Properties

Applies to: all inline-level FOs

Values: auto | use-script | no-change | reset-size | ideographic | alphabetic | hanging | mathematical | central | middle | text-after-edge | text-before-edge | inherit

Default: auto

elevation

The vertical direction from which the listener should perceive the reader's voice. `<angle>` is a number in the range –90 to 90 followed by the letters deg. The value 0deg is directly in front.

Group(s): Common Aural Properties

Applies to: all elements

Values: <angle> | below | level | above | higher | lower | inherit

Default: inherits from the parent

Initial: level

empty-cells

Whether to draw borders around cells that have no content.

Group(s): Table Properties

Applies to: table-cell

Values: show | hide | inherit

Default: inherits from the parent

Initial: show

end-indent

The width of space, padding, and border at the end edge.

Group(s):	Common Margin Properties-Block
Applies to:	all block-level FOs
Values:	<length> | <percentage> | inherit
Percent:	refers to the inline-progression-dimension of the containing reference-area
Default:	inherits from the parent
Initial:	0pt

ends-row

Starts a new row after the table cell, provided that the table cell has no parent table row.

Group(s):	Table Properties
Applies to:	table-cell
Values:	true | false
Default:	false

extent

The width of the region as measured from the edge of the page toward the edge of the body region.

Group(s):	Pagination and Layout Properties
Applies to:	region-before, region-after, region-start, region-end
Values:	<length> | <percentage> | inherit
Percent:	refers to the corresponding height or width of the page-viewport-area.
Default:	0.0pt

external-destination

The URI for an external resource to display when a user activates the link.

Group(s):	Properties for Dynamic Effects Formatting Objects
Applies to:	basic-link
Values:	<uri-specification>
Default:	empty string

float

The edge where the formatter should place this floating element.

Group(s): Float-related Properties

Applies to: float

Values: before | start | end | left | right | none | inherit

Default: none

flow-name

The name of the region into which the formatter will place this content.

Group(s): Pagination and Layout Properties

Applies to: flow, static-content

Values: <name>

Default: None. Supply a value.

font

Shorthand for `font-family`, `font-size`, `font-weight`, `font-style`, `font-variant`, and `line-height`.

Group(s): Shorthand Properties

Applies to: all elements

Values: [[<font-style> || <font-variant> || <font-weight>]? <font-size> [/ <line-height>]? <font-family>] | caption | icon | menu | message-box | small-caption | status-bar | inherit

Default: see individual properties

font-family

A list of font family names to constrain selection of a font for text, in which `<family-name>` is a group of related fonts with the same design, such as Helvetica, Times Roman, Baskerville, or Symbol. Values for `<generic-family>` are serif, sans-serif, cursive, fantasy, and monospace.

Group(s):	Common Font Properties
Applies to:	all elements
Values:	[[<family-name> | <generic-family>],]* [<family-name> | <generic-family>] | inherit
Default:	inherits from the parent
Initial:	the implementation selects an initial font family

font-selection-strategy

Whether the font may change within a block of text to accommodate characters present in one font but absent in another.

Group(s):	Common Font Properties
Applies to:	all elements
Values:	auto | character-by-character | inherit
Default:	inherits from the parent
Initial:	auto

font-size

The size of characters.

Group(s):	Common Font Properties
Applies to:	all elements
Values:	xx-small | x-small | small | medium | large | x-large | xx-large | larger | smaller | <length> | <percentage> | inherit
Percent:	refers to the parent element's font size
Default:	inherits from the parent
Initial:	medium

font-size-adjust

Use this property to adjust the size of any substituted font to maintain a similar X height to the specified font.

Group(s):	Common Font Properties
Applies to:	all elements
Values:	<number> | none | inherit
Default:	inherits from the parent
Initial:	none

font-stretch

Whether the font appears compressed or expanded horizontally.

Group(s):	Common Font Properties
Applies to:	all elements
Values:	normal | wider | narrower | ultra-condensed | extra-condensed | condensed | semi-condensed | semi-expanded | expanded | extra-expanded | ultra-expanded | inherit
Default:	inherits from the parent
Initial:	normal

font-style

Whether characters slant.

Group(s):	Common Font Properties
Applies to:	all elements
Values:	normal | italic | oblique | backslant | inherit
Default:	inherits from the parent
Initial:	normal

font-variant

Whether font selection should find a font with lowercase characters that look like capitals.

Group(s): Common Font Properties
Applies to: all elements
Values: normal | small-caps | inherit
Default: inherits from the parent
Initial: normal

font-weight

Whether letters of the font appear dark and bold or thin and light.

Group(s): Common Font Properties
Applies to: all elements
Values: normal | bold | bolder | lighter | 100 | 200 | 300 | 400 | 500 | 600 | 700 | 800 | 900 | inherit
Default: inherits from the parent
Initial: normal

force-page-count

The condition under which the formatter may add a page to the `page-sequence` in addition to the pages required to format the content of the flow.

Group(s): Pagination and Layout Properties
Applies to: page-sequence
Values: auto | even | odd | end-on-even | end-on-odd | no-force | inherit
Default: auto

format

A format string for page numbers within this page sequence.

Group(s): Properties for Number-to-String Conversion
Applies to: page-sequence
Values: <string>
Default: 1

glyph-orientation-horizontal

The orientation of glyphs when the block progression direction is top to bottom or bottom to top.

Group(s):	Writing-Mode-Related Properties
Applies to:	character
Values:	0deg | 90deg | 180deg | 270deg | inherit
Default:	inherits from the parent
Initial:	0deg

glyph-orientation-vertical

The orientation of glyphs when the block progression direction is left to right or right to left.

Group(s):	Writing-Mode-Related Properties
Applies to:	character
Values:	auto | 0deg | 90deg | 180deg | 270deg | inherit
Default:	inherits from the parent
Initial:	auto

grouping-separator

The grouping separator to use with page numbers within this page sequence. The `<character>` is any Unicode character.

Group(s):	Properties for Number-to-String Conversion
Applies to:	page-sequence
Values:	<character>
Default:	no separator

grouping-size

The size of groups separated using the `grouping-separator` in page numbers within this page sequence.

Group(s):	Properties for Number-to-String Conversion
Applies to:	page-sequence
Values:	<number>
Default:	no grouping

height

The optimum height of the content rectangle.

Group(s):	Area Dimension Properties
Applies to:	all elements but nonreplaced inline elements, table columns, and column groups
Values:	<length> | <percentage> | auto | inherit
Percent:	refers to the height of the containing block if specified; otherwise treated as auto
Default:	auto

hyphenate

Enable or disable hyphenation of words in order to break lines.

Group(s):	Common Hyphenation Properties
Applies to:	block, character
Values:	false | true | inherit
Default:	inherits from the parent
Initial:	false

hyphenation-character

The character used to render a hyphen, in which `<character>` is a Unicode character.

Group(s):	Common Hyphenation Properties
Applies to:	block, character
Values:	<character> | inherit
Default:	Inherits from the parent
Initial:	the Unicode hyphen character U+2010

hyphenation-keep

Whether a word may be hyphenated across a column or page.

Group(s): Block and Line-Related Properties
Applies to: block
Values: auto | column | page | inherit
Default: inherits from the parent
Initial: auto

hyphenation-ladder-count

The number of consecutive lines that may end with a hyphen.

Group(s): Block and Line-Related Properties
Applies to: block
Values: no-limit | <number> | inherit
Default: inherits from the parent
Initial: no-limit

hyphenation-push-character-count

The minimum number of characters from a word that may appear on a new line after a hyphen.

Group(s): Common Hyphenation Properties
Applies to: block, character
Values: <number> | inherit
Default: inherits from the parent
Initial: 2

hyphenation-remain-character-count

The minimum number of characters from a word which may appear at the end of a line before a hyphen.

Group(s): Common Hyphenation Properties
Applies to: block, character
Values: <number> | inherit
Default: inherits from the parent
Initial: 2

id

An identifier unique to all other occurrences of `id` in the document.

Group(s):	Miscellaneous Properties
Applies to:	all elements
Values:	<id>
Default:	The formatter generates a unique to value.

indicate-destination

Whether to somehow to highlight the destination upon display when a user activates the link.

Group(s):	Properties for Dynamic Effects Formatting Objects
Applies to:	basic-link
Values:	true | false
Default:	false

initial-page-number

The method for to determining the number of the first page in the `page-sequence`.

Group(s):	Pagination and Layout Properties
Applies to:	page-sequence
Values:	auto | auto-odd | auto-even | <number> | inherit
Default:	auto

inline-progression-dimension

The size of the content to rectangle in the `inline-progression-dimension`.

Group(s):	Area Dimension Properties
Applies to:	elements that produce areas
Values:	auto | <length> | <percentage> | <length-range> | inherit
Percent:	refers to the inline-progression-dimension of the closest ancestor block if specified; otherwise treated as auto
Default:	auto

internal-destination

The identifier (`id`) of a to FO within the document to display when the user activates the link.

Group(s):	Properties for Dynamic Effects Formatting Objects
Applies to:	basic-link
Values:	empty string	<idref>
Default:	empty string

intrusion-displace

Method for wrapping to content around a side float.

Group(s):	Float-Related Properties
Applies to:	block, block-container, table-and-caption, table, table-caption, list-block, list-item.
Values:	auto	none	line	indent	block	inherit
Default:	inherits from the parent
Initial:	

keep-together

Whether to keep the to content of this element together within a line, a column, or a page.

Group(s):	Keeps and Breaks Properties
Applies to:	block-level FOs, inline FOs, table-caption, table-row, list-item, list-item-label, and list-item-body
Values:	<keep>	inherit
Default:	inherits from the parent
Initial:	.within-line=auto, .within-column=auto, .within-page=auto

keep-with-next

Whether to keep to this element together with the next element within a line, a column, or a page.

Group(s):	Keeps and Breaks Properties
Applies to:	block-level FOs, inline FOs, list-item, and table-row
Values:	<keep> | inherit
Default:	.within-line=auto, .within-column=auto, .within-page=auto

keep-with-previous

Whether to keep this to element together with the previous element within a line, a column, or a page.

Group(s):	Keeps and Breaks Properties
Applies to:	block-level FOs, inline-level FOs, list-item, and table-row
Values:	<keep> | inherit
Default:	.within-line=auto, .within-column=auto, .within-page=auto

language

The written language of the to text content, in which `<language>` is a language code defined in IETF. RFC 3066, "Tags for the Identification of Languages." Available at `http://www.ietf.org/rfc/rfc3066.txt`.

Group(s):	Common Hyphenation Properties
Applies to:	block, character, page-sequence
Values:	none | <language> | inherit
Default:	inherits from the parent
Initial:	none

last-line-end-indent

Extra space which must appear at the end of the last line.

Group(s): Block and Line-Related Properties
Applies to: block
Values: <length> | <percentage> | inherit
Percent: refers to the inline-progression-dimension of the closest ancestor block-area that is not a line-area
Default: inherits from the parent
Initial: 0pt

leader-alignment

The alignment point for the content of leaders.

Group(s): Leader and Rule Properties
Applies to: leader
Values: none | reference-area | page | inherit
Default: inherits from the parent
Initial: none

leader-length

The length of a leader in the `inline-progression-dimension`.

Group(s): Leader and Rule Properties
Applies to: leader
Values: <length-range> | <percentage> | inherit
Percent: refers to the inline-progression-dimension of content-rectangle of parent area
Default: inherits from the parent
Initial: leader-length.minimum=0pt, .optimum=12.0pt, .maximum=100%

leader-pattern

The content of a leader.

Group(s): Leader and Rule Properties

Applies to: leader

Values: space | rule | dots | use-content | inherit

Default: inherits from the parent

Initial: space

leader-pattern-width

The length in the `inline-progression-dimension` of each repeated element in a leader.

Group(s): Leader and Rule Properties

Applies to: leader

Values: use-font-metrics | <length> | <percentage> | inherit

Percent: refers to the inline-progression-dimension of content-rectangle of parent area

Default: inherits from the parent

Initial: use-font-metrics

left

Specifies the offset of a block's left edge from the left edge of the referenced element.

Group(s): Common Absolute Position Properties and Common Relative Position Properties

Applies to: absolute or relative positioned elements

Values: <length> | <percentage> | auto | inherit

Percent: refers to the width of the containing block

Default: auto

letter-spacing

Extra space to insert between each character of text.

Group(s): Character Properties

Applies to: all elements

Values: normal | <length> | <space> | inherit

Default: inherits from the parent

Initial: normal

letter-value

Resolves ambiguity in letter formatting. Whether to use "a, b, c, ..." or "i, ii, iii, ..." for example.

Group(s): Properties for Number-to-String Conversion
Applies to: page-sequence
Values: auto | alphabetic | traditional
Default: auto

linefeed-treatment

How the formatter interprets Unicode character U+000A (linefeed).

Group(s): Block and Line-Related Properties
Applies to: all descendants of flow or static-content
Values: ignore | preserve | treat-as-space | treat-as-zero-width-space | inherit
Default: inherits from the parent
Initial: treat-as-space

line-height

Sets the half leading used in line-height calculations.

Group(s): Block and Line-Related Properties
Applies to: all elements
Values: normal | <length> | <number> | <percentage> | <space> | inherit
Percent: refers to the font size of the element itself
Default: inherits from the parent
Initial: normal

line-height-shift-adjustment

Whether line-height calculations account for baseline shift.

Group(s): Block and Line-Related Properties
Applies to: Bbock
Values: consider-shifts | disregard-shifts | inherit
Default: inherits from the parent
Initial: consider-shifts

line-stacking-strategy

The strategy used to determine the distance from one line to the next within a block.

Group(s):	Block and Line-Related Properties
Applies to:	block
Values:	line-height | font-height | max-height | inherit
Default:	inherits from the parent
Initial:	max-height

margin

Shorthand for `margin-top`, `margin-bottom`, `margin-left`, and `margin-right`.

Group(s):	Shorthand Properties
Applies to:	all elements
Values:	<margin-width>{1,4} | inherit
Percent:	refers to the width of the containing block
Default:	see individual properties

margin-bottom

The width of space at the bottom edge.

Group(s):	Common Margin Properties-Block and Common Margin Properties-Inline
Applies to:	all elements
Values:	<margin-width> | inherit
Percent:	refers to the width of the containing block
Default:	0pt

margin-left

The width of space at the left edge.

Group(s):	Common Margin Properties-Block and Common Margin Properties-Inline
Applies to:	all elements
Values:	<margin-width> | inherit
Percent:	refers to the width of the containing block
Default:	0pt

margin-right

The width of space at the right edge.

Group(s): Common Margin Properties-Block and Common Margin Properties-Inline

Applies to: all elements

Values: <margin-width> | inherit

Percent: refers to the width of the containing block

Default: 0pt

margin-top

The width of space at the top edge.

Group(s): Common Margin Properties-Block and Common Margin Properties-Inline

Applies to: all elements

Values: <margin-width> | inherit

Percent: refers to the width of the containing block

Default: 0pt

marker-class-name

Designates the name of a group of elements, each labeled with a marker for retrieval with `retrieve-class-name`.

Group(s): Properties for Markers

Applies to: marker

Values: <name>

Default: None. Supply a value.

master-name

The name of the page master for reference by the `page-sequence`.

Group(s): Pagination and Layout Properties

Applies to: simple-page-master, page-sequence-master

Values: <name>

Default: None. Supply a value.

master-reference

Reference the master name of a page master or sequence of page masters.

Group(s): Pagination and Layout Properties

Applies to: page-sequence, single-page-master-reference, repeatable-page-master-reference, conditional-page-master-reference

Values: <name>

Default: None. Supply a value.

max-height

The maximum height of the content rectangle.

Group(s): Area Dimension Properties

Applies to: all elements except nonreplaced inline elements and table elements

Values: <length> | <percentage> | none | inherit

Percent: refers to the height of the containing block

Default: 0pt

maximum-repeats

The maximum number of times to use this master or set of alternative masters before moving to the next master in the sequence.

Group(s): Pagination and Layout Properties

Applies to: repeatable-page-master-reference, repeatable-page-master-alternatives

Values: <number> | no-limit | inherit

Default: no-limit

max-width

The maximum width of the content rectangle.

Group(s): Area Dimension Properties

Applies to: all elements except non-replaced inline elements and table elements

Values: <length> | <percentage> | none | inherit

Percent: refers to the width of the containing block

Default: none

media-usage

Whether to treat the output medium as a bounded page, an infinite scroll bounded in one dimension, or a single page with no boundaries.

Group(s):	Pagination and Layout Properties
Applies to:	root
Values:	auto | paginate | bounded-in-one-dimension | unbounded
Default:	auto

min-height

The minimum height of the content rectangle.

Group(s):	Area Dimension Properties
Applies to:	all elements except nonreplaced inline elements and table elements
Values:	<length> | <percentage> | inherit
Percent:	refers to the height of the containing block
Default:	0pt

min-width

The minimum width of the content rectangle.

Group(s):	Area Dimension Properties
Applies to:	all elements except nonreplaced inline elements and table elements
Values:	<length> | <percentage> | inherit
Percent:	refers to the width of the containing block
Default:	The implementation determines a minimum width.

number-columns-repeated

Repeats a column specification some number of times starting with the column indicated by `column-number`.

Group(s):	Table Properties
Applies to:	table-column
Values:	<number>
Default:	1

number-columns-spanned

The number of columns occupied by a table cell.

Group(s):	Table Properties
Applies to:	table-column, table-cell
Values:	<number>
Default:	1

number-rows-spanned

The number of rows occupied by a table cell.

Group(s):	Table Properties
Applies to:	table-cell
Values:	<number>
Default:	1

odd-or-even

Whether the formatter may use the master to typeset an odd page, an even page, or either.

Group(s):	Pagination and Layout Properties
Applies to:	conditional-page-master-reference
Values:	odd | even | any | inherit
Default:	any

orphans

The minimum number of lines that must be left before a page break.

Group(s):	Keeps and Breaks Properties
Applies to:	block-level elements
Values:	<integer> | inherit
Default:	inherits from the parent
Initial:	2

overflow

Whether to render content visible outside of the clipping rectangle and whether to supply scroll bars for exposing clipped content.

Group(s):	Layout-Related Properties
Applies to:	block-level and replaced elements
Values:	visible | hidden | scroll | error-if-overflow | auto | inherit
Default:	auto

padding

Shorthand for `padding-top`, `padding-bottom`, `padding-left`, and `padding-right`.

Group(s):	Shorthand Properties
Applies to:	all elements
Values:	<length> | inherit
Percent:	refers to the width of the containing block
Default:	see individual properties

padding-after

The width of padding on the after edge.

Group(s):	Common Border, Padding, and Background Properties
Applies to:	block and inline elements
Values:	<length> | <length-conditional> | inherit
Percent:	refers to the width of the containing block
Default:	0pt

padding-before

The width of padding on the before edge.

Group(s):	Common Border, Padding, and Background Properties
Applies to:	block and inline elements
Values:	<length> | <length-conditional> | inherit
Percent:	refers to the width of the containing block
Default:	0pt

padding-bottom

The width of padding on the bottom edge.

Group(s):	Common Border, Padding, and Background Properties
Applies to:	all elements
Values:	<length> | inherit
Percent:	refers to the width of the containing block
Default:	0pt

padding-end

The width of padding on the end edge.

Group(s):	Common Border, Padding, and Background Properties
Applies to:	block and inline elements
Values:	<length> | <length-conditional> | inherit
Percent:	refers to the width of the containing block
Default:	0pt

padding-left

The width of padding on the left edge.

Group(s):	Common Border, Padding, and Background Properties
Applies to:	all elements
Values:	<length> | inherit
Percent:	refers to the width of the containing block
Default:	0pt

padding-right

The width of padding on the right edge.

Group(s):	Common Border, Padding, and Background Properties
Applies to:	all elements
Values:	<length> | inherit
Percent:	refers to the width of the containing block
Default:	0pt

padding-start

The width of padding on the start edge.

Group(s): Common Border, Padding, and Background Properties

Applies to: block and inline elements

Values: <length> | <length-conditional> | inherit

Percent: refers to the width of the containing block

Default: 0pt

padding-top

The width of padding on the top edge.

Group(s): Common Border, Padding, and Background Properties

Applies to: all elements

Values: <length> | inherit

Percent: refers to the width of the containing block

Default: 0pt

page-break-after

Shorthand for `break-after` and `keep-with-next`.

Group(s): Shorthand Properties

Applies to: block-level elements, list-item, and table-row

Values: auto | always | avoid | left | right | inherit

Default: auto

page-break-before

Shorthand for `break-before` and `keep-with-previous`.

Group(s): Shorthand Properties

Applies to: block-level elements, list-item, and table-row.

Values: auto | always | avoid | left | right | inherit

Default: auto

page-break-inside

Equivalent to `keep-together`.

Group(s):	Shorthand Properties
Applies to:	block-level elements
Values:	avoid | auto | inherit
Default:	inherits from the parent
Initial:	auto

page-height

The height of the page available for content formatted with this master.

Group(s):	Pagination and Layout Properties
Applies to:	simple-page-master
Values:	auto | indefinite | <length> | inherit
Default:	auto

page-position

Whether the formatter may use this master to typeset the first, last, neither first nor last, or any page of the page sequence.

Group(s):	Pagination and Layout Properties
Applies to:	conditional-page-master-reference
Values:	first | last | rest | any | inherit
Default:	any

page-width

The width of the page available for content formatted with this master.

Group(s):	Pagination and Layout Properties
Applies to:	simple-page-master
Values:	auto | indefinite | <length> | inherit
Default:	auto

pause

Shorthand for `pause-before` and `pause-after`. Specify `<time>` as a `<number>` followed by ms for milliseconds or s for seconds.

Group(s):	Shorthand Properties
Applies to:	all elements
Values:	[<time> | <percentage>]{1,2} | inherit
Percent:	see individual properties
Default:	see individual properties

pause-after

Time the reader must pause after reading the content. Specify `<time>` as a `<number>` followed by ms for milliseconds or s for seconds.

Group(s):	Common Aural Properties
Applies to:	all elements
Values:	<time> | <percentage> | inherit
Percent:	refers to the rate of speech
Default:	depends on user agent

pause-before

Time the reader must pause before reading the content. Specify `<time>` as a `<number>` followed by ms for milliseconds or s for seconds.

Group(s):	Common Aural Properties
Applies to:	all elements
Values:	<time> | <percentage> | inherit
Percent:	refers to the rate of speech
Default:	depends on user agent

pitch

Whether the reader's voice sounds high or low, where `<frequency>` is a `<number>` followed by Hz for Hertz or kHz for kiloHertz, designating the average frequency of the voice. 120Hz sounds male. 210Hz sounds female.

Group(s):	Common Aural Properties
Applies to:	all elements
Values:	<frequency> | x-low | low | medium | high | x-high | inherit
Default:	inherits from the parent
Initial:	medium

pitch-range

Whether the reader's voice sounds animated or monotonic.

Group(s):	Common Aural Properties
Applies to:	all elements
Values:	<number> | inherit
Default:	inherits from the parent
Initial:	50

play-during

A sound the reader must produce while reading the content.

Group(s):	Common Aural Properties
Applies to:	all elements
Values:	<uri-specification> mix? repeat? | auto | none | inherit
Default:	auto

position

Shorthand for `absolute-position` and `relative-position`.

Group(s):	Shorthand Properties
Applies to:	all elements, but not to generated content
Values:	static | relative | absolute | fixed | inherit
Default:	static

precedence

Whether the region extends to the corners of the page or allows any `region-start` or `region-end` to extend to the corners in its place.

Group(s):	Pagination and Layout Properties
Applies to:	region-before, region-after
Values:	true | false | inherit
Default:	false

provisional-distance-between-starts

Modifies the start location of the list item body.

Group(s):	Miscellaneous Properties
Applies to:	list-block
Values:	<length> | <percentage> | inherit
Percent:	refers to the inline-progression-dimension of the closest ancestor block-area that is not a line-area
Default:	inherits from the parent
Initial:	24.0pt

provisional-label-separation

Modifies the spacing between list item labels and the list item body.

Group(s):	Miscellaneous Properties
Applies to:	list-block
Values:	<length> | <percentage> | inherit
Percent:	refers to the inline-progression-dimension of the closest ancestor block-area that is not a line-area
Default:	inherits from the parent
Initial:	6.0pt

reference-orientation

Defines which edge of the page is the top.

Group(s):	Layout-Related Properties
Applies to:	block-container, inline-container, simple-page-master, region-*, table
Values:	0 | 90 | 180 | 270 | -90 | -180 | -270 | inherit
Default:	inherits from the parent
Initial:	0

ref-id

Refers to the `id` attribute of some FO in the document.

Group(s):	Miscellaneous Properties
Applies to:	page-number-citation
Values:	<idref> | inherit
Default:	None. Supply a value.

region-name

The name of the region for reference by the `flow-name` property of a flow or static-content FO.

Group(s):	Pagination and Layout Properties
Applies to:	region-body, region-start, region-end, region-before, and region-after
Values:	xsl-region-body | xsl-region-start | xsl-region-end | xsl-region-before | xsl-region-after | xsl-before-float-separator | xsl-footnote-separator | <name>
Default:	"xsl-" prefixed to the name of the FO; for example, xsl-region-body

relative-align

Group(s):	Area Alignment Properties
Applies to:	list-item, table-cell
Values:	before | baseline | inherit
Default:	inherits from the parent
Initial:	before

relative-position

Whether the formatter offsets the position of the element relative to where it would otherwise place the element.

Group(s):	Common Relative Position Properties
Applies to:	all block-level (except block-container) and inline-level FOs
Values:	static | relative | inherit
Default:	static

rendering-intent

The method for rendering colors on the output device.

Group(s):	Color-Related Properties
Applies to:	color-profile
Values:	auto | perceptual | relative-colorimetric | saturation | absolute-colorimetric | inherit
Default:	auto

retrieve-boundary

Whether to limit the search for a matching marker within a page, a page-sequence, or to the entire document.

Group(s):	Properties for Markers
Applies to:	retrieve-marker
Values:	page | page-sequence | document
Default:	page-sequence

retrieve-class-name

Designates the group of elements that have the same `marker-class-name` property value on their marker.

Group(s):	Properties for Markers
Applies to:	retrieve-marker
Values:	<name>
Default:	None. Supply a value.

retrieve-position

Designates which marked element to retrieve.

Group(s): Properties for Markers
Applies to: retrieve-marker
Values: first-starting-within-page | first-including-carryover | last-starting-within-page | last-ending-within-page
Default: first-starting-within-page

richness

Whether the reader has a rich voice that carries or a soft voice that does not.

Group(s): Common Aural Properties
Applies to: all elements
Values: <number> | inherit
Default: inherits from the parent
Initial: 50

right

Specifies the offset of a block's right edge from the right edge of the referenced element.

Group(s): Common Absolute Position Properties and Common Relative Position Properties
Applies to: absolute or relative positioned elements
Values: <length> | <percentage> | auto | inherit
Percent: refers to the width of the containing block
Default: auto

role

Identifies the XML source element that produced the XSL FO markup.

Group(s): Common Accessibility Properties
Applies to: all descendants of flow or static-content
Values: <string> | <uri-specification> | none | inherit
Default: none

rule-style

The pattern used to render a rule.

Group(s): Leader and Rule Properties
Applies to: leader
Values: none | dotted | dashed | solid | double | groove | ridge | inherit
Default: inherits from the parent
Initial: solid

rule-thickness

The thickness of a rule.

Group(s): Leader and Rule Properties
Applies to: leader
Values: <length>
Default: inherits from the parent
Initial: 1.0pt

scaling

Whether any scaling of an imported graphic element should preserve the aspect ratio of that element.

Group(s): Area Dimension Properties
Applies to: external-graphic, instream-foreign-object
Values: uniform | non-uniform | inherit
Default: uniform

scaling-method

The method for scaling an imported graphic element.

Group(s): Area Dimension Properties
Applies to: external-graphic, instream-foreign-object
Values: auto | integer-pixels | resample-any-method | inherit
Default: auto

score-spaces

Whether `text-decoration` affects spaces between words.

Group(s): Miscellaneous Properties
Applies to: bidi-override, character, initial-property-set, page-number, page-number-citation
Values: true | false | inherit
Default: Inherits from the parent
Initial: true

script

A category for characters that share similar typesetting characteristics, especially their baseline. ISO 15924, "Code for the Representation of Names of Scripts," defines values for `<script>`. The value `auto` causes use of the script associated with each character in the Unicode standard.

Group(s): Common Hyphenation Properties
Applies to: block, character
Values: none | auto | <script> | inherit
Default: inherits from the parent
Initial: auto

show-destination

Whether to display the destination of a link in the current view or open a new view when the user activates the link.

Group(s): Properties for Dynamic Effects Formatting Objects
Applies to: basic-link
Values: replace | new
Default: replace

size

Shorthand for `page-width` and `page-height`.

Group(s): Shorthand Properties
Applies to: the page context
Values: <length>{1,2} | auto | landscape | portrait | inherit
Default: see individual properties

source-document

Identifies the XML source document that produced the XSL FO markup.

Group(s): Common Accessibility Properties
Applies to: all FOs that may be contained within flow or static
Values: <uri-specification> [<uri-specification>]* | none | inherit
Default: none

space-after

The width of space at the after edge.

Group(s): Common Margin Properties-Block
Applies to: all block-level FOs
Values: <space> | inherit
Default: space.minimum=0pt, .optimum=0pt, .maximum=0pt, .conditionality=discard, .precedence=0

space-before

The width of space at the before edge.

Group(s): Common Margin Properties-Block
Applies to: all block-level FOs
Values: <space> | inherit
Default: space.minimum=0pt, .optimum=0pt, .maximum=0pt, .conditionality=discard, .precedence=0

space-end

The width of space at the end edge.

Group(s): Common Margin Properties-Inline
Applies to: all inline-level FOs
Values: <space> | <percentage> | inherit
Percent: refers to the inline-progression-dimension of the closest ancestor block-area that is not a line-area
Default: space.minimum=0pt, .optimum=0pt, .maximum=0pt, .conditionality=discard, .precedence=0

space-start

The width of space at the start edge.

Group(s): Common Margin Properties-Inline
Applies to: all inline-level FOs
Values: <space> | <percentage> | inherit
Percent: refers to the inline-progression-dimension of the closest ancestor block-area that is not a line-area
Default: space.minimum=0pt, .optimum=0pt, .maximum=0pt, .conditionality=discard, .precedence=0

span

Whether the block should span columns.

Group(s): Layout-Related Properties
Applies to: block descendents of flow
Values: none | all | inherit
Default: none

speak

Suppress reading or force reading character by character.

Group(s):	Common Aural Properties
Applies to:	all elements
Values:	normal | none | spell-out | inherit
Default:	inherits from the parent
Initial:	normal

speak-header

Whether the reader should repeat header information for a table with each cell or once before a series of cells.

Group(s):	Common Aural Properties
Applies to:	elements that have table header information
Values:	once | always | inherit
Default:	inherits from the parent
Initial:	once

speak-numeral

Whether the reader should speak a series of digits as a single number or as individual digits.

Group(s):	Common Aural Properties
Applies to:	all elements
Values:	digits | continuous | inherit
Default:	inherits from the parent
Initial:	continuous

speak-punctuation

Whether the reader should indicate punctuation with pauses or speak them literally.

Group(s):	Common Aural Properties
Applies to:	all elements
Values:	code | none | inherit
Default:	inherits from the parent
Initial:	none

speech-rate

How slowly or quickly the reader speaks.

Group(s):	Common Aural Properties
Applies to:	all elements
Values:	<number> | x-slow | slow | medium | fast | x-fast | faster | slower | inherit
Default:	inherits from the parent
Initial:	medium

src

The source URI of a graphic or color profile.

Group(s):	Miscellaneous Properties
Applies to:	external-graphic, color-profile
Values:	<uri-specification> | inherit
Default:	None. Supply a value.

start-indent

The width of space, padding, and border at the start edge.

Group(s):	Common Margin Properties-Block
Applies to:	all block-level FOs
Values:	<length> | <percentage> | inherit
Percent:	refers to the inline-progression-dimension of the containing reference-area
Default:	inherits from the parent
Initial:	0pt

starting-state

Whether to use this `multi-case` for the initial display of a `multi-switch`.

Group(s):	Properties for Dynamic Effects Formatting Objects
Applies to:	multi-case
Values:	show | hide
Default:	show

starts-row

Starts a new row before the table cell, provided the table cell has no parent table row.

Group(s):	Table Properties
Applies to:	table-cell
Values:	true I false
Default:	false

stress

Describes the degree of stress given "stress" words, such as "very" or "significantly."

Group(s):	Common Aural Properties
Applies to:	all elements
Values:	<number> I inherit
Default:	inherits from the parent
Initial:	50

suppress-at-line-break

Whether the formatter should display the character if it occurs at a line break.

Group(s):	Character Properties
Applies to:	character
Values:	auto I suppress I retain I inherit
Default:	auto

switch-to

Identifies the `multi-case` to display when the user activates this `multi-toggle`. A `<name>` refers to the value of `case-name` on a `multi-case`.

Group(s):	Properties for Dynamic Effects Formatting Objects
Applies to:	multi-toggle
Values:	xsl-preceding I xsl-following I xsl-any I <name>[<name>]*
Default:	xsl-any

table-layout

Specifies whether column widths are fixed using table-column specifications or calculated automatically according to the content of the table.

Group(s):	Table Properties
Applies to:	table
Values:	auto | fixed | inherit
Default:	auto

table-omit-footer-at-break

Whether to format the footer at the bottom of a page when the table continues on the following page.

Group(s):	Table Properties
Applies to:	table
Values:	true | false
Default:	false

table-omit-header-at-break

Whether to format the header at the top of a page when the table started on the preceding page.

Group(s):	Table Properties
Applies to:	table
Values:	true | false
Default:	false

target-presentation-context

Specific reference to content within the resource identified by the external destination of a `basic-link`.

Group(s):	Properties for Dynamic Effects Formatting Objects
Applies to:	basic-link
Values:	use-target-processing-context | <uri-specification>
Default:	use-target-processing-context

target-processing-context

Start location for processing content within the resource identified by the external destination of a `basic-link`.

Group(s): Properties for Dynamic Effects Formatting Objects
Applies to: basic-link
Values: document-root | <uri-specification>
Default: document-root

target-stylesheet

The URI of an XSL style sheet. Use with `external-destination` to process the destination with the given style sheet and display the transformed result.

Group(s): Properties for Dynamic Effects Formatting Objects
Applies to: basic-link
Values: use-normal-stylesheet | <uri-specification>
Default: use-normal-stylesheet

text-align

Selects left, center, right, or full-justified text in a block.

Group(s): Block and Line-Related Properties
Applies to: block-level elements
Values: start | center | end | justify | inside | outside | left | right | <string> | inherit
Default: inherits from the parent
Initial: start

text-align-last

Selects alignment for the last line of text in a block.

Group(s): Block and Line-Related Properties
Applies to: block
Values: relative | start | center | end | justify | inside | outside | left | right | inherit
Default: inherits from the parent
Initial: relative

text-altitude

Override the height reported by the current font.

Group(s):	Writing-Mode-Related Properties
Applies to:	block, character, leader, page-number, page-number-citation
Values:	use-font-metrics | <length> | <percentage> | inherit
Percent:	refers to the font's em-height
Default:	use-font-metrics

text-decoration

Whether to decorate text with underline, overline, line-through, or blink.

Group(s):	Character Properties
Applies to:	all elements
Values:	none | [[underline | no-underline] || [overline | no-overline] || [line-through | no-line-through] || [blink | no-blink]] | inherit
Default:	None. (Inline FOs inherit from any parent block FO.)

text-depth

Override the depth reported by the current font.

Group(s):	Writing-Mode-Related Properties
Applies to:	block, character, leader, page-number, page-number-citation
Values:	use-font-metrics | <length> | <percentage> | inherit
Percent:	refers to the font's em-height
Default:	use-font-metrics

text-indent

Extra space that must appear at the start of the first line.

Group(s):	Block and Line-Related Properties
Applies to:	block-level elements
Values:	<length> | <percentage> | inherit
Percent:	refers to the width of the containing block
Default:	inherits from the parent
Initial:	0pt

text-shadow

Marks to appear around the edges of text characters.

Group(s): Character Properties

Applies to: all elements

Values: none | [<color> || <length> <length> <length>? ,]* [<color> || <length> <length> <length>?] | inherit

Default: None. (Inherits the color property.)

text-transform

Changes to the capitalization of text characters.

Group(s): Character Properties

Applies to: all elements

Values: capitalize | uppercase | lowercase | none | inherit

Default: inherits from the parent

Initial: none

top

Specifies the offset of a block's top edge below the top edge of the referenced element.

Group(s): Common Absolute Position Properties and Common Relative Position Properties

Applies to: absolute or relative positioned elements

Values: <length> | <percentage> | auto | inherit

Percent: refers to the height of the containing block

Default: auto

treat-as-word-space

Whether the formatter treats the character as a space character.

Group(s): Character Properties

Applies to: character

Values: auto | true | false | inherit

Default: auto

unicode-bidi

Whether to embed a new writing direction or override the writing directions implicit in Unicode characters.

Group(s):	Writing-Mode-Related Properties
Applies to:	all elements
Values:	normal ǀ embed ǀ bidi-override ǀ inherit
Default:	normal

vertical-align

Shorthand for `alignment-baseline`, `alignment-adjust`, `baseline-shift`, and `dominant-baseline`.

Group(s):	Shorthand Properties
Applies to:	inline-level elements and table-cell
Values:	baseline ǀ middle ǀ sub ǀ super ǀ text-top ǀ text-bottom ǀ <percentage> ǀ <length> ǀ top ǀ bottom ǀ inherit
Percent:	refers to the line-height of the element itself
Default:	baseline

visibility

Whether to render the content or merely reserve the space it would occupy if rendered.

Group(s):	Miscellaneous Properties
Applies to:	all elements
Values:	visible ǀ hidden ǀ collapse ǀ inherit
Default:	inherits from the parent
Initial:	visible

voice-family

A list of voice family names in which `<specific-voice>` is the name for a voice installed on the system, such as "romeo," "juliet," or "announcer." Values for `<generic-voice>` are `male`, `female`, or `child`.

Group(s):	Common Aural Properties
Applies to:	all elements
Values:	[[<specific-voice> | <generic-voice>],]* [<specific-voice> | <generic-voice>] | inherit
Default:	inherits from the parent
Initial:	depends on user agent

volume

Describes how loud the reader sounds.

Group(s):	Common Aural Properties
Applies to:	all elements
Values:	<number> | <percentage> | silent | x-soft | soft | medium | loud | x-loud | inherit
Percent:	refers to the inherited value
Default:	inherits from the parent
Initial:	medium

white-space

Shorthand for `linefeed-treatment`, `white-space-collapse`, `white-space-treatment`, and `wrap-option`.

Group(s):	Shorthand Properties
Applies to:	block-level elements
Values:	normal | pre | nowrap | inherit
Default:	inherits from the parent
Initial:	normal

white-space-collapse

How the formatter interprets multiple, contiguous XML white space characters.

Group(s):	Block and Line-Related Properties
Applies to:	all descendants of flow or static-content
Values:	false | true | inherit
Default:	inherits from the parent
Initial:	true

white-space-treatment

How the formatter interprets XML white space characters.

Group(s):	Block and Line-Related Properties
Applies to:	all descendants of flow or static-content
Values:	ignore | preserve | ignore-if-before-linefeed | ignore-if-after-linefeed | ignore-if-surrounding-linefeed | inherit
Default:	inherits from the parent
Initial:	ignore-if-surrounding-linefeed

widows

The minimum number of lines that must be left after a page break.

Group(s):	Keeps and Breaks Properties
Applies to:	block-level elements
Values:	<integer> | inherit
Default:	inherits from the parent
Initial:	2

width

The optimum width of the content rectangle.

Group(s):	Area Dimension Properties
Applies to:	all elements except nonreplaced inline elements, table-rows, and row groups
Values:	<length> | <percentage> | auto | inherit
Percent:	refers to the width of the containing block
Default:	auto

word-spacing

Extra space to insert between each word of text.

Group(s): Character Properties
Applies to: all elements
Values: normal | <length> | <space> | inherit
Default: inherits from the parent
Initial: normal

wrap-option

Whether line breaking will occur when a line exceeds the width of the content rectangle.

Group(s): Block and Line-Related Properties
Applies to: block, inline, page-number, page-number-citation
Values: no-wrap | wrap | inherit
Default: inherits from the parent
Initial: wrap

writing-mode

Specifies the block and inline progression directions.

Group(s): Writing-Mode-Related Properties
Applies to: block-container, inline-container, simple-page-master, region-*, table
Values: lr-tb | rl-tb | tb-rl | lr | rl | tb | inherit
Default: inherits from the parent
Initial: lr-tb

xml:lang

Shorthand for country and language.

Group(s): Shorthand Properties
Applies to: block, character, page-sequence
Values: <country-language> | inherit
Default: see individual properties

z-index

Establish the order of stacking for absolute or relative positioned elements.

Group(s): Miscellaneous Properties

Applies to: absolute or relative positioned elements

Values: auto | <integer> | inherit

Default: auto

Index

A

B

C

D

E

F

G

H

I

M

N

O

P

Q - R

S

T

U

V - W

X-Y-Z

Other Related Titles

XML Internationalization and Localization
Yves Savourel
0-672-32096-7
$49.99US/$74.95CAN

Strategic XML
W. Scott Means
0-672-32175-0
$34.99US/$52.95CAN

Voice Application Development w/VoiceXML
Rick Beasley, Mike Farley, John O'Reilly, and Leon Squire
0-672-32138-6
$49.99US/$74.95CAN

JAX: Java APIs for XML Kick Start
Aoyon Chowdhury and Parag Choudhary
0-672-32434-2
$39.99US/$52.95CAN

SAMS
www.samspublishing.com

XML Distributed Systems Design
Ajay M. Rambhia
0-672-32328-1
$49.99US/$74.95CAN

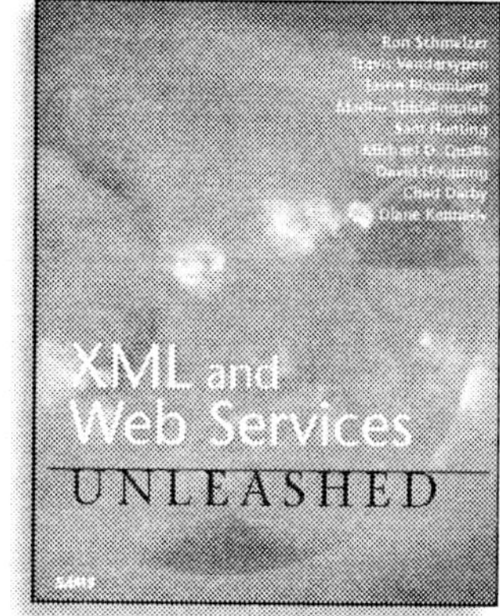

XML and Web Services Unleashed
Ron Schmelzer, Jason Bloomberg, et al.
0-672-32341-9
$49.99US/$74.95CAN

Building Web Services with Java, Making Sense of XML, SOAP, WSDL, and UDDI
Steve Graham, Toufic Boubez, et al.
0-672-32181-5
$44.99US/$69.99CAN

All prices are subject to change.